STEADFAST

STEADFAST

365 DAYS OF DEVOTION

ABINGDON PRESS | NASHVILLE

2026

STEADFAST 2026
365 DAYS OF DEVOTION

Continued on page 396.

CONTENTS

Introduction

"How can I know God's will for my life?" As a pastor, I have been asked this question many times over. I think it is a good question to ask and shows a desire to be obedient to the Lord. It is also a question that seems as if it ought to have a complicated answer, but it doesn't. How can you know God's will for your life? Spend time with God through Scripture and prayer.

Throughout compiling the devotions for this book, it has been my prayer that they would serve as a tool to help you deepen your relationship with God. By developing the habit of daily study and prayer, you will grow in God's grace and find yourself open to the Holy Spirit's leading.

As this book came together, the word *steadfast* came to take on significance for me. In these devotions, I see time and time again stories of God being steadfast toward us. The writers behind these devotions repeatedly share their stories as well as the stories of the Bible of God's loving, unending faithfulness toward us, especially when we do not deserve it.

I hope that as you spend 2026 immersing yourself in God's Word, you will find your faithfulness toward the Lord growing to match the Lord's faithfulness toward you. May your love for God and your neighbor likewise be steadfast.

Jarrod S. Davis,
Editor

JANUARY

CONTRIBUTORS:

*Michelle Morris
(January 1–January 26)*

*Susan Groseclose
(January 27–January 31)*

JANUARY 1

God's Holy Presence

Joshua 5:10-15

Where do you feel God's holy presence?

In the wilderness, God provided manna for the Israelites to eat. In Canaan, the Israelites ate food "[produced] in the land." In the wilderness and in Canaan, the Israelites experienced God's abiding love and holy presence. God's presence was made known to Moses in a burning bush, and God was with him as he led the Israelites through the wilderness. God's presence was made known to Joshua as a "commander of the Lord's heavenly force" and called him to be the new leader in Canaan. Moses and Joshua were instructed to remove their shoes when they were standing in God's presence (Exodus 3:5; Joshua 5:15).

Find a comfortable place to reflect on God's holy presence in your life. If you wish, take off your shoes and feel the ground underneath. Take a few deep breaths. As you breathe in, invite God's Spirit to fill you. As you breathe out, release any worries or concerns that you are carrying. Slowly reread Joshua 5:15. Reflect on the places where you have recently experienced God's holy presence. God provided manna in the wilderness and food from the land in Canaan.

What is God providing in your life today? How do you experience God's abiding love? God promised to be with Moses and Joshua. Where do you need to trust God? Slowly reread Joshua 5:15 as an affirmation that God's presence abides with you and goes with you, wherever you are.

> I lift up my praise to you, O God, for I know
> that I am standing on holy ground. Amen.

Experience God's Presence

Exodus 26:31-35

Where is your sacred space?

One of my sacred spaces is underneath the lighted cross on the grounds of Lake Junaluska Conference and Retreat Center in North Carolina. The cross sits atop a hill overlooking the lake, surrounded by the mountains. As a child, my family would gather each summer at this cross. As an adult, I periodically journey to the foot of this cross to encounter God's presence. In the light of the cross, I find the peace and illumination that I came seeking. I breathe a prayer of thanksgiving for the time of rest in God's arms, the renewal and refreshment of my soul, and the assurance that God will walk with me throughout the days ahead.

For the Israelites, the ark of the covenant was a sacred place. Today's Scripture gives instructions for the veil, which was made to hide the chest with the covenant, thus separating the holy from the holiest. In the Israelites' journey through the wilderness, the priests and Levites carried the ark of the covenant as a constant reminder that God was present with them. Do you have a sacred space? Are there specific rituals, prayers, or devotional materials that you use to shape a sacred space? In what ways have you grown closer to God and others by spending time in this space? If this hasn't been part of your practice, could you benefit from crafting such a place?

*Loving God, just as the Israelites experienced you
in the wilderness, lead me to those places
where I can be in your presence. Amen.*

SATURDAY, JANUARY 3
A Safe Place

Psalm 9:7-13

What safe spaces are you co-creating with God?

In today's reading, the psalmist proclaims, "The LORD is a safe place for the oppressed—a safe place in difficult times." We are reminded that God doesn't abandon us; rather, we are safe in God's presence during life's difficulties, especially those who are oppressed or experiencing an injustice.

What are the safe places in your life? How does feeling safe allow you to trust God? Reflect on a time that you felt unsafe. How did that experience lead you to mistrust God or others?

As followers of Jesus, we too provide that safe space for those who are oppressed or experiencing difficulty. I have worked in congregations that provided safe spaces for those experiencing homelessness, poverty, and food insecurity; recovery for persons dealing with the opioid crisis; safe sanctuaries for immigrants and refugees; ministries with persons with disabilities or living with HIV/AIDS or with Alzheimer's or other forms of dementia. In all these places of ministry, persons experience safety where they can then experience and trust that God is with them.

How are you providing a safe space for another person to experience God? How is your church providing a safe space for those who experience an injustice?

God of Justice, show me ways to develop safe relationships
where your people can trust your abiding love. Amen.

Listen and Speak Carefully

Ecclesiastes 5:1-7

When you worship God, how do you listen and speak carefully?

Our first instruction is to listen. One of my spiritual guides taught me the art of deep, holy listening. She called it listening with the "ear of your heart." So often, we are thinking about our next statement or we are focused on our next task rather than listening. To practice listening with the "ear of your heart," find a comfortable, quiet spot. Choose a Scripture passage to read, or describe to Jesus a situation or decision where you are struggling. Using your imagination, "listen" to what Jesus has to say to you. If your mind wanders, set those thoughts aside to pay attention to later.

"Don't be quick with your mouth" is the second instruction. Not only are we called to deep, holy listening, but God also calls us to speak carefully to one another. In difficult, courageous conversations, this instruction becomes even more important.

Listening and speaking go hand in hand. I often have to remind myself to allow the silent space of listening to ponder my expectations and perceptions, seek to understand another, then carefully choose what I say. Thus, what I say is not only a reaction but is informed and formed out of Christ's love for all people.

In your worship, how do you speak and listen to God? How do you listen for God's guidance in your life? How are your conversations Christlike?

Holy God, open my heart to listen
and my mouth to speak carefully. Amen.

MONDAY, JANUARY 5

Cut to the Chase

Genesis 15:1-7

Can you question the Lord's faithfulness?

These few verses tell us a tremendous amount about the relationship between God and Abram. We might think that there was little intimacy between the two of them because God told Abram that he should not be afraid and that God was Abram's protector, as if Abram didn't already know that.

Abram's reaction, however, does not seem to be one of fear. Abram asked a question (maybe an accusation?) about God's ability to fulfill God's promises since Abram still had no heir. Bold.

Are we allowed to challenge God like that? I think we are. Abram regularly put a challenge before God. Moses asked God all kinds of questions. Job threw down the gauntlet. And Jesus prayed for a different path from the garden, if it were God's will. The important thing about such challenges is that they do one very important thing: they preserve an honest relationship between us and God.

I tell youth to go ahead and pray for a new iPhone or whatever it is they want. Just don't expect that God will answer you in the way you think. The point is that they are creating a relationship with God that will allow them to bring their authentic worries and dreams to God. So should we all.

Lord God, let me bring my heart to you so that
we can be closer than we have ever been. Amen.

TUESDAY, JANUARY 6

Darkness and Light

Genesis 15:8-20

When have you felt that the darkness was too deep and terrifying?

Today is Epiphany, the day after the twelfth day of Christmas, marking the arrival of the wise men and the inclusion of the Gentiles into the story of Jesus. Epiphany and this passage have me thinking about how God shows up in our lives. This passage in Genesis is the "cutting of the covenant." The ritual sacrifice here, where the animals were divided and then God passed through them, could signal many things: the division in Creation that was covered by God, the use of animals in sacrifices dedicated to the Lord, the bringing together of God and humanity, and so forth.

In this moment, however, I want to focus on the darkness in this event. Falling asleep after sunset, "a terrifying and deep darkness settled over" Abram. In his sleep, he was promised that his descendants would be enslaved! Then, the sun set (again?), darkness deepened, and the Lord appeared as light, a fiery flame in a smoking vessel. Now Abram got the promise of the land for himself and his descendants. Now there was light in the darkness.

The tension between light and darkness in this passage reflects the same reality that Epiphany speaks to. The world opened to God when Jesus shone into the world. Just as the light came and cut the darkness for Abram, assuring him of God's presence, Christ's light cuts the darkness for all of us.

Lord Jesus, let me live looking for your light,
even when the darkness seems deep and terrifying. Amen.

Wednesday, January 7

Whose Worship Exactly?

2 Samuel 6:12-23

When have you seen spiritual leaders abuse power?

This is either one of the high points of David's faith journey or a first step toward the corruption of that faith. Perhaps, in truth, it is both. Was David celebrating God, or was he showing off? How often do we fool ourselves into thinking we are doing the Lord's will when we are doing what brings glory to us instead? Maybe for a time it brings glory to God and us, but it can be difficult to recognize.

We have all known people, and have certainly known religious leaders, who put on a great show of their piety. This usually starts from a place of true faith. Something happens along the way, though. Maybe they begin to understand the power of God more fully, and then maybe they experience that power. Maybe they take some of that power, and then maybe they use some of that power. But maybe they abuse power.

This passage should remind us of the temptations of power, and especially power claimed in God's name. We should walk carefully with it, pausing every six steps not to make a sacrifice but to remember whose power it is.

Almighty God, let me always be humble
in the presence of your power. Amen.

Don't Try to Prove It!

2 Samuel 7:1-17

What does God expect of your relationship with God?

I am routinely baffled that God wants to be in relationship with us. My heart is not as pure and true as I want it to be.

Yesterday, we read a passage about David bringing the ark of the covenant into Jerusalem. Yes, maybe David was being super pious, but he was doing so in questionable ways. His motives might have been less than pure.

God must have known that, yet God gave David this covenant, a promise of a dynasty that will be established forever. This is a change from how the Lord treated Saul. Saul's rule was highly conditional.

This Davidic covenant is more about God recognizing us. God realizes that we fail when we have part of the bargain to fulfill. So God made a covenant where the work is on God, not on us. While I appreciate the graciousness about covenant here, I also long to rise to some expectations. I wish I could be what God sees in me. I know David wished that too, as is evidenced in several psalms. The point is not David's faith, though, but God's faith in and for David.

Resting in that assurance can be difficult. God knew it would be difficult for David. God gave him an opportunity not to prove himself by denying David the chance to build God's temple. God told David, "Love me, and don't prove it to me. It is enough that I love you." May we all receive the gift of not proving ourselves worthy to God.

Loving God, thank you for loving me. Amen.

FRIDAY, JANUARY 9

David's Praise

2 Samuel 7:18-29

When has it been easy for you to praise God, and when has it been difficult?

David is credited with penning many of the psalms. If this prayer is any indication, he had a real gift for praise.

Praise is not always easy, but praise is our response. We are all supposed to do it. David did it well. Granted, in this passage, when he was heaping glory on God, saying, "No one can compare to you, no god except you," God had just promised him a dynasty. When God seems to work things to my benefit, I can come up with fantastic words, too.

David was also good with words when things went terribly wrong. He was good at words of repentance and at words of praise for God within that repentance. Look at Psalm 51, a psalm of repentance after sinful deeds. David praised God as compassionate, righteous, and the God of salvation. He knew he had sinned, but he also knew that God was still God, still the God of praise and promise.

There are times in our lives when praise comes easily, and there are times when we feel lost, when we know we have messed up, when the world seems aligned against us. But God is still God. God is still with us, still providing, still loving us. God still seeks to be in relationship with us. We are still inheritors of the promise. Amid it all, we are still called to praise.

Lord, give me a heart of praise like David's,
and let me lift glory to you in all things. Amen.

Cloud Versus Temple

1 Kings 8:12-21

How do you hold on to God?

As Christians, we teach that God lives in heaven, in our church buildings, beside us, and in our hearts. We affirm that God is present in all of creation. But does God want a house, or do we want a house for God?

If we pay attention as we read today's passage, God never asked for a house. God instead relented that the people needed God to have a house. By having such a house, the people of Israel would look like the other tribes around them. But that was a concern of people, not of God. In fact, building a temple like the other gods would imply that God needed to compete. Building a temple would tie God down to a geographic location. It would seem they were trying to tame and domesticate God, thus creating "haves" and "have-nots": those who could travel to the Temple would have God; those who couldn't, didn't.

We are desperate to hold on to God. That desire is built on a lack of trust. Without the building, we don't trust that God will stay in our lives. We don't trust ourselves to be worthy and to stick around. We don't trust our neighbors to stick to the program, so God will stay. Finally, we don't trust God to keep God's promise and love us anyway.

Perhaps the very buildings we build to honor God keep us from honoring God. The concrete temples we make to God become what we love. Is it possible that we think they allow us to love God, but perhaps instead they distract us from loving and trusting God more fully?

God of fire and God of cloud, help me
to trust you more fully. Amen.

SUNDAY, JANUARY 11

A Gift from the Lord?

Psalm 127:1-5

Can you stand in places of joy and pain simultaneously?

A lot of the psalms were written in a time when the Israelites were still a small, somewhat vulnerable tribe of people. They were written when the Israelites understood that immortality came from having children, and before people had little more than a rudimentary understanding of reproduction. All those combine to result in a psalm that touts what a blessing children are, that they are directly put in wombs by God, and that having bunches of them proves you are happy and God loves you.

I can't read this psalm without thinking of the people who struggle to have a child. I cannot look them in the eye and think, God must not want to bless you. Then I think about people like me, who had one child and then took medical steps not to have another. My first and only pregnancy was a high-risk one, and I couldn't take the chance of leaving one or two children behind in trying to have another. Of course, some people choose not to have any children at all.

So what do I do with this psalm? First, I do thank God for all the children in this world. Then, I also use this psalm to remind me of the people who are experiencing loss and the depth of pain and disconnection they may feel. That is much of life. We stand between the celebration and the heartache, the joy and the pain, and we try to do so with caring, concern, and attentiveness to the other. May this psalm cause such reflection in you as well.

Lord of bounty and famine, let me be present
to all people in all places in all times of life. Amen.

MONDAY, JANUARY 12

Love in the Midst of Loss

Ruth 1:1-14

How do you need people to help you navigate loss?

One day I was visiting an incredibly kind, good-hearted couple at the church I served; we would bury their son in a few days. The heartbreak of loss was tempered only by the fact that their son's children were in the room with us, tying them to hope for the days ahead. Less than six months later, we were burying their grandchild. She had been in that living room, sharing words about her father. Where was the hope now? How could this couple go from one devastating loss to the next? They had not finished grieving the loss of their son when they had to grieve the death of their granddaughter.

Naomi certainly found herself in such a state. With the death of her sons, Naomi's life was in great jeopardy. She felt she was cursed. She did not want to drag anyone else down in the muck with her.

Yet Ruth was there for her. Ruth chose to stay and walk with her through her grief. She would accompany Naomi in her emotional, spiritual, and literal journey.

We all face troubles in this life. None of us must face those alone. There are always people willing to walk beside us. We might be tempted to push them away, but that is not good for us or for the ones who want to walk with us. They are often hurting, too. God designed us to be companions to one another. Let's honor that design and walk through life together, even when that walk puts us in long funeral lines.

> Holy Companion, let me see those who are
> hurting and walk with them, and let me see
> those who are willing to walk with me. Amen.

Tuesday, January 13

Ruth's Pledge to Naomi

Ruth 1:15–2:3

What sacrifices do you make for covenantal love?

When couples get married, they don't always anticipate that the plans they made early on might change. After pursuing college degrees, changing careers, having children or struggling to have a child, moving from one location to another, life may look different than it did on their wedding day. This also happens when God makes a call on their lives and they accept that call.

This is especially true when one person's calling dictates much of what life looks like for the family. It's easy to forget what the other spouse put aside so the other person can follow God's call. But it's important to remember a spouse's sacrifice and be thankful for the willingness to be supportive.

Ruth's words, a gift and a promise to Naomi, are a covenant, not of paper or political alliance, but of heart. Making such a promise and living it are two different things. Ruth was willing to live a different way in a different place and stay with her mother-in-law even if it put her own livelihood at risk. That is never easy. Making that kind of commitment takes a strong will and deep love because it invites us to set aside our self-centered, self-oriented natures. It invites us to love our neighbor.

This story of Ruth and Naomi always reminds me of marriage, of the covenant people make with each other and the life they live together, good times and bad. May we all have and be such steadfast companions in this life, as well as in marriage, in friendship, or whatever our relationships are.

Loving God, help me to love at least one other person
with the depth of true covenant. Amen.

God Behind the Scenes

Ruth 2:17-23

When have you thought a coincidence might be God working for you?

God was not an obvious character in Ruth. However, that does not mean God was not shaping the story. In this passage, we get a glimpse of God in the background. Was it a coincidence that Ruth ended up in the field of one of her redeemers? Was it a coincidence that Boaz just happened to take notice of her and offer her protection and sustenance? Or was God more present in this story than we think?

Naomi seemed to notice God's presence here, though she named that reality subtly. She called on the Lord to bless Boaz for his kindness and encouraged Ruth to continue gleaning in that field. In the next chapter, Naomi orchestrates the plan to take this budding relationship further. Naomi seemed to detect that there was more going on. She perceived God was at work.

Has something ever happened to you that made you feel God was present? Sometimes we write off the idea that God is working in our lives by chalking it up to coincidence. Sometimes it feels like just a random occurrence. I always try to remember that what looks like a coincidence could be a God-incident. God is at work in our lives. God got so "up in our business" God became one of us as Jesus! So the next time you feel as if things are unusually working out, stop for a moment and thank God for the blessing and for God's behind-the-scenes presence.

God, thank you for the surprising ways
you show up. Amen.

Thursday, January 15
Let's Talk about Sex

Ruth 3:1-11

Can the Bible help you talk about sex in a healthy way?

Sometimes in the Bible, a reference to feet is a reference to genitalia. When Naomi told Ruth to clean herself up and then watch for a chance to uncover Boaz's feet, she was telling her daughter-in-law to have sex with Boaz. The hope here was to take the relationship to the next level.

This is a complicated passage for readers of the Bible. On one hand, this is an expression of the union of two loving people. On the other hand, it is a scene of seduction between two unmarried parties. On the third hand, it is an act of a desperate woman who needed to provide for herself and her family.

Is sex any less complicated today? Sex is a gift God gives us and is supposed to be about intimate love and care. It perpetuates human existence. All that is good, but sex also gets all tangled up in our sinfulness. It is used to abuse and manipulate, to keep some in power and some oppressed, and at times causes damage to our bodies and souls.

This passage gives us an opportunity to have a frank discussion about the challenges of sex and sexuality. The church can give the world a healthy understanding of sex that has no shame but also recognizes how precious a gift sex is. We can recover the aspect of covenant that could be present in sex and give people tools to set healthy limits and counteract the damage and abuse that too often occurs. But first, we must be willing to have the talk.

> Creator God, help me to recognize the gift of sex
> and to guide others into healthy patterns. Amen.

Let's (Kinda) Talk about Sex, Part 2

Ruth 4:1-13

How has God worked through strange circumstances?

This whole scene probably strikes us as weird, so let's explain the details. The city gate was where people conducted important business. It looks like what was happening here was the observation of levirate marriage. *Levir* is the Latin word meaning "husband's brother." According to Deuteronomy 25:5-10, it was a man's responsibility to marry his brother's widow if his brother died with no heirs. If he refused, the widow pulled off the man's sandal, spat in his face, and he was then known as the head of the house whose sandal was removed. The purpose of levirate marriage was to preserve property lines and protect vulnerable widows.

There is a clue that this was an observation of levirate marriage. Ruth 4:12 refers to Tamar and Judah in Genesis 38. When Tamar's husband died without leaving her with children, his brother refused to have children with her, and her father-in-law stalled on giving her to his third son, she dressed as a prostitute and slept with her father-in-law and had his child. She was judged righteous for it.

In Jesus' genealogy, we find Tamar and Ruth. Theirs are stories off the beaten paths, yet in both, the women are heralded as heroes. Through both, the redemption of the world happens. Even in situations difficult to understand, God works for good and sees purpose in and for all of us.

> Wise and clever God, let me see you at work
> in the situations I don't understand. Amen.

SATURDAY, JANUARY 17

The Families We Have

Ruth 4:14-20

How has your family changed over the years?

My mom has lived through a lot of loss. She was one of 21 brothers and sisters. She is in her 60s and has buried 18 brothers and sisters. We also lost my dad this past fall. She must feel alone sometimes.

But my mom is also the family's great aunt. I mean that in both senses of the word: She is the elder generation, and she is a fantastic aunt. Every baby born into our family gets a baby quilt from her. To 21 brothers and sisters and three generations beneath hers, each quilt is unique. What a significant undertaking that is! Every spring or summer, Mom visits as many of her nieces and nephews as she can. In a world when many of us struggle to keep up with one another, she shows up and hugs your neck.

Like Naomi learned to do, my mom does not mire herself too long in loss. She grieves, she is lonely for her brothers and sisters, but she also celebrates the future in all the new family being born. She, like Naomi, sees all those babies as hers to help raise in some way. I am grateful to have a mom who loves so abundantly. She teaches me more about God than she will probably ever know. I pray we can all love as she does.

Loving God, remind me to celebrate the family I have in all its unexpected and wonderful glory. Amen.

God's Loyal Love

Psalm 89:19-20, 28-37

When have you thought you were "above the law"?

In Walter Brueggemann's *Reality, Grief, Hope: Three Urgent Prophetic Tasks*, he talks about how the Israelites became accustomed to the idea of chosenness and did not expect the Temple to be destroyed. Because of the covenant God made with David, that David's dynasty was everlasting, the Israelites thought that they were something special, above the laws of nature and humanity.

But that covenant promise was never about people. It was about the God who made that promise. God could and would remain loyal to David. God could and would love David and David's descendants for all time. Because of that love, however, God would also give David and David's descendants the freedom to choose a path that led them away from God. This psalm speaks to that reality. God would love David for all time. However, if his children chose to reject God's instructions, they would face consequences.

Thankfully, we worship a God who is loyal despite our faults and infinitely creative. As the covenant appears broken, our clever and creative God has plans to save the world through one who is in David's family and in God's own, establishing the throne forever through Jesus Christ.

Lord God, I am so grateful that when my love fails,
your love remains steadfast. Amen.

Monday, January 19

A True Promise

Psalm 132:11-18

How do you keep a promise?

God promised to establish David's throne forever, but this psalm puts conditions on that covenant. Why does this psalm recount the covenant differently? It could be for practical purposes. In the ancient world, people were more likely to recall things from memory than look at a scroll and quote it exactly. Or maybe it was written after David's death.

Soon after David died, the kingdom was divided into two. Both kingdoms were eventually conquered. That was the definitive end of the Davidic dynasty as it was understood at the time. This psalm just deals with reality as it happened.

Did God break the promise? No. Anytime a promise is made between two parties, both parties have a part they must uphold. In the case of David's descendants, the piece they had to uphold was to continue a relationship with God. Things went south straight out of the gate when Solomon married so many foreign wives, and worship became corrupted. It only got worse from there.

God's promise was true. God would not remove the Davidic line from reign. What God would allow, however, was the line itself to choose to throw it away. As soon as a deep and abiding relationship with God quit being a priority, the promise was broken, not by the one who made the promise, but by the ones who received the promise. God has promised to always love us. We received that promise through Jesus, but we still must choose to accept that love.

Loving Jesus, sign of the Davidic promise,
let me always be ready to receive your love. Amen.

Persisting in Grace

Jeremiah 31:2-7

When have you been surprised by hope?

This section of Jeremiah was likely composed during the Babylonian exile, after Jerusalem was captured. The people were shocked: The promise of an eternal reign for the family of David was ended; the Temple was in ruins; many families were uprooted from their ancestral homes and transplanted to a foreign land that did not acknowledge God. Yet the prophet said, "Sing joyfully. . . . Raise your voices with praise!"

Have you ever found yourself in despair, wondering what was coming next, unsure of the future or even what tomorrow would hold, and certain persons encouraged you amidst all that trauma? Did you look at them as if they did not understand your despair or as if they had lost their minds?

Christian hope is sublimely ridiculous. Who looks at a cross, an implement of execution, and says, "Yeah, that is the symbol I want to represent my faith"? Well, we do because we know we are not at the end of the story.

Christians know the persistence of grace. No matter what we are going through, God persists in loving us. God will neither abandon us nor leave us to utter destruction. It may look bad, but our story will never have an unhappy ending as long as we persist in God's grace. Jeremiah reminds us of that here, and Jesus reminds us of that in his whole gospel story. It remains true despite our desperate circumstances.

Lord of grace, let me always find myself
persisting in you as you persist in me. Amen.

Wednesday, January 21

In With the New

Jeremiah 31:27-30

What destructive pattern of living do you have that needs to be changed?

A genogram is like a family tree on steroids. You lay out your family tree, but also track things such as family feuds, divorces, abuse, and addictions, as well as healthy patterns of differentiation. One of the things that my genogram revealed was that patterns showed up across generations. That usually happens in a genogram. Without airing my family's dirty laundry, things that happened to people before they had children, and that were never spoken about around the children, also happened to the children anyway.

This is how I came to terms with the announcement that God will punish the third and fourth generation for the sins of their parents (Deuteronomy 5:9). I understand that verse less as something God is doing and more in terms of the reality that, in our broken and sinful state, we create destructive patterns that we pass down. The only way we are set free is to deliberately seek a new pattern. This passage in Jeremiah calls us to such work.

When we take on the role of a child of God, we have the freedom to choose who we can be. Of course, that also means we can choose not to choose God, but such a decision will be ours and not one that has been passed down to us. What a compelling vision: to be free of old broken patterns of life! Through the guidance of Scripture and the Holy Spirit and the power of grace, we live new lives.

Lord, let me live into your reign so that I might
be freed from old, broken ways of being. Amen.

Thursday, January 22

Seriously? Another One?

Jeremiah 31:31-37

How many chances do you need to have a good relationship with God?

I am tired of talking about "covenant." I'm running out of things to say. If we haven't gotten it by this point, then we aren't going to get it. Or I am not going to be able to explain it. Or both. This whole experience of trying to come at covenant in different ways is exhausting. But now I have just a small taste of what God must experience in relationship with us.

God made a series of covenants. Some of those covenants were made with a family (as with Noah). Some were made with one man (as with Abraham). Some were made with the whole community (as at Sinai). Some were made to a lineage (as with David). They all had problems.

God knew the Israelites had made decisions that would lead to destruction. God could have walked away right then and there, but no, that's not what happened. Why? Maybe it is simply because God loves the people, and that would be enough. But also, God's hope springs eternal. God wouldn't give up. Maybe this would be the one. Maybe making a covenant during exile would so deeply reveal God's commitment that they would be unable to resist that kind of love. They would seal those words on their hearts and live as God's people now and forever. Maybe, but no. Even after writing these devotional readings on covenant, I don't totally have it yet either. How about you? Yet God still doesn't give up on us.

God, I don't know why you keep believing in me, even
when I struggle to believe in you, but thank you. Amen.

FRIDAY, JANUARY 23

A Fuller Table

1 Corinthians 11:17-26

Can you experience Communion with people unlike you?

Gathering in a community mission worship service were people with long-term careers, plus a man bumming a lighter off the guy beside me; a woman with three young kids who shared her husband's experience going through rehab; and another woman who shared her struggles with drug abuse.

I was aware of my position as a highly-educated person who was invited into this place, and I wondered how I would enter it true to myself and still able to relate. It was messy. I was probably more aware of trying to make the place inclusive than they were about needing to be included. They were more comfortable than I was, but gradually their hospitality invited me in. We closed the evening with Communion, when I realized how perfect this was. It was a hodge-podge of humanity. But as we passed around the bread, there was enough. No one was given more than anyone else, and no one was restricted from the meal.

In 1 Corinthians, Paul reminds the people that this "received tradition" is one that makes space for all people. This supper we share together is not for some to have more and some less. I am reminded that I usually take Communion with people who have more than we need. But the Communion of the early church was a cross-section of the community. May we remember to get out of our shiny buildings and go to places where the fullness of the body of Christ can be known.

Lord Jesus, may I always find myself gathered
around a table with your whole family. Amen.

Out with the Old

Hebrews 8:6-13

How do you react when things you value change?

After Hurricane Katrina, many predicted that the Creole culture of New Orleans would be gone forever. Gradually, their accents and language, their whole way of living, would be swallowed by the cultures of the places they were displaced to. Only determined effort could keep Creole culture alive. So people worked at preserving the music, stories, food, and lifestyles. It is still too early to say if the efforts will hold. It is an act of faith, and faith does not always show us results right away. There is grief over what is lost and intentionality to live into the new.

Jesus brought a new covenant to a people who would soon be scattered. He brought it to a people whose old ways of doing things would be challenged. Where humans had failed to keep aligned with the covenant and keep it always on our hearts, Jesus would not fail. Now, instead of us working to show our obedience to God, Jesus lived that obedience. Now, instead of us having to work at being in relationship with God, Jesus would incarnate that reality for us.

For those who follow him, we do write the Word on our hearts, for Jesus is the Word. As we learn more about that Word, the culture the Word gives birth to in us is better than the one we lost. We grieve the old covenant that is gone, but at the same time, we must be intentional about the newness of life we are given in Christ.

Jesus, I am so grateful for the new life
you are creating in me. Amen.

SUNDAY, JANUARY 25

A New Path of Faith

Hebrews 9:13-18

How do you understand Jesus' sacrifice?

Hebrews was likely written after the fall of the Temple in AD 70. It was probably written to Jews who had been displaced all over the Mediterranean world prior to or shortly following that destruction. They faced a tremendous faith crisis. What were they supposed to do when there was no Temple?

As the Temple fell, the synagogues rose in prominence. But synagogues tended to start out in homes, and those were not conducive to sacrifices. While money had for a long time been a means of making a sacrifice (sometimes in the form of buying an animal to sacrifice), it now became the de facto means of offering a sacrifice in Jewish circles. Hebrews, however, makes a different case. For those who followed Jesus, Jesus became the fulfillment of the blood sacrifice requirement. His willingness to offer himself stood in place of all other such sacrifices. The letter to the Hebrews helped Jesus' story make sense for the time and place in which his followers found themselves.

With his act of sacrifice, Jesus sealed the new covenant. Where the covenant with Moses was demanding, the covenant with David fractured, and the covenant with Jeremiah unfulfilled, the new covenant, sealed with the blood of Jesus, would hold, not because of our fidelity but because of his. Thank you, Jesus, for sealing our relationship with God. Thank you for giving us a new path. Thank you for the new covenant.

Lord Jesus, you gave your life for us.
For that we can only and always be grateful. Amen.

MONDAY, JANUARY 26

MONDAY, JANUARY 26

Finding Fellow Followers

Genesis 14:17-24

How can other Christians keep us focused on our faith?

Within the context of this passage, Melchizedek's importance is two-fold. First, he was a contrast to the king of Sodom, who was interested in material gain and may not have been trustworthy, judging by Abram's refusal to be in debt to that king. Sodom's king was focused on the political reality before him. Melchizedek, on the other hand, turned a political/military event into a religious moment. He brought Abram bread and wine and blessed him. The contrast of a greedy political figure and a generous religious one is stark.

Melchizedek's other purpose is far more important. He was the first figure Abram encountered since leaving Ur who also worshiped one God on high. Melchizedek signaled to Abram that God continued to be with him as he was making his way in the Promised Land. He was blessed by a priest of the Most High God. The next thing that would happen to Abram was a sealing of the covenant with that God.

The king of Sodom was trying to establish a political covenant with Abram, and Abram rejected it, instead giving his honor and allegiance to God and those who shared in serving God. We, too, are challenged in our faith to find ways to navigate our social and political realities while still maintaining our commitment to God. Perhaps this story reminds us that allies in that fight are all around us. We just have to be open to seeing them, relating with them, and being blessed by them.

Most High God, help me to see others who serve you
and to cultivate relationships of support with them. Amen.

TUESDAY, JANUARY 27

God-Qualified

2 Corinthians 3:4-14

Have you ever noticed God working through you?

This passage in 2 Corinthians is empowering. It encourages us to recognize that our relationship with Christ can give us great confidence. The Spirit will gift us with the power to do great things. But this passage also reminds us not to get too big for our britches. Those gifts the Spirit gives flow from God. When we are standing in the reality of our covenant with God, then the work we do on God's behalf is empowered by God, not us. We agree to the relationship, we agree to be open to direction, and as such can then do incredible things. We must always remember that power flows from God to us.

While it is contrary to our American myth of the "self-made" person, it is comforting to me to know that I do not have to do it all. I get to cooperate in what God is doing. Each of us who agrees to covenant with God is now called, and God will equip us to do the work.

I need to remember this passage from 2 Corinthians when I think I don't have it in me to give anymore. I never had it in me. I am a conduit of God's power for the world. I also need to remember this passage when I do think that I am all that and a bag of chips. I need to remember that I have been most "effective" in ministry when I stepped aside and let the Spirit work. God's power is immense, and God calls us to share in that power. But we should always be attentive to where it flows from and who it flows for.

Lord, let me be a conduit of your peace
and work in this world. Amen.

WEDNESDAY, JANUARY 28

Where There's Smoke . . .

Judges 6:11-24

How have you been surprised by God?

Gideon was going about his business, using a winepress to thresh grain, when this stately gentleman suddenly appeared. I say "stately" because Gideon kept saying, "With all due respect, my LORD," though I detect a hint of sarcasm.

The fact that Gideon asked for a sign means that he did not quite believe this visitor and his claims. He was testing for the truth. I want us to recover some of the comedy of this scene. Gideon showed up with his goat and flour. The stranger gave him specific instructions about what to do with the sacrifice. I can just see the smirk on Gideon's face as he did what the stranger instructed. Then, God wiped that smirk right off Gideon's face as the sacrifice burst into flames from fire that sprang forth from a rock!

This wonderful, hilarious, real story of someone encountering God in a way he didn't expect helps us to be open to the surprise of God. God shows up in our lives and sometimes asks us to do something we think is beyond us. Because it is so outlandish, we tend to doubt the veracity of the request. So God will show us just how possible all our supposed impossibilities are, demonstrating that there is fire behind the smoke. All we have to do is be open to the experience, even if we want the proof. We must then be willing to make the commitment God is calling us to make.

Surprising Lord, help me to hear your truth and to trust
in the fire behind the smoke of your call on my life. Amen.

Thursday, January 29
Missing the Signs

2 Kings 20:1-11

In hindsight, when have you seen God's work in your life?

When we read this story in 2 Kings, we don't read it as an ancient audience might have heard it. We miss some of the signs, particularly the fig bandage. In the ancient world, figs were used for medical diagnosis and prognosis. They were placed on a hurting area, and then the skin and the figs were checked to determine if healing was occurring.

Verse 7 says that the fig bandage was placed on Hezekiah, "and he started getting better." Yet he still wanted a sign that he would make it up to the Temple. God, through Isaiah, would grant him another sign, this one significantly harder to miss: God moved the sun to reverse the motion of the shadows.

The text does not pass judgment on Hezekiah for his request. This passage speaks of a God who goes to great lengths to preserve a relationship, particularly with someone who was trying to be faithful, and who was vulnerable enough to weep before God. It also speaks of a God who is constantly sending us signs and signals to point us in God's direction. We haven't even mentioned the fact that God raises up prophets to communicate God's will for us, too.

So when you wonder if God is hearing your prayers, maybe take a step back and look with new eyes at your surroundings. Perhaps God is communicating with you through that friend who offers sound advice, through your physician, or in any number of ways. Be thankful for the creative ways God continues to speak to and through us.

> God, let me see with your eyes and not mine the
> future you have planned for me. Amen.

The People Contribute Too Much

Exodus 36:4-19

What do you expect when you give to your church?

I witnessed a miracle when we undertook a sanctuary renovation and no one left the church. The trustees assigned a subcommittee of strongly opinionated women to make decisions as the process unfolded. Those women kept their eyes on God; each of them made or agreed to a decision that surprised her because it was not her usual preference. When put in the context of what was best for the church and for worship of God, the decisions were clear.

That is not always the case when it comes time to build or renovate a sanctuary. It is usually not easy, because people feel passionately about the places they dedicate to God. Generally, that is a good thing; we should give our best to God. Unfortunately, what sometimes happens is that people forget that the purpose is to give to God and instead seek their own glory. People sometimes give to show off. Sometimes people bring things to the church as a show of generosity. It is done without thought of if it is needed or not. A lot of church rooms are filled with things donated to clear room in our houses; God receives our leftovers.

We should have the courage in the church, like the workers here in this passage, to sometimes stop and declare, "The people are contributing way too much material for doing the work that the LORD has commanded us to do." We should give what is needed and called for to bring glory to God, and nothing else.

Beautiful God, let me give to you what is practical
and needed for your glory, not mine. Amen.

SATURDAY, JANUARY 31

Holy Encounter to Restore Justice

Acts 7:30-36

Where is God calling you to works of justice?

As part of his defense, Stephen emphasized that God called Moses to be the leader and the deliverer of the Israelites. On the surface, we recognize that God called Moses to lead the Israelites out of slavery. But on a deeper level, God called Moses to works of justice. God called Moses to go where it was risky. God called Moses to extend God's compassion by responding to the Israelites' cries for deliverance. God called Moses to speak on behalf of the Israelites. God called Moses to stand up against Pharaoh's policies of oppression. God called Moses to restore the Israelites' dignity. God called Moses to make a difference in the lives of the Israelites, leading them to put their trust in God and to experience a new life in God's Promised Land. Ultimately, God called Moses to restore God's *shalom*: peace and wholeness to God's people.

We, too, are called to works of justice. Often, our work for justice begins with awakening our hearts to the injustices around us. Consider today's news and name the places where persons are oppressed and discriminated against. Prayerfully consider where God is calling you to work for justice. How might you extend God's compassion, especially to those on the margins of society? How can you be a voice for the voiceless? Where is God calling you out of your comfort zone? How can you change unjust policies? How can we work to restore God's *shalom*?

God of justice, open my heart to see and hear the cries of
your people. Lead me to work for your shalom. Amen

FEBRUARY

CONTRIBUTORS:

Susan Groseclose
(February 1–February 23)

Clara Welch
(February 24–February 28)

Celebrating God's Presence

Psalm 16:1-11

How do you celebrate God's presence in your life?

At times, I immediately experience God's presence: when a red cardinal sits atop the bird feeder; when I sit on the beach gazing into the vast horizon; when I drive down the street in the light of a full moon, I am reminded of my smallness and God's greatness. At other times in the midst of my busyness, I must stop, reflect, and name those times I experience God's presence.

The psalmist affirms that we live with the assurance that God will not abandon us (verse 10). We are heirs of God's kingdom (verse 6) and will be filled with joy in God's presence (verse 11). But sometimes, our awareness is lacking.

The Examen prayer practice is a way to awaken ourselves to God's presence. At the end of the day, reflect on where you have experienced God. Thank God for those moments of joy in God's presence. Name the time you felt far away from God. Ask for forgiveness when you have harmed another, and acknowledge where you have been harmed. Lean into God's guidance and instructions in those times of uncertainty. As you drift off to sleep, close your eyes in the assurance of God's abiding presence.

Loving God, your abiding presence is ever with me.
Hold me in your love and care. Amen.

Holy Renewal

Exodus 2:11-25

When have you experienced God's restoration?

After Moses killed the Egyptian and hid his body, he realized that other Hebrews had seen his actions and knew him to be a murderer. Out of fear and to save his own life, Moses fled to Midian. Throughout the years in Midian, God remembered Moses and planned to restore his status as leader of the Israelites. God worked through Moses' failures and personal flaws to fulfill God's purposes.

In today's Scripture reading, we become aware not only of God's redemptive power, but we also get a glimpse of ways that God used Moses' character and experiences to prepare him for future purposes. At Moses' core, he had a heart of justice. Even though Moses wrongly killed the Egyptian, he was attempting to rescue his fellow Hebrew from harm and abuse. Moses' sense of justice meant he was a leader who would stand up against Pharaoh, advocate on behalf of the Israelites, and lead the Israelites through the wilderness for 40 years.

How has God used a personal flaw or failure of yours for God's purposes? How has an experience prepared you for your future?

Redeeming God, forgive me when I have wronged another,
and restore me to your purposes. Amen.

TUESDAY, FEBRUARY 3

Unexpected Holiness

Exodus 3:1-12

Where has God surprised you?

God's call of Moses was totally unexpected. I imagine Moses had numerous feelings during this encounter: astonishment, curiosity, confusion, uncertainty, and excitement mixed with fear. I can imagine that when God said, "I am the God of your father, Abraham's God, Isaac's God, and Jacob's God," Moses felt a sense of awe that he was in the presence of his covenant-making God. Yet Moses was afraid and hid his face from God. I can imagine that God's description of seeing the oppression and hearing the cries of his fellow Hebrew people touched Moses' soul with empathy and compassion. I can imagine Moses' total surprise yet reluctance when God called him to lead the Israelites.

Have you ever been afraid to get too close to God? How does God get your attention? For me, it has often been a personal health crisis, the loss of a job, or a significant family circumstance for me to move beyond my self-centeredness and control to rely on God. At other times, it has been a hymn or Scripture passage that has touched the depths of my soul.

God called Moses to face Pharaoh, even though he didn't feel qualified. When has God surprisingly called you despite your feelings of inadequacy or uncertainty?

Surprising God, I open myself to your
divine presence and holy revelation. Amen.

God's Presence in the Sanctuary

Exodus 40:1-11

How do you experience God's presence in your church's sanctuary?

The Mennonite Information Center in Lancaster, Pennsylvania, has a full-scale replica of the wilderness Tabernacle. Looking at this replica, I was amazed. Even as a replica, it feels holy, a sacred space for God's presence.

The wilderness Tabernacle was God's dwelling place. It was set up in the center of the Israelites' camp so that God was central to the Israelites' lives. The Israelites offered their burnt offerings to God in the courtyard. The high priests offered the people's prayers and blessings to God in the holy place. The ark of the covenant held the stone tablets that God gave to Moses but remained hidden behind the veil, the holiest of holies. Each object in the Tabernacle had a specific place. Moses was to anoint the dwelling and each of the objects to make them holy.

The Tabernacle was also the meeting place between God and the Israelites. It was not a place where the Israelites gathered to worship but a place where God met with God's people through their burnt offerings. (Exodus 29:42-43).

What objects or design of your church's sanctuary help you experience God's presence? What fond memories in this sacred place call you into God's living presence?

O God, your presence dwells within me. Let me experience
your living presence in my worship. Amen.

Thursday, February 5

Anointed for Service

Exodus 40:12-15

Who is God calling you to serve?

I am named for both of my grandmothers. These women were influential in my life. Not only did they freely express their love and warmth, but they also taught me the power of prayer. Each day, they prayed for me. They sang praises for God's abiding love and grace. They reminded me that God was always with me. They assured me that God was working for good in any of life's circumstances. Now I continue their legacy of prayer and pointing others to God.

In today's reading, God instructs Moses to anoint Aaron and his sons as priests "for all time in every generation." They had the responsibility of conducting the rituals and ceremonies at the altar (Numbers 18:7), offering sacrifices to God on the people's behalf. Other Levites who were not descendants of Aaron served as aides to the priests.

Just as Aaron, his sons, and the Levites were set apart for specific ministry in the Tabernacle, God calls pastors and deacons to serve in specific ministries within our churches and in our communities. Yet we are all called by God and anointed through our baptismal waters for ministry and service in the world. Who needs to experience the love of Christ through you? With whom do you need to share God's good news? Who needs you to stand with them?

Creating God, you call us to be coworkers with you.
Show me how to share your love and justice today. Amen.

Evoking God's Presence

Exodus 40:16-33

How do the baptismal font and Communion altar evoke God's presence?

Just as the wilderness Tabernacle evoked God's presence for the Israelites, the baptismal font and the Communion table can evoke God's presence in our worship.

Sometimes the baptismal font is placed in the center of the altar area or even in the center of the congregation, representing that God is central in our lives and worship. At other times, the baptismal font is placed near a door into the sanctuary, signifying that we enter God's presence.

Receiving and celebrating Holy Communion also bring us into God's presence. What are your thoughts when you see the bread and cup on the sanctuary's altar table? What evokes God's holy presence? The Communion elements? the smell of the bread or taste of the juice? the familiar liturgy? How do you experience God's presence as you receive Communion?

Spend time thinking about where these items (the baptismal font and the Communion altar) are located in the sanctuary where you most often worship. What does their presence communicate to you about our relationship with God? Where does God meet with you?

Holy God, I seek your presence.
Let me meet you in my worship. Amen.

God Dwells With Us

Exodus 40:33-38

What tangible ways do you celebrate God's presence?

Some people wear crosses around their necks or carry a Bible. Others might wear a t-shirt with a slogan indicating their loyalty to God. Those who are ordained often wear collars or stoles as a symbol of God's presence. What other objects have you seen that indicate God's presence?

The cloud was a tangible expression of God's presence for Moses and the Israelites. God used the cloud to guide the Israelites. The cloud enveloped and filled the meeting tent, representing that God was fully present with the people. God's presence filling the Tabernacle was the final act in setting up the tent and the climax to the Book of Exodus.

God was present with the Israelites during their deliverance from Egypt, including their confrontation with Pharaoh, the plagues, and crossing the Red Sea. God was present with the Israelites by providing manna, quail, water, new life, new commands, and new direction as they journeyed through the wilderness toward the Promised Land.

As Christians, we experience firsthand the indwelling of God's presence. Think for a moment about all the different ways you have experienced God's presence in your life. Spend a few moments in prayer expressing your appreciation and thanksgiving for God working in and through your life.

Ever-present God, thank you for dwelling in my life.
Continue to guide and point me in the Way. Amen.

God Does Not Desert Us

2 Timothy 4:14-22

How do you sense God's presence in difficult situations?

Who in your life is difficult to get along with? Who has caused harm to you personally or to persons in your church?

Today's reading includes Paul's mention that Alexander had really hurt him. Paul also warned Timothy about Alexander, saying that he opposed and rejected the teachings of God. We don't have any specific details about Alexander, although he could have been the same person Paul mentioned in Acts 19:33 or 1 Timothy 1:20. Paul also affirmed to Timothy that, despite his persecution, imprisonment, and desertion by others, God was always on his side. Paul gave encouragement to Timothy to continue carrying God's message to the world, no matter the situations or circumstances he faced.

Whenever you find your frustration or anger with a person or situation overtaking your emotions, take time to sit quietly in prayer with God. Pray for the other person, asking God to soften your heart and melt your anger. Pray for God's guidance and wisdom. When needed, seek out others for support or guidance to respond in a just, safe manner.

Abiding God, remind me that you never desert
me and that you are always with me. Amen.

Monday, February 9

God's Peace Sustains Us

Philippians 4:1-9

How do you experience God's peace?

When we rejoice in God's loving, abiding presence, we can experience God's peace. Paul encourages all believers to be gentle with one another and not anxious. Rather than argue, present your requests to God in prayer. Live with the assurance that God's peace transcends our understanding. Shift your thoughts to things that are holy, just, pure, lovely, and worthy of praise, rather than things that cause division.

It is often easier to argue a point than to build loving relationships. When we fail to guard our words carefully, our speech can easily become hateful and abusive. Sometimes our fear or loss of control results in disagreements. It can be easier to focus on what we believe is right or wrong rather than to listen to one another. It can be difficult to gather as the body of Christ in prayer, trusting God's power and peace.

In those times, take a few moments to follow these steps:

- Focus on, feel, and sink into the feelings, emotions, thoughts, and sensations in your body.
- Welcome God in those feelings, emotions, thoughts, or sensations by saying, "Welcome."
- Let go by repeating the following sentences, "I let go of the desire for security, affection, control. I let go of the desire to change this feeling/sensation."

Welcoming God, enter into my difficult relationships and grant me your peace. Amen.

Integrity

Psalm 26:1-12

How do you walk with integrity?

We receive a wealth of information each day: television, radio, and news reports; newspapers and magazines; emails, websites, and search engines; and one-on-one conversations. How do we sort through the different perspectives to figure out the truth? It is hard to determine what information is factual, what is partially factual, and what is false.

Psalm 26 describes David's desire for integrity, the characteristic of being reliably honest and truthful in one's actions. David was not proclaiming sinless perfection but asking God for forgiveness and pleading for personal integrity. His actions were motivated by God's love and truth. He wanted his life to demonstrate the truth of God's love.

Just as David's actions were motivated by God's love and truthfulness, those same values motivate us to walk with integrity. When we are honest and keep our promises; when we are compassionate and have empathy for others; when we live and act out of God's love and truthfulness, never compromising these values, we walk with integrity. Reflect on your relationships and actions today. How have you walked with integrity? When have you taken a wrong step? Ask for God's forgiveness, trusting that God forgives us and shows us how to be loving and truthful.

> Forgiving God, lead me to be holy and walk
> with integrity. May I be a witness to your
> love and truthfulness. Amen.

WEDNESDAY, FEBRUARY 11

Righteousness

Isaiah 56:1-8

How do you live a righteous life?

The focus of some churches is on personal holiness, while the focus of other churches is on social holiness. Both are good and important. A righteous life finds a balance between personal and social holiness.

Isaiah 56:1-8 challenges the people of God to be holy and righteous, to do what is right and maintain justice, and to keep the sabbath. Righteousness is based on the act of doing what is right. Taking just actions leads to a life pleasing to God. It involves a balance of personal and social holiness.

John Wesley prescribed Christians three simple rules: Do no harm; do all the good you can; and stay in love with God. Discipleship is a balance between acts of devotion, acts of worship, acts of compassion, and acts of justice. It is a balance of loving God and loving others. It is a balance of inward practices growing in holiness and outward practices of showing love to all those whom God loves.

How do you know that your actions are right and pleasing to God? How do you keep sabbath in a way that witnesses to your devotion and worship of God? How do you welcome the stranger in your life and in your church? How do you balance the compassion of God's people with standing with those who live on the margins of society?

Holy God, lead me in your righteous ways.
Show me how to fully love you and
love all your people. Amen.

Thursday, February 12

Kingdom People

Matthew 5:3-12

How do you strive to live the Beatitudes?

As we look closely at each beatitude, we gain a deeper understanding of our relationship with God and one another. Those who are "hopeless," Jesus said, recognize their need for God and receive the Kingdom. Recognizing our need for God, we can accept even our imperfections, knowing that we are included as family. When we grieve, we learn that God will comfort us. We become better able to show empathy. We are willing to humbly give up control, live without overpowering others, and be gentle, for Jesus promised that we will inherit the earth. We aim to meet these standards not on our own but through God's power.

As part of God's family, we want to seek out God's will more than our own because Jesus promises that our lives will be full. We lead others to a deeper life with Christ. Rather than being judgmental, we learn to mercifully enter the pain of others, feeling and suffering alongside them, for we, too, have received that same mercy. We seek to live with a "pure heart," without pretending to be someone we are not, knowing that we will see God. We seek and work for peace, working out our differences without hurting others. By our actions, we show that we are children of God.

Loving God, I seek to live as part of your family.
Walk with me as I practice each of these beatitudes. Amen.

FRIDAY, FEBRUARY 13

Salt and Light

Matthew 5:13-16

What does it mean to be salt and light to others?

Salt has many uses. Salt in our bodies affects blood pressure, sleep, and digestion. Salt aids against muscle cramping. It lowers the boiling point of water and can aid in cleaning. Salt can also help extinguish a grease fire, de-ice a driveway, and kill poison ivy. Saltwater can soothe a sore throat and help treat gum disease, infections, sores, and wounds.

Light is equally useful. It shines into darkness to guide our paths. It is necessary for the photosynthesis of plants and for the biomolecular synthesis after we eat to give our bodies energy. Because of light, our eyes can see. Light makes colors possible. Light maintains our circadian rhythms.

Following the Beatitudes in Jesus' Sermon on the Mount, he instructed his followers to be "salt of the earth" and "light of the world." Like salt, we season our relationships with love (Mark 9:49-50) and speak graciously and insightfully (Colossians 4:6). We are like salt when we offer healing and preservation by acting in kind and just ways. Just as salt makes us thirsty, we can lead others to thirst for a deeper relationship with Christ. Like light, we are to shine our love of Jesus Christ in our thoughts, words, actions, and relationships with all people.

Loving Lord, show me how to be
salt and light to others. Amen.

SATURDAY, FEBRUARY 14

Wisdom

Matthew 7:24-29

How can you be a wise builder?

Think about a difficult time or situation in your life. For me, it was multiple job losses in a period of a few years. It was only through the foundation of prayer, trusting in God's faithfulness, and caring family and friends that I was able to stand firm and not feel that I was sinking in this life storm.

Jesus gives us this analogy of the foolish builder who builds his house on sand and the wise builder who builds on rock. The foolish builder's house did not withstand the storms, but the wise builder's house remained standing.

What does a weak foundation of sand look like in our lives? What does a strong foundation with Jesus look like in our lives? A characteristic of being holy is hearing the word of God and putting those words into practice. It's not enough simply to know Scripture; we must apply what Scripture teaches us, follow Christ's commands and example, and express our faith in our loving, just actions. We are to embody the words of Scripture into our daily lives.

A strong foundation requires trust in God and God's faithfulness and building a strong relationship with Christ through prayer, devotion, and acts of compassion and justice. It is nurtured through a loving, caring faith community.

> God, give me wisdom to build a strong foundation
> that can withstand the storms of life. Amen.

SUNDAY, FEBRUARY 15

Wear God's Armor

Ephesians 6:10-18

How does God's armor fit you?

In Paul's letter to the church at Ephesus, he explained the characteristics of God's holy people by calling on Christ's followers to put on God's armor. Clothed like this, we are "strengthened by the Lord and his powerful strength" and are prepared to "stand against the tricks of the devil" and live faithfully in a world that is often dark and evil.

Paul named six pieces of armor, six qualities of a holy people: the belt of truth, the breastplate of justice, shoes enabling us to spread the good news of peace, the shield of faith, the helmet of salvation, and the sword of the Spirit.

When we wear God's armor, we resist evil and stand strong in God's power. Equipped in this way, we are ready to face whatever comes our way. When we feel weak, we know we have for our immediate use God's powerful strength.

Paul was in prison when he wrote this letter. He believed that we are not fighting against one another but against all the forces of evil. These may be issues of discrimination, injustices, abuses of power, or other forces that move our focus from God and God's love. How can we use God's armor against these forces in our communities?

Holy God, I want to wear your armor.
Teach me how to be truthful, righteous,
peaceful, and a faithful witness
of your salvation and love. Amen.

Honorable

Psalm 24:1-6

What does it mean to have clean hands and a pure heart?

Psalm 24, a processional psalm, emphasizes God's sovereign reign and our need for God's salvation and righteousness. It is only with clean hands and a pure heart that we can enter God's holy sanctuary and holy presence. In God's eyes, our hearts are pure when our thoughts, attitudes, and motives are of God. We are clean when the work we do with our hands is loving and just. Because of Christ's sacrifice and the salvation he offers, we not only can enter into God's holy presence, but we also become part of God's reign and kingdom.

When our hearts are pure and our actions are loving and just, we are known as being honorable. Persons who are honorable believe in truth and are honest not only in their thoughts but in their actions. Honorable persons are morally and ethically fair and worthy of respect. Honorable persons believe in doing the right thing and strive to live up to these high principles, even when no one is watching.

What are the ways that you live an honorable life? What does it mean for us to be a holy people living in God's reign? What are we called to be? What are we called to do?

God of salvation, give me clean hands and a pure heart,
and enable me to love all of your creation. Amen.

Tuesday, February 17
Holy Purpose

Isaiah 11:1-5

What is your purpose in God's kingdom?

Isaiah promised a ruler who would come from the lineage of David. Like David, the "Lord's spirit" will rest on him: "a spirit of wisdom and understanding . . . of planning and strength, . . . of knowledge and fear of the Lord." This ruler will undertake God's purposes and be righteous and faithful in his actions. He will "judge the needy with righteousness, and decide with equity for those who suffer." Righteousness and faithfulness will guide his actions.

Isaiah spoke of this as a future promise, which we understand as fulfilled in Jesus. We see in Jesus the highest expressions of righteousness and faithfulness. Through our relationship with Jesus, we get a glimpse of God working in the world and what our purpose is in the Kingdom.

What stories about Jesus' righteousness and faithfulness come to mind as you read verses 2-5? The Gospels are full of the stories of Jesus' life, teachings, death, and resurrection that illustrate his purpose for showing us how to be faithful, loving, and just in our actions. As followers of Jesus, we join Christ in the world to fulfill God's holy purpose to be righteous and faithful. What will you do today to witness to God's righteousness and faithfulness?

> Living God, show me today how to live faithfully
> and righteously, showing love and working for
> justice in your kingdom. Amen.

Among the Weeds and Thistles

Genesis 3:8-19

Where have you experienced hope in hardship?

Notice that God issues only two curses in this story: The first to the snake that started the chain of disobedient acts and the second to "the fertile land." The man and the woman were not cursed. Remember, "God created humanity in God's own image" (Genesis 1:27). Despite our sin, we are not cursed. God continues to call us to be the bearers of the divine image in the world.

In the midst of suffering the consequences of their actions, there is hope. The woman will bear children. The man and woman will know the joy of having a family. Life will go on. Yes, "weeds and thistles will grow" in the fields, making farming difficult, yet there will be plants to eat and grains from which to make bread.

We may sometimes believe the "weeds and thistles" growing around us will take over. But when we look closely among the weeds and thistles, we see new life sprouting up.

Verse 19 reminds us of words the minister may say during the imposition of ashes on Ash Wednesday: "Remember that you are dust, and to dust you shall return." The minister may also say, "Repent, and believe the gospel." When we repent of our sin, God forgives us. We may be of the dust, but it is from the dust that new life grows. We have the sure hope of Jesus.

Merciful God, help me to be mindful of your love, even
when I feel surrounded by weeds and thistles. Amen.

Thursday, February 19

Holy Requirements

Micah 6:6-8

How do you walk humbly, love kindness, and do justice?

In Matthew 18:21-35, Jesus tells a story wherein a master releases a servant and forgives his debt of ten thousand bags of gold, but that servant throws a fellow servant in jail till his much smaller debt is paid. The parable challenges us to see the face of God in one another, to faithfully love others, and to obey and follow God, who treats us lovingly and justly.

This reminds me of the requirements we read in Micah. The Lord made a case against Israel's sinfulness, then reminded them of God's gracious acts on their behalf. Israel asked, "With what should I approach the Lord?" Then Micah responded with a prescription for how to live our lives as God's holy people: "Do justice, embrace faithful love, and walk humbly with your God."

To do justice is to see that each person is created in God's image, to stand against evil and stand alongside those who have been wronged. To embrace faithful love is to see and act out of God's love and compassion, to be the hands and feet of Christ. To walk humbly with our God means to think of others before ourselves, to see one another with the eyes of God, and to dedicate our daily lives to the Lord. How are you obeying these holy requirements?

God of mercy and justice, forgive me when I fail
to obey you. Teach me how to act justly, embrace
faithful love, and walk humbly with you. Amen.

Holy Responsibility

Matthew 25:31-46

Are you an unresponsive goat or a compassionate sheep?

Jesus' teaching in Matthew 25 may startle and surprise. In fact, we may unexpectedly find ourselves on the side of the reluctant, unresponsive goats. I can almost hear our complaints: "Jesus, this must be some mistake! I'm in the wrong place. I should be with the sheep. I've attended church regularly. I've studied the Bible and prayed. I have written checks to numerous causes and organizations."

Our personal holiness is based on how well we see the face of God in one another, especially those who are marginalized. Jesus calls us to make visible Christ's compassion in the world as we provide food, clothing, and housing to those who are the most vulnerable in our community; as we visit the sick and the prisoner; as we love the least loveable; as we show radical hospitality to friend and stranger; and as we give hope to the hopeless by dismantling systems of injustice. God holds us responsible and accountable for our compassionate love for others.

We have all at times been goats, neglecting opportunities to see Christ in the other and to serve compassionately. But we have also at times been sheep. The grace is that we have been given a glimpse of the Kingdom, and we know the standards by which God holds us accountable. So will you be a goat or a sheep?

Merciful Christ, lead me to see your face in others
and to love with your compassion. Amen.

SATURDAY, FEBRUARY 21

Holy Time

Isaiah 61:1-7

What blessings are in the time of the Lord's favor?

Isaiah proclaimed a new age; God's people will receive the Lord's favor. This age ushers in judgment but also blessings. Isaiah announced good news to the poor, hope for the brokenhearted, release to the captives, and liberation for prisoners. Mourners exchange sackcloth and ashes for crowns of beauty, oil of joy, and mantles of praise. God renews and restores deserted places.

Many people in our world live in poverty. Some are financially poor and have little hope for getting out of the vicious cycles of poverty. Others may be rich monetarily but are destitute spiritually, attempting to fill the emptiness in their souls. Some are brokenhearted from life's circumstances or from abuse they have endured. Others are imprisoned, politically oppressed, or psychologically captive to their decisions or addictions. Yet Isaiah promises that the blessings of the Lord's favor will usher in a new life.

God promises to restore and change the lives of God's people so that we can rejoice. The time of the Lord's favor continues! God's blessing is available for all of us. It is our responsibility to receive and accept these blessings. It is our purpose to be ministers who bring forth God's restoration.

Ever-loving God, your time is now!
Fill me with your joyful blessings.
Open my life to share these same
blessings with others. Amen.

Holy Righteousness

Isaiah 61:8-11

How do you prepare for God's righteous presence?

Isaiah declared that at the time of God's favor, the hearts of God's people will be full of joy, and they will be clothed in victory and righteousness like a bridegroom and bride are adorned for their wedding. Just as we prepare for a wedding, Isaiah called the Israelites and us to prepare our hearts to receive God's blessings. We prepare for when others will know of God's love of justice and hate of robbery or dishonesty; persons will be paid fairly; and all persons will be blessed. We prepare for a time when God's righteousness and praise will be known among all the nations.

Recently, the choir at my church sang Chris Tomlin's "Even So, Come." This song reflects on the time of Christ's coming, when we will see justice, newness, and the faithful and true Lord. The song compares the church, ready for Jesus' coming, to a bride "waiting for her groom." We have the promise that God ushers in a new day of righteousness. All of us are inherited by God: claimed, called, and blessed. Our holy purpose is to be ready to receive our King!

How do we, God's people, prepare ourselves to receive God's righteousness? What spiritual practices prepare us to listen, hear, and discern God's call in our lives? How do we receive and witness to God's love and righteousness?

Holy One, I joyfully anticipate your presence.
Open my heart to receive your righteousness. Amen.

Monday, February 23

God's Holy Partners

Luke 4:14-21

How do you proclaim God's love and justice?

In Luke 4, Jesus entered the synagogue in his hometown. This carpenter's son sat among those who had known him as a young boy. Now he sat among them as a teacher. He read aloud from Isaiah 61:1-7 and then announced that he was the Messiah who had come to fulfill this prophecy. Jesus' proclamation was direct and radical. No wonder some who heard him that day wanted to throw him over the cliff.

What does it mean for Jesus to preach good news to the poor, to proclaim release to the prisoners, to recover sight of the blind, to liberate the oppressed, and to proclaim the year of the Lord's favor? Jesus' actions were not to applaud those who were powerful and wealthy but to love and befriend those who were outcast and powerless in the community. Jesus taught a way of justice where all persons are valuable and included. Jesus came to liberate and free all persons from sin by his death on the cross. We are called and challenged to his kind of holiness.

Reflect on the people, experiences, and situations you encountered last week. Consider when you could have acted more faithfully. Ask for God's forgiveness, and commit yourself to radically loving others and acting for justice.

Holy and forgiving God, I commit myself to be your partner
who radically loves others and works for justice. Amen.

TUESDAY, FEBRUARY 24

Brand-New Again

Psalm 104:24-30

How do you experience God's ongoing acts of creation?

When our daughter was born, my husband and I found ourselves on brand-new ground. Our tiny baby was a new creation, and we excitedly embraced our roles as parents. Then, all too quickly, we were attending her graduation from veterinary school and helping her move to another state. I felt sadness and loss; our family life was changing. The house felt empty. Yet while God was moving with our daughter to new ground, God was making "the surface of the ground" my husband and I still lived on "brand-new again."

The psalmist praised God for the things God has done, proclaiming, "The earth is full of your creations." All of God's creations are filled when God's hand is open and terrified when God's face is hidden. Perhaps we have all experienced times when we felt God's face was hidden, but through Christ, we know that God is always with us. God was present at the time of Creation and continues to be a creative presence in the world. As we move, God moves with us. When we feel we have come to a dead end or an empty house, we can trust God's creative work in our lives. God offers us what we need "on time." God continues to "make the surface of the ground brand-new again," covering it with possibility and hope.

Creating God, thank you for the new opportunities and
hope you offer me in each stage of my life. Amen.

WEDNESDAY, FEBRUARY 25
A Prohibition and a Promise

Genesis 3:1-7

How does focusing on God's promise of life help you remain obedient to God?

In Genesis, God created a home for the first man and woman. God gave the first humans a vocation: tending the garden. God instructed, "Eat your fill from all of the garden's trees; but don't eat from the tree of the knowledge of good and evil, because on the day you eat from it, you will die!" (Genesis 2:16-17). There is a blessing in this prohibition, the blessing of life! It might have been worded, "Do not eat from this tree and you will live!" God's plan for creation is life, not death.

When the snake tempted Eve to desire the "delicious food" she saw on the tree, he promised she would gain wisdom by eating this food. The man and woman ate, choosing death over life. Adam and Eve's disobedience destroyed the perfect relationship that had existed between them and God.

Jesus asked his disciples, "Why would people gain the whole world but lose their lives?" (Matthew 16:26). We do not always understand why God sets the boundaries as God does, yet we can be assured that God has our best interests in mind. When we choose the path of obedience, we are choosing the path of life God desires for us.

> Merciful God, help me remain focused
> on you and your promise of life! Amen.

Sent Out of the Garden With Love

Genesis 3:20-24

How do you experience God's love and protection daily?

God's response to Adam and Eve's disobedience may seem harsh, yet God's love for humankind is evident throughout this story. God made clothing for them before sending them out of the garden. God "stationed winged creatures wielding flaming swords to guard the way to the tree of life" to protect them from the temptation to return and eat its fruit. This text clearly shows that only God is immortal, in contrast to humans, who are mortal creatures. God took the human from "the fertile land." Our mortal lives could end as the author of Ecclesiastes suggests, "all are from the dust; all return to the dust" (Ecclesiastes 3:20).

But as followers of Christ, we know that dust is not the future God intends for us. Eternal life is a gift of God's love and grace. It is not something we can attain on our own. When we place our faith in Christ, we accept our mortality and anticipate the gift of everlasting life. Paul wrote, "Since we have been made righteous by his grace, we can inherit the hope for eternal life" (Titus 3:7). Paul assures us that this "hope does not disappoint us" (Romans 5:5, NRSV). God protected the first man and woman from eating the forbidden fruit of the tree of life. Through Christ, God protects us from our sin and offers us salvation.

Loving, merciful God, thank you for the gift of my mortal life and the promise of eternal life through Christ. Amen.

FRIDAY, FEBRUARY 27

Expelled From God's Mountain to Dust

Ezekiel 28:11-19

Have you been tempted to exalt yourself instead of God?

People with a lot of wealth, power, and influence can use these things to help others in significant ways. Yet people often choose instead to exalt themselves, a decision that can bring harmful consequences. The Lord instructed Ezekiel to "sing a lament for the king of Tyre." The king had been "the image of perfection" until he committed the sin of exalting himself instead of God. The king's self-centered interests led to "oppressive business practices" and impurity in the sanctuaries. When the king put his own interests ahead of the interests of his people, he lost everything. God "expelled [him] from God's mountain."

The king of Tyre is depicted as "a winged creature . . . installed as a guardian" on the mountain. This imagery reminds us of the "winged creatures" God stationed "to guard the way to the tree of life" (Genesis 3:24). The king of Tyre became enamored with his "beauty" and "exalted" himself instead of God. He lost his relationship with God, the one who gives and sustains life.

The secular world beckons us to honor ourselves. We are called to give all honor and glory to God. When we do this, God offers us abundant life, here on earth and in God's eternal kingdom.

Eternal God, help me remain focused on you and
live my life in a way that brings honor to you. Amen.

SATURDAY, FEBRUARY 28

Holy Praises

Psalm 146:1-10

What is your spiritual legacy?

When we move from one stage of life to another, we often must discover a new purpose. Sometimes these transitions are easy, while at other times they are difficult. In any case, the psalmist reminds us to sing God's praises. And in every case, we can leave a legacy to those who come behind us.

What does it mean to praise God throughout our entire life? Praising God involves more than joy and glee. It is also the confidence that God remains with us through all our sadness, anger, confusion, happiness, and any other feelings we may have. What does it mean to put our trust in God and not in ourselves or others? God is the ultimate source of our trust. We live out of the promise of Romans 8:38-39 that nothing will separate us from God's love. We move into the future with the assurance that God walks with us.

What is our purpose in God's kingdom? God invites us to join in giving justice to the oppressed, feeding the hungry, freeing the prisoner, restoring health to those who suffer, loving the righteous, protecting the immigrant, caring for the orphan and widow, and turning the ways of the wicked. What a legacy we would leave by doing these things!

Whatever phase of life you're in, how will you spend your time and talents in ways that glorify God?

God of love and justice, I sing your praises
through my words and my actions. Amen.

MARCH

CONTRIBUTORS:

Clara Welch
(March 1–March 29)

Michael Whitcomb-Tavey
(March 30–March 31)

The Tree of Life for Us

Revelation 2:1-7

What helps you endure challenges and hold fast to Christ's love?

The text for this lesson is a letter from Christ to the church in Ephesus. Christ complimented the "works . . . labor, and . . . endurance" of the Ephesian Christians. The letter acknowledges their faithfulness in the midst of challenges, specifically evildoers, false apostles, and persecution. The Ephesian church could not "tolerate evildoers" (verse 2, NRSV), and it did not listen to false apostles who were in truth "liars." The "Nicolaitans" may have been false apostles. The letter does not mention details about the persecution but acknowledges that the church "put up with a lot."

Paul wrote in Galatians 6:9, "So let us not grow weary in doing what is right, for we will reap at harvest time, if we do not give up." The church in Ephesus had "not grown weary" (verse 3, NRSV). In fact, the letter mentions its "endurance" twice. Yet despite these compliments, there is a "But."

On the surface, the Ephesian Christians were doing things right but had "let go of the love" and forgotten "the high point" when they first knew Christ. Have you ever felt this way? Christ called the Ephesian Christians to "change your hearts and lives and do the things you did at first." In other words, we are called to remember Christ's love for us and our love for Christ as we seek to live as faithful followers. When we do this, we will "emerge victorious to eat from the tree of life, which is in God's paradise."

God, let me hold fast to your love so I may eat
from the tree of life in your paradise. Amen.

MONDAY, MARCH 2

God Listens

Psalm 61:1-5

In what ways have you received assurance that God is listening to your prayers?

The psalmist cried out, "God, listen to my cry; pay attention to my prayer!" The author of Psalm 61 had experienced God's action on his behalf in the past as a "refuge, a tower of strength in the face of the enemy." Now he felt separated from God, for he cried out "from the very ends of the earth."

The psalmist's "rock that is higher than I am" refers to a place of refuge. It may have been a reference to God, for God had been "a tower of strength," or it may have been a reference to the temple or another safe place. Psalm 27:5 proclaims that God "will shelter me in his own dwelling during troubling times; he will hide me in a secret place in his own tent; he will set me up high, safe on a rock." The psalmist cried out with confidence that God was listening. He affirmed that God had "heard" and answered his prayer.

In what ways is this psalmist's prayer similar to your prayer? What images would you use to describe how it feels to be separated from God? What images describe the ways God has been a refuge for you in the past? When we are overwhelmed, frightened, or troubled, we long to feel sheltered in God's loving presence. From Old Testament times to the present, God's people have witnessed to the truth that God is listening to us. We can pray with confidence that God will indeed hear and respond to our prayers.

Merciful God, thank you for listening to my prayers and sheltering me in your loving presence. Amen.

TUESDAY, MARCH 3

Jesus Prays for Himself

John 17:1-5

How do you glorify God the Father and Jesus the Son?

At first glance, Jesus' request that God glorify him may seem a little out of character. But even Jesus' request to be glorified was for the sake of others. Jesus accepted the purpose for his life "so that he could give eternal life to everyone [God] gave him." Jesus gives us eternal life through his death and resurrection. After Jesus entered Jerusalem for the Passover Festival, he said, "The time has come for the Human One to be glorified" (John 12:23). He was speaking about the painful death he would endure on the cross, saying, "I assure you that unless a grain of wheat falls into the earth and dies, it can only be a single seed. But if it dies, it bears much fruit . . . This is the reason I have come to this time. Father, glorify your name!" (John 12:24, 27-28). Jesus knew his glorification called for his self-sacrifice. God's glorification of Jesus the Son will call forth the people's praise and worship of God the Father.

The Gospel of John opens with, "In the beginning was the Word and the Word was with God and the Word was God. The Word was with God in the beginning" (John 1:1-2). In this prayer with his disciples, Jesus acknowledged his oneness with the Father, saying, "glorify me in your presence with the glory I shared with you before the world was created."

How do you give glory to the Father and the Son? What opportunities do you have each day to give glory to your Lord and Savior? Do your actions demonstrate Christ's glory?

Holy God, let my words and my actions
bring glory to you every day. Amen.

Jesus Prays for His Disciples

John 17:6-19

How do you feel when you know someone else is praying for you?

When our loved ones go out into the world, we are concerned for them. Whether we are seeing our child off for the first day of kindergarten or the first day of college, we are aware that we will not be with them to protect them. We pray that God will watch over them.

Jesus prayed this prayer on the night he was arrested. He knew his time with his disciples was coming to an end, and he would not be physically present to protect them. Jesus prayed to the Father, "I'm no longer in the world, but they are in the world. . . . When I was with them, I watched over them in your name . . . and I kept them safe." Now Jesus beseeched God to "watch over them in your name, . . . keep them safe from the evil one."

Just as Jesus did not "belong to this world," his disciples did not "belong to this world." They, like Jesus, were "sent . . . into the world" to witness to Christ and make disciples.

Yesterday, we considered Jesus' prayer, "Father, . . . Glorify your Son" (John 17:1). Jesus is glorified through his sacrifice on the cross "so that they also would be made holy." The disciples were "made holy" because "they received . . . and . . . believed" the word of God proclaimed in Jesus. We are "made holy" when we believe the truth of God's word proclaimed in Jesus. We share in Christ's holiness when we follow Jesus' example.

Holy God, thank you for drawing us into a relationship with
you as we pray for others and ourselves. Amen.

Thursday, March 5

Jesus Prays for Those Who Believe in Him

John 17:20-26

How do you respond to Jesus' prayer for his believers, which includes you?

As Jesus looked ahead to the end of his time on earth, he prayed for the people God had given him. He prayed first for his disciples, whom he had "sent . . . into the world" (John 17:18). Then he said, "I'm not praying only for them but also for those who believe in me because of their word." As Jesus faced the cross, he prayed for us! The disciples who had known him during his life on earth responded to his resurrection with a powerful witness. Believers through the generations have continued to witness to the truth of God's word and make disciples of Jesus Christ.

Jesus prayed for a continuing relationship with God's people after his earthly life. He prayed, "I want those you gave me to be with me where I am." He prayed that God's people would see his glory, know God's love, and experience oneness with God and Christ. Jesus also promised to continue to be involved in the life of God's people, saying, "I've made your name known to them and will continue to make it known so that your love for me will be in them, and I myself will be in them."

When we accept the call to make disciples for Jesus Christ, we invest ourselves in the lives of others. We share the love of Christ with our families, the people in our churches and communities, and with others God places in our path.

Holy and ever-present God, thank you for
inviting me to be one with you in Christ. Amen.

"Not What I Want"

Matthew 26:36-39

How do you pray in times of suffering?

After the Last Supper, "Jesus went with his disciples to a place called Gethsemane" on the Mount of Olives, a place where they had gathered before. On this night, Jesus prayed a difficult prayer. Jesus knew his time to finish his work on earth had come, and "he began to feel sad and anxious." Other translations read "grieved and agitated" (NRSV); "sorrowful and troubled" (NIV); "sorrowful and very heavy" (KJV). Jesus said, "I'm very sad. It's as if I'm dying." Other translations read, "I am deeply grieved" (NRSV); "overwhelmed with sorrow" (NIV); "exceeding sorrowful" (KJV).

These are strong emotions. We find comfort in knowing that when we experience these emotions, Jesus knows exactly how we feel. Jesus prayed, "If it's possible, take this cup of suffering away from me." We pray similar prayers as we ask God to take away the causes of our suffering. It takes courage to continue our prayer as Jesus prayed, "However—not what I want but what you want."

God did not take away Jesus' cup of suffering. God gave Jesus all that he needed to stay the course. The result was life! Life for Jesus as our risen Christ and eternal life for us as redeemed children of God. God gives us all that we need to endure suffering. When we trust God's loving and faithful presence, we experience new life in Christ, even in the midst of suffering.

Merciful God, thank you for your faithful love that sustains me through times of suffering. Amen.

SATURDAY, MARCH 7

"Let It Be What You Want"

Matthew 26:40-46

How have you prayed about the difficult things you felt God calling you to do?

Jesus prayed three times that the Father, if possible, take away his cup of suffering (Matthew 26:39, 42, 44). We hear the plea in his words: "Take this cup of suffering away from me." Do we also detect a question, "Is there not another way?"

Jesus made his plea three times. Have you ever done that? Have you ever asked, just one more time, with the hope that the answer will be different? We noted in yesterday's reading that it took courage for Jesus to pray his next words, and again, he prayed them three times: "However—not what I want but what you want" (verse 39); "then let it be what you want" (verse 42); "he . . . prayed the same words for the third time" (verse 44).

God's will was for Jesus to respond faithfully to fulfill God's call for his life. It is God's will that we remain faithful in the face of suffering and hardship. God wants us to trust God for the courage, strength, and wisdom we need when the road ahead of us is frightening and difficult.

When we are suffering, we can cry out to God as Jesus did. We may never understand why suffering is part of our lives, yet we can always trust God to be with us. We are called to follow the example of Jesus and place our faith in God every day through all circumstances.

Loving and faithful God, thank you for remaining
awake and listening to my prayers. Thank you for
your faithful presence every day of my life. Amen.

Divine Strength

Luke 22:39-43

When has God given you the strength to face a frightening or difficult experience?

On the night of his arrest, Jesus shared his last supper with his disciples. He broke bread with them and shared the cup, saying: "This is my body, which is given for you. . . . This cup is the new covenant by my blood, which is poured out for you" (Luke 22:19-20). Jesus' time of ministry on earth was behind him, and the cross was before him. He went to the Mount of Olives and prayed.

Our hearts go out to our Savior as we read, "He was in anguish and prayed even more earnestly" (verse 44). We can only imagine what the disciples were thinking and feeling. While they did not fully understand until after the Resurrection, they had been Jesus' companions in ministry for three years. Luke says they were "overcome by grief."

God did not take away Jesus' "cup of suffering." God also did not leave Jesus to endure his suffering alone, for "a heavenly angel appeared to him and strengthened him." It is interesting that Luke records that the angel strengthened Jesus before Jesus "prayed even more earnestly."

We learn from Jesus the importance of honest prayer. We can ask God to strengthen us to express our heartfelt anguish and fear in prayer. We can trust that God will hear us and give us all that we need to face challenges and suffering that may be before us.

Grant me strength, O Lord, to pray my deepest anguish
to you, trusting that you will hear my prayer. Amen.

MONDAY, MARCH 9

Water in the Wilderness

Exodus 17:1-7

When have you asked, "Is the Lord with me or not?"

After escaping Egypt, the Israelites "traveled for three days in the desert and found no water. When they came to Marah, they couldn't drink Marah's water because it was bitter. . . Moses cried out to the LORD, and the LORD pointed out a tree to him. He threw it into the water, and the water became sweet" (Exodus 15:22-23, 25). God provided water and tested the faith of the Israelites, calling them to obedience.

In this text from Exodus 17, the availability of water is again the issue. Instead of trusting God, "the people argued with Moses" and demanded water. Notice the turn in Moses' question back to them: "Why are you testing the LORD?" God had "tested" the Israelites' faith by calling them to obedience. Now the people were "testing" God's faithfulness to provide for them.

Have you ever wondered if God was testing you? Have you ever felt that you were testing God, waiting to see if God would indeed remain faithful?

God promises to provide healing for our suffering. Healing may not come in the form or the time frame we hope for. Healing may not come in this lifetime but in the promise of eternal life in. God remained faithful to the Israelites despite their testing and arguing, and God remains faithful to us. God faithfully provides water in the desert and everything else we need as we journey ahead in faith.

Healing God, help me remain faithful and
obedient even in times of great thirst. Amen.

Faithfully Facing Fear

Numbers 14:1-4

What helps you face your fear and step into the unknown with faith?

The Israelites found the report of "powerful people" inhabiting the Promised Land to be alarming. Caleb said, "We must go up and take possession of it, because we are more than able to do it" (Numbers 13:30). The men who accompanied Caleb on the scouting expedition did not share his confidence and said, "We can't go up against the people because they are stronger than we are" (13:31). Unfortunately, the Israelites gave in to fear and rebelled against God and Moses, saying, "Let's pick a leader and let's go back to Egypt" (Numbers 14:4).

We can't blame them for being afraid. In their minds, they were making a choice between suffering at the hands of unknown inhabitants in an unknown land and suffering at the hand of the Egyptians in a land that was familiar to them. On the other hand, they had experienced God's faithful love many times over. Why could they not trust God to take them safely into the Land of Promise? They allowed their fear of suffering in the unknown to overpower their faith in God.

We may at times be tempted to accept familiar suffering rather than step into the unknown. When God offers us new opportunities, God promises to be with us through our fear. God calls us to step out in faith and trust God's promises.

> Faithful God, help me to trust you when you
> call me to new opportunities. Let my faith in
> you be stronger than my fear. Amen.

WEDNESDAY, MARCH 11

Rebelling Against God

Psalm 78:12-22

When have you been tempted to rebel against God?

Psalm 78 was written so that future generations "will know these things . . . to put their hope in God—never forgetting God's deeds, but keeping God's commandments—and so that they won't become like their ancestors: a rebellious, stubborn generation, . . . whose heart wasn't set firm and whose spirit wasn't faithful to God." The text for today's reading begins with recalling the "wonders" or plagues God inflicted on the Egyptians that influenced Pharaoh to let them go. The psalmist listed the ways God provided for the Israelites' needs in the wilderness and then declared the Israelites' disobedient response, "but they continued to sin against God, rebelling against the Most High in the desert." They sinned and rebelled "because they had no faith in God, because they didn't trust his saving power."

We live in a broken and imperfect world, and sometimes we experience suffering and challenges. We have the same choice the Israelites had: We can blame God, or we can trust God's presence and provision in all circumstances. When we find it hard to trust God, we can count our blessings of God's faithfulness in the past. We can seek out Christian friends who will support and encourage us. An ancient psalmist declared, "Because God's faithful love toward us is strong, the LORD's faithfulness lasts forever!" (Psalm 117:2). This is a truth we want to remember and share!

> Ever-present God, help me remember that your faithfulness is forever and that I can trust you to provide for my needs in all circumstances. Amen.

Craving More

Psalm 78:23-30

How much is enough?

The author of Psalm 78 proclaimed God's mighty acts of delivering Israel from bondage and providing for the people's needs in the wilderness (verses 12-16). But Israel lacked "trust" in God's "saving power" (verses 17-22). After God answered the people's cry for water, they did not respond with words of thanksgiving but with more demanding questions: "Can he give bread too? Can he provide meat for his people?" (verse 20). Despite their unfaithfulness, "God gave them exactly what they had craved."

Exodus recorded, "Then the LORD said to Moses, 'I'm going to make bread rain down from the sky for you. The people will go out each day and gather just enough for that day' " (Exodus 16:4). The psalmist reported that they "were completely satisfied." But instead of thanking God, "they didn't stop craving." The object of their craving was their own self-satisfaction and not God's will.

God desires a relationship with the people, so much so that God never gave up on the Israelites and even gave the Son for our salvation. Deep down, don't we long for a relationship with God? We can trust God to give us "enough" of what we need, whether it be courage, wisdom, sustenance, comfort, or something else. We can also share with God our craving for "more," more time in prayer, more ways to offer our praise and thanksgiving, more awareness of God's presence and faithful love.

> Holy God, thank you for providing "enough" and for
> answering my longing for more of your love. Amen.

Friday, March 13

The Bronze Snake

Numbers 21:4-9

Where do you look for God's healing?

In this text from Numbers, we see that the Israelites were at it again, complaining about the lack of water and food in the desert. We know that God did provide food and water, yet the Israelites were not thankful for the simple sustenance and declared, "We detest this miserable bread."

This time, "the LORD sent poisonous snakes" with a deadly bite. The Israelites confessed their sin and asked Moses to pray for God to "send the snakes away from us." God did not "send the snakes away." Instead, God offered healing from the venomous bite.

When we face hard times, it is natural that we pray for God to remove the cause of our suffering. We know, however, that while God does not always remove the source, God provides help and healing in countless ways. God grants comfort in the midst of grief, courage to face surgeries and medical treatments, and guidance to face uncertain paths.

Where do you look when you need to be reminded of God's healing power? For these Israelites in the wilderness, it was to a pole holding the likeness of a poisonous snake. For us, it may be the cross in a church, the beauty of God's creation, a memory of God's past faithfulness, or the Bible on our bedside table. Evidence of God's faithful love and presence is all around us. All we need to do is place our faith in God and "look."

God of healing and hope, thank you for always
responding faithfully to my need. Amen..

SATURDAY, MARCH 14

"How Are These Things Possible?"

John 3:9-15

How have you experienced heavenly things you don't understand?

Nicodemus was not so quick to dismiss Jesus. He went to Jesus privately and stated what he had seen, "Rabbi, we know that you are a teacher who has come from God, for no one could do these miraculous signs that you do unless God is with him" (John 3:2). Jesus knew Nicodemus was searching and he responded by saying, "Unless someone is born anew, it's not possible to see God's kingdom" (John 3:3). Nicodemus questioned how it was possible to be born a second time. Even after Jesus' explanation, Nicodemus was confused. He asked again, "How are these things possible?"

Jesus recalled a symbol from the Israelites' history that Nicodemus would be familiar with: the snake that "Moses lifted up . . . in the wilderness." Jesus stated that he, too, would "be lifted up." The snake represented God's healing power for the ancient Israelites. Jesus' death on the cross is a visible sign of God's healing power and the promise of "eternal life" for "everyone who believes in him."

Where have you seen "miraculous signs" and glimpses of "God's kingdom" on earth? Perhaps you have witnessed healing, an answer to prayer, or "the peace of God that exceeds all understanding" (Philippians 4:7) after giving your worries to God. "How are these things possible?" They are possible through "God's Spirit" and Jesus Christ, who was "lifted up" for us.

> Loving God, thank you for the promise of eternal life
> through Christ, who was "lifted up" for me. Amen.

The Wilderness Generation

1 Corinthians 10:1-13

How does the faithfulness of former generations help you remain faithful?

The manna and water that nourished the people in the wilderness were real food and drink they could touch and taste. Paul called them "spiritual food" and "spiritual drink" because God provided them. This bread and water, like "the cloud," reminded the people of God's presence. We are reminded of the bread and juice of Holy Communion, real food and drink that symbolize Christ's presence. With this in mind, Paul wrote that the spiritual rock that provided water "was Christ."

Paul's tone quickly changed in verse 5 when he recalled the disobedience of the wilderness generation. He warned the church in Corinth not to "crave evil things . . . worship false gods . . . practice sexual immorality . . . test Christ," or "grumble." For the wilderness generation the penalty for these sins was death.

The Corinthian Christians faced the temptations of idolatry and faithlessness. Paul encouraged them to trust God to "supply a way out so that you will be able to endure it." God remained faithful to the wilderness generation, and the Israelites who remained obedient entered the Promised Land. Through Christ, God provides a way for us to enter God's kingdom. God is present with us and supplies what we need to resist temptation and remain faithful.

Thank you, God, for your eternal faithfulness
to each generation. Supply me with what I
need to follow you. Amen.

Do Not Follow the Way of Sinners

Proverbs 1:10-17

What helps you remain focused on following the way of God?

In Proverbs 1, the Hebrew word for "sinners" may also be translated "one who misses the mark." In this context, sin is "to miss the mark" of being who God calls us to be. The message is simple: "Don't let sinners entice you. Don't go when they say: Come with us." The sinners' goal is twofold: (1) to have "fun," causing the "innocent" to suffer and (2) stealing "wealth" and "money." These sinners do not obey God's commandment to love. They seek to satisfy their self-centered cravings at the expense of others. The author voices the instruction again, "keep your feet from their way, because their feet run to evil."

We "miss the mark" when we follow the way of sinners. We "hit the bull's-eye" when we follow the way of God. We know that only Jesus was able to follow God's way perfectly. To borrow imagery from archery, there will be times when we don't quite hit the bull's-eye, and sometimes we may miss the target altogether! But when we place our faith in God and crave God's will for our lives, we can trust God's forgiveness when we miss. We can look to God for guidance and know that our lives are secure in God's faithful love.

Loving God, steady my aim and guide me as
I follow your way for my life. Amen.

TUESDAY, MARCH 17

Vacant, Cleaned, Decorated

Matthew 12:43-45

How do you keep sin from moving into your life?

Jesus told a parable about "when an unclean spirit leaves a person." The "unclean spirit" in this parable represents sin. Just as weeds can return and take over a cleared garden plot, sin can return and reclaim a person's life. In Jesus' story, the unclean spirit "wanders through dry places looking for a place to rest." Finding none, it returns to its former dwelling. The unclean spirit must have been delighted to find the home was not only "vacant" but also "cleaned up and decorated." It moves back in bringing "with it seven other spirits more evil than itself." We can imagine the unclean spirits making the dwelling a party house for sin, while the "person is worse off at the end than at the beginning."

John the Baptist announced, "Change your hearts and lives! Here comes the kingdom of heaven!" (Matthew 3:2). It is not enough to rid our lives of sin. We must change our "hearts and lives" and fill our "house" (Matthew 12:44) with love for God and neighbor. When we do this, our practices, including generosity and prayer, become genuine expressions of our devotion to God.

Just as we must tend a flower garden to keep out the weeds and encourage healthy plant growth, we must tend our hearts and lives to keep out sin and grow in our relationship with God. If the person in Jesus' parable had done this, the unclean spirit would have found a No Vacancy sign when it returned to its former dwelling.

Merciful God, help me clean my heart of sin and
fill my heart with love for you. Amen.

Joyful Endurance

James 1:2-4, 13-15

In what ways have you relied on God to help you endure hardship and temptation?

When my husband was diagnosed with cancer, I did not respond with joy! I remember crying and feeling frightened. As my husband and I persevered through medical center hallways and the frightening world of cancer and treatments, we trusted God to be with us. We felt our ability to endure grow stronger as we continued to look to God to help us.

The Greek noun for "test" in this passage has two meanings. In verse 2, it signifies an external hardship. We are all faced with external hardships that can range in scope from minor inconveniences to major crises. James instructs us to view these hardships "as occasions for joy" because "the testing of your faith produces endurance."

In verse 13, James has another meaning in mind for the Greek word "test": an inner impulse to evil. James was quick to say that this is not from God. The source of this temptation is a person's "own cravings" to fulfill his or her self-centered desires.

God is the source of "every good [and] perfect gift," and God's "character" never changes. God does not test or tempt us with evil. Instead, God promises to be with us through all that we face. When we place our faith in God, we find the courage to turn away from sin and the strength to endure every hardship. Our faith grows stronger as God remains with us through these challenges.

Merciful God, we thank you for your continuing
faithfulness and your gift of joy, even in hardship. Amen

Thursday, March 19

Not by Bread Alone

Deuteronomy 8:1-10

How do your experiences of God's faithfulness help you continue to walk in God's ways?

God spoke a promise to the Israelites: God would bring them "to a wonderful land" where there would be no shortage of food and no lack of anything. Yet at times, the Israelites lost faith and sinned, disobeying God.

This text does not say we do not need bread to live. When speaking about food and clothing, Jesus said, "Your heavenly Father knows that you need them" (Matthew 6:32). The text says that to live the life God desires for us, we also need God's Word. God's Word calls us to obedience so we may know God's blessings. God's commandment instructs us in the way we are to live with God and one another. God's Word calls us to depend on God and to trust God's promises of presence, provision, healing, and hope.

Moses encouraged the people to "remember the long road on which the Lord your God led you during these forty years in the desert so he could humble you, testing you to find out what was in your heart: whether you would keep his commandments or not." Moses offered assurance that God would indeed fulfill the promise. During challenging times, we may concern ourselves with our physical needs and forget to listen to God. When we open our hearts to God, we often find that it is in the midst of trying times that we experience God's grace and love more deeply.

Loving and faithful God, help me live according to what
you say to me. Thank you for your abundant gifts of
mercy and love, figs and honey. Amen.

FRIDAY, MARCH 20

The Lord Is Present and Passionate

Deuteronomy 6:10-19

What helps you continue to revere and serve the Lord when you are tempted to turn away?

When we have a change in circumstances, we may find ourselves facing a whole new set of temptations that can draw us away from God. God called Moses to lead the people out of bondage and through the wilderness. God also called Moses to prepare the people for their new life in the Promised Land. In this text, Moses warns the Israelites of the new temptations they will face in the land God promised.

Moses said, "Watch yourself! Don't forget." The Israelites would find established towns, well-stocked houses, and an abundance of food in the new land. These would be welcome changes after their wilderness journey. They would need to remember that these gifts of stability and abundance were from God and not the fruit of their own labor.

Moses warned that they would also encounter "other gods . . . of the people around you." He told them, "The LORD your God, who is with you and among you, is a passionate God." Today's "other gods," such as wealth, power, and popularity, are not "passionate" for us. Do we want to devote our lives to things that care nothing for us?

Moses called the people to "Revere . . . serve . . . and take . . . solemn pledges in [God's] name." In these ways, they would show their allegiance to the Lord. In what ways do you show your gratitude and loyalty to our ever-present and passionate Lord?

Thank you, God, for living among us and remaining with us.
Thank you for your steadfast love. Amen.

SATURDAY, MARCH 21

One Who Is Tempted as We Are

Hebrews 4:11-16

How do you find comfort in knowing that Jesus can "sympathize" with your weakness?

We may wonder if the Israelite wilderness generation would have behaved differently if they had known the story of their failure would be repeated to future generations. The author of Hebrews references Psalm 95: "So, as the Holy Spirit says, Today, if you hear his voice, don't have stubborn hearts as they did in the rebellion, on the day when they tested me in the desert. . . . Because of my anger I swore: 'They will never enter my rest!'" (Hebrews 3:7-8, 11). By "rest," the author means the ability to rest in God today and our future hope of eternal rest in glory.

As Christians, we make daily choices about our obedience to God. Hebrews points out that there can be no fudging on our part because of "God's word." Humans cannot hide any disobedience from God "because God's word is living [and] active." God's word "penetrates" and judges "the heart's thoughts and intentions."

The author of Hebrews offers encouragement, reminding us that Jesus also faced temptation and can "sympathize with our weaknesses." Just as God remained faithful to the Israelites and led them into the Land of Promise, God remains faithful to us. Through Jesus, "we can receive mercy and find grace when we need help." God sees our disobedience. God also sees our struggle and repentance and responds with mercy and grace.

Thank you, God, for your mercy and grace. Help me align
my thoughts and intentions with your will. Amen.

Jesus Faithfully Resists Temptation

Matthew 4:1-11

How does Jesus' experience of temptation in the wilderness help you remain faithful?

We, like the Israelites, are tempted to turn away from God's will. We find comfort in knowing Jesus understands our temptation firsthand.

The tempter tested Jesus' obedience to God in three ways. First, knowing Jesus "was starving," he told Jesus to perform a miracle and create bread for himself instead of trusting God to provide for his physical needs. Second, the tempter told Jesus to "throw" himself off "the highest point of the temple" to test God's promise of protection. Third, the tempter offered Jesus worldly kingdoms and glory in exchange for Jesus' worship.

Jesus resisted the tempter's demands and quoted God's instructions: "People won't live only by bread, but by every word spoken by God"; "Don't test the Lord your God"; "You will worship the Lord your God and serve only him."

It is hard to resist temptation. Sometimes we may feel too weak. Sometimes the pull to satisfy our selfish desires and embrace the world's values is strong. Jesus experienced these same temptations and knows how we feel. When we share our struggles in prayer, we are pouring out our hearts to one who has walked this road before us. We trust God to provide us with courage and strength so we may follow Jesus' example and resist the tempter's influence.

Holy God, thank you for Jesus, who lived among us
and knows the temptations we face. Help me follow
his example and remain faithful. Amen.

Editor's Note for March 23–27

Devotions for this week use Scriptures from the end of 2 Kings. There is a lot of history in these books, and it can get confusing. To help clarify, here is an abbreviated summary of the end of Israel and Judah's monarchies.

In 931 BC, after the death of King Solomon, the kingdom was divided into two nations: Israel in the North and Judah in the South. Judah kept to the Davidic dynasty with the coronation of Solomon's son, Rehoboam, as well as maintaining Jerusalem as the capital, complete with the Temple. Israel crowned Jeroboam their new king.

Neither kingdom remained faithful to the covenant of God, and the Lord sent several prophets to speak warnings against these nations, including Elijah, Elisha, Isaiah, and Jeremiah. Nevertheless, with only two exceptions, the kings of Israel and Judah refused to listen, choosing to do what was right in their own eyes and seek power in political and military alliances with bordering nations.

Israel was conquered by Assyria and taken into exile in 722 BC. These are the "lost tribes" of Israel, which were never restored. Babylon conquered Assyria in 612 BC then set its eyes on Judah. Judah became a vassal state for Babylon under King Jehoiakim. Relying on untrustworthy alliances, Jehoiakim rebelled against Babylon in 601 BC and was taken captive. When King Zedekiah likewise rebelled against Babylon, King Nebuchadnezzar laid siege to Jerusalem from 588 BC until Jerusalem's fall in 586 BC. Judah was subsequently left desolate, almost all its people taken into captivity or fled. Judah and Jerusalem would not be restored until 537 BC, after Persia conquered Babylon.

Trouble in the Promised Land

2 Kings 23:34–24:7

When have you witnessed pain and loss that occurred as a result of sin?

After Israel fell to Assyria in 722 BC, the kingdom of Judah was ruled by two kings who "did what was right in the LORD's eyes" (2 Kings 18:3, 22:2): Hezekiah (715-687 BC) and Josiah (640-609 BC). Unfortunately, two kings who "did what was evil in the LORD's eyes" (2 Kings 21:2, 20), Manasseh and Amon, ruled between them. Manasseh was so evil that "the LORD didn't turn away from the great rage that burned against Judah on account of all that Manasseh had done to make him angry. The LORD said, 'I will remove Judah from my presence just as I removed Israel'" (2 Kings 23:26-27).

King Josiah died in battle against the Egyptians, and his son Jehoahaz was anointed king. Pharaoh Neco took Jehoahaz prisoner, "imposed a fine on the land" (2 Kings 23:33), and made Jehoiakim king. Unlike his father, Josiah, Jehoiakim "did what was evil in the LORD's eyes." He submitted to Pharaoh Neco and then to Babylon's King Nebuchadnezzar. When he later rebelled, the Lord was not with him "on account of all the sins that Manasseh had committed" (2 Kings 24:3). When Jehoiakim died, the nation of Babylon controlled the Promised Land.

Sin has painful consequences and leaves us feeling separated from God. Yet sin does not need to be the end of our story. God accepts our true repentance and forgives us.

Merciful Lord, thank you for your forgiveness.
Help me do what is right in your eyes. Amen.

Leaving the Promised Land

2 Kings 24:8-17

When have you or someone you know experienced closed doors and lost opportunities because of sin?

Judah lost the Promised Land after Josiah's death. First, Pharaoh Neco took control, then "King Nebuchadnezzar of Babylon attacked" (2 Kings 24:1). Jehoiakim "submitted to him for three years" (verse 1) before rebelling. After Jehoiakim died, his son Jehoiachin became king. Three months into his reign, "the officers of Babylon's King Nebuchadnezzar attacked Jerusalem and laid siege to the city." Jehoiachin surrendered. King Nebuchadnezzar exiled King Jehoiachin's family and "all the officials, all the military leaders," as well as skilled soldiers, workers, and tradespeople. Only the "poorest of the land's people" were left behind.

The people of Judah associated God's presence with the Temple in Jerusalem. To their way of thinking, they were losing land and God's presence when they were exiled to Babylon. What were they thinking as they walked away from Jerusalem to an unknown land? Were they remembering God's promises? Were they remorseful about their sin against God?

Sinful actions can lead to broken relationships and lost opportunities. This text from 2 Kings 24 does not include words of hope. We will see, however, that God did not turn forever from God's people. With God, there is always hope!

Holy Lord, "Cast me not away from thy presence. . . .
Restore unto me the joy of thy salvation"
(Psalm 51:11-12, KJV). Amen.

Judah's Last King

2 Kings 24:18–25:7

What do you do with undeserved second chances?

King Zedekiah followed in the footsteps of Jehoiakim and Jehoiachin and "did what was evil in the LORD's eyes." He refused to turn his heart and the hearts of the people of Judah back to the Lord. He ignored the prophets until he wanted something from God.

Zedekiah rebelled against Babylon, believing the Egyptian army would help him. Zedekiah sent messengers to the prophet Jeremiah with a plea for the Lord: "Please pray for us to the LORD our God" (Jeremiah 37:3). The Lord's response was not what Zedekiah wanted to hear: "Pharaoh's army that came to assist you is heading back to Egypt. The Babylonians will return and attack this city. They will capture it and burn it down" (Jeremiah 37:7-8). Zedekiah was captured, forced to witness his sons' death, and taken away in chains.

God wanted Israel to honor God as their king. Before granting their request for a human king, God warned them of the risks (1 Samuel 8). Most kings of Israel and Judah did not obey the first commandment, "You must have no other gods before me" (Deuteronomy 5:7) or the commandment to "love the LORD your God with all your heart, all your being, and all your strength" (Deuteronomy 6:5). Still today, we see the suffering that occurs when these commandments are broken. What helps you remain obedient to the commands to love and honor God? How can you encourage others to remain faithful to God?

> Loving God, I offer you my undivided worship
> and my faithful love. Amen.

THURSDAY, MARCH 26
Destruction, Desolation, Departure

2 Kings 25:8-21

When have you felt separated from God?

King Solomon oversaw the building of the Temple and the palace in Jerusalem. He started construction of the Temple 480 years "after the Israelites left Egypt" and "built it in seven years" (1 Kings 6:1, 38). Solomon also oversaw the work of making all the equipment for the Temple. God said, "Regarding this temple that you are building: If you follow my laws, enact my regulations, and keep all my commands faithfully, then I will fulfill for you my promise that I made to your father David. I will live among the Israelites. I won't abandon my people Israel" (1 Kings 6:11-13).

After Zedekiah was exiled, the commander of the Babylonian guard, Nebuzaradan, was given the task of destroying Jerusalem, including the palace, Temple, and Temple equipment. If any of the exiles looked back as they were being forced to leave, they saw their Promised Land and the Holy City in ruins, smoldering and desolate.

When the Temple was built, God promised to live among the people if they faithfully obeyed God's commands. The people chose to distance themselves from God through their disobedience. As a result, God was distanced from the people by sending them away from the Promised Land. Did the exiles see any hope for reconciliation? We read this story as post-Resurrection Christians. We know that, yes, God offers us opportunities for repentance and reconciliation with God.

God of hope, thank you for offering me the
gift of reconciliation with you. Amen.

Undeserved Mercy

2 Kings 25:22-30

When have you experienced mercy and compassion?

Before fleeing to Egypt, the Judean leadership asked Jeremiah to pray on their behalf, saying, "May the LORD your God show us where we should go and what we should do" (Jeremiah 42:3). Jeremiah prayed, then shared God's word: "If you live in this land, I will build you up. . . . I will be merciful to you" (Jeremiah 42:10, 12). They didn't trust this promise of mercy. They "departed for Egypt because they were afraid of the Chaldeans," despite God's warning that they would "die by the sword, famine, and disease" (Jeremiah 42:17).

But do we detect a glimmer of hope? Nebuchadnezzar's son freed Judah's king Jehoiachin and treated him with kindness. Did this mean God had not forgotten God's people and that their suffering in exile would end? Perhaps the exiles remembered God's promise to David: "Your throne will be established forever" (2 Samuel 7:16). Perhaps they found hope in the prophetic words in Deuteronomy: "The LORD will scatter you among the nations. . . . You will seek the LORD your God from there, and you will find him . . . you will obey his voice. . . . God is a compassionate God. He won't let you go" (Deuteronomy 4:27, 29-31).

As we observe our world today, we see the suffering that occurs when people follow their way instead of God's way. We, like the exiles of Israel and Judah, may find hope in the prophetic words of Deuteronomy: God is compassionate and won't let us go. When we seek God, we will find God

> Merciful God, forgive me for rebelling against your will.
> Thank you for your compassion. Amen.

SATURDAY, MARCH 28

An End in Sight

2 Chronicles 36:17-21

How have you experienced God's gifts of hope and rest?

Leviticus 26 describes the blessings the people will receive if they live faithfully (verses 1-13) and the punishments they will endure if they disobey (verses 14-39). One of the punishments was exile and the devastation of their land. God said, "While it is devastated and you are in enemy territory, the land will enjoy its sabbaths. . . . it will have the rest it didn't have during the sabbaths you lived in it" (verses 34-35). Second Chronicles 36 reports that during Judah's exile, "the land finally enjoyed its sabbath rest" (verse 21).

The prophet Jeremiah spoke God's word of hope concerning the Exile, saying, "These nations will serve the king of Babylon for seventy years" (Jeremiah 25:11). God also said through Jeremiah, "When Babylon's seventy years are up, I will come and fulfill my gracious promise to bring you back to this place" (Jeremiah 29:10). Second Chronicles 2:20 was written after the nation of Persia conquered Babylon and the exiles had been allowed to return home. The writer mentions the fulfillment of Jeremiah's prophecy and the completion of the "seventy years."

God's words to the exiles bring comfort to us today: "I know the plans I have in mind for you, declares the LORD; they are plans for peace, not disaster, to give you a future filled with hope" (Jeremiah 29:11). We do not always know how long a time of suffering or trial will last, but we can trust God's promise of hope and rest in God's steadfast love.

Thank you, God, for your promise of hope
and your steadfast love. Amen.

Like the Garden of Eden

Ezekiel 36:33-38

What images symbolize hope for you?

After the people of Judah were exiled to Babylon, the Promised Land "seemed a wasteland to all who passed by." Ezekiel proclaimed to the people in exile that God would cleanse the people of their guilt and "cause the cities to be inhabited." God would allow the people to return, to rebuild, and to farm, so the desolate land would "become like the garden of Eden." God would allow the people to repopulate the land and increase so they would again be "the holy flock" God initially called them to be. In this way, God would show "the house of Israel" and "the nations" that God is the Lord.

We find many symbols of hope in a garden, especially in the spring. For God's people in exile, "the garden of Eden" was a symbol of hope. Isaiah prophesied, "The LORD will comfort Zion; he will comfort all her ruins. He will make her desert like Eden and her wilderness like the LORD's garden" (Isaiah 51:3). Garden imagery is included in descriptions of heaven in the Book of Revelation. Christ promises, "The tree of life . . . is in God's paradise" (Revelation 2:7).

Just as God delivered the people from exile and brought new life to their devastated land, God delivers us from our times of suffering and offers us new life with new opportunities. Where do you see signs of God's healing and hope? How have you experienced God's merciful love and faithfulness?

> Holy and merciful God, thank you for beautiful
> gardens and your amazing gift of hope. Amen.

MONDAY, MARCH 30

All Alone?

Psalm 22:1-11

How do your feelings affect the perception of your reality? How do they shape your beliefs?

When we think that feelings or circumstances are an indicator of our standing with God, then we can erroneously assume that God has abandoned us when those feelings or circumstances seem to indicate such. David seems to suggest that he went through a similar experience. According to verses 1-2 and 6-8, David felt abandoned by God because of the difficult circumstances in which he found himself.

However, according to verses 3-5 and 9-10, David recognized that, despite his personal feelings, God had not abandoned him. David rightly recognizes that God is holy. In verses 4-5, David makes an implicit statement regarding God's trustworthiness, explaining that God has proved to be trustworthy in the past. He states that his ancestors trusted God, and in their despair, God delivered them. Regardless of the many circumstances in which David found himself or the feelings associated with those circumstances, he knew that God was with him. God had not forgotten or abandoned him.

Such a message is informative for our walk with God. God is a redemptive God. God's salvation, enacted on the cross, proves that God has neither abandoned us nor forsaken us. That reality stands true no matter our circumstances or feelings. Be encouraged. God has not forsaken you!

Dear Lord, there are times in my life in which I feel
as though you have abandoned me. However, I know
that you have not. Thank you. Amen.

God Is Faithful

Psalm 22:12-18

How did God respond to Jesus' death on the cross?

Although this psalm does not explicitly point to the cross, we draw comparisons between it and the Christ event. For example, verses 14 and 17 recall for us the suffering Jesus endured during his flogging and his subsequent carrying of the cross (Matthew 27:24-26, 31). The Romans had no set limit for a scourging, so it is quite possible that during the flogging, Jesus' muscles and bones were exposed.

When Jesus uttered, "My God, my God, why have you left me?" (Matthew 27:46), he was pointing to this psalm, which begins with that same thought. People sometimes think these words indicate that God forsook Jesus on the cross due to humankind's sins. However, standard Jewish practice was to use one or two lines from a passage of Scripture to point to the entirety of that passage. Thus, in this case, Jesus was pointing to the entirety of Psalm 22. Considering that verse 24 is an affirmation of God's faithfulness when the afflicted cried out to God, Jesus' words affirm God's faithfulness toward him rather than God's rejection of him. As such, Jesus' words declare victory over his oppressors who brutally tortured and crucified him. Psalm 22 begins with despair but ends with God's faithfulness. This Holy Week, I encourage you to reflect on Psalm 22 as a psalm of victory, not defeat.

Dear God, you are faithful. Even in the midst
of what appeared to be the ultimate defeat,
Jesus was victorious. Praise God! Amen.

APRIL

CONTRIBUTORS:

*Michael Whitcomb-Tavey
(April 1–April 26)*

*Sue Mink
(April 27–April 30)*

Direct Access

Hebrews 9:1-12

What grants you access to God?

The Tabernacle represented God's presence among the people. The Tabernacle had three parts, each representing closer access to God. First, was the outer court, which any Israelite could enter. Next, was the inner court. Only priests had access to this location. Then came the "Most Holy Place," which represented the closest point of contact with God, otherwise known as the "dwelling place of the Most High." Only the high priest had access to this part of the Tabernacle. A curtain covered the entrance into this location, separating it from the inner and outer courts. As such, only the high priest had direct access to God.

Jesus changed all that, however. Hebrews 9:11-12 describes Christ "securing our deliverance for all time." The fallible high priests before him had to make continual sacrifices on behalf of the people. These sacrifices were imperfect. Christ, the perfect High Priest, offered himself as the perfect sacrifice for the sins of humanity. This sacrifice was so perfect, so complete, that there is now no need for any further sacrifices. Moreover, due to this perfect sacrifice, the sanctuary curtain was torn in two (Matthew 27:45-51). From that point on, nothing excludes access to the "Most Holy Place" for the people of God. All of God's people now have direct access to God's dwelling place. Therefore, all of God's people, due to the sacrifice of Christ, can have a close and intimate relationship with God.

Dear God, thanks to Christ, I have access to you. I have a relationship with you. Thank you. Amen.

MAUNDY THURSDAY, APRIL 2
Insulted and Taunted

Mark 15:22-32

Were you ever convinced of a belief about God that you later found out was wrong?

In Jesus' day, everybody "knew" the proper identity and role of Messiah: The Messiah was a person appointed as a divine agent by God as a conquering king. He would overthrow the Roman government, defeat all of Israel's enemies, and reestablish the Davidic kingdom. This Messiah conquered with a sword and an army.

This belief is one of the reasons why, quite often, the disciples were so confused about things Jesus said. Jesus claimed he was the Messiah. And quite consistently, Jesus stated that he would die and be subsequently resurrected. But the disciples refused to believe him. The disciples were simply dumbfounded at the idea of this Messiah being defeated and dying. In more pithy terms, Jesus was not the Messiah they had expected.

Thus, when Jesus was crucified, many of the religious elites mocked Jesus. Such mockery was rooted in a complete misunderstanding of the identity and role of Messiah. The New Testament reveals that the true role of the Messiah was to reconcile humanity into right relationship with God. In this crucified Messiah, through Jesus' death and resurrection, there is peace between God and humanity.

> Dear Jesus, through your death and resurrection,
> I have been reconciled to God. Praise you! Amen.

GOOD FRIDAY, APRIL 3

A New Reality

Mark 15:33-37

What good did Christ's death accomplish?

Mark 15:37 is stark: "Jesus let out a loud cry and died." The Bible is quite clear throughout its pages that Jesus died on a cross. For example, Paul commanded the church to emulate Christ, who, although he was fully God, became human and submitted himself to death on a cross (Philippians 2:5-11). He also stated that through Jesus' death, we can have life (1 Thessalonians 5:9-10). Peter said that Jesus' death is sufficient for the forgiveness of sins (1 Peter 3:18).

The death of Christ created a new reality: salvation. Jesus' death and resurrection freed and saved us from enslavement to sin (Colossians 2:13-15; Hebrews 2:14-15), and it brought about forgiveness of sin. Jesus' death released us from the just penalty of the law, which was established by God. These new realities make it possible for the people of God to live holy lives (1 Thessalonians 4:1-3; 1 Peter 1:16), as well as approach God in confidence and peace (Hebrews 4:14-16).

However, these new realities are not the summation of salvation. Christ's death brings about reconciliation between God and people. Reconciliation means "the restoration of friendly relations." In other words, by Jesus' death, the people of God have become friends with God. People no longer need to be estranged from God. As a result, the people of God can enjoy unmitigated peace with God. Right relationship is thus restored between God and people due to the death that Jesus Christ suffered on a cross.

Dear God, I have been forgiven, and I can live a holy life.
I have a relationship with you. Thank you! Amen.

A Surprising Confession

Mark 15:38-41

In what ways can religion blind you from recognizing God?

The phrase "God's Son" or "Son of God" appears four times in Mark's Gospel. It first appears at the beginning of Mark as an explanation of its plot (Mark 1:1). It then appears in Mark 3:11 and 5:7, where the focus is on demonic spirits acknowledging Jesus Christ as the Son of God. The fourth time it appears is in this passage. Interestingly, then, only one person confesses Christ as the Son of God throughout the entire Book of Mark. Unlike Matthew, where an Israelite professes Jesus as the Son of God (Matthew 16:16), Mark presents a Gentile as the one who recognizes and professes Jesus as the Son of God. And he was not just any Gentile, but a Roman centurion, whom the Israelites would have despised because he represented the Roman government, which oppressed the people of Israel.

This profession boldly creates a contrast in the Book of Mark, where the people of God are consistently unable to recognize Jesus as the Son of God. Instead, it was a despised Gentile who could recognize him as the Son of God. That plot point challenges the people of God. Sometimes, those able to recognize God most clearly are the despised, outcast, and disenfranchised. Sometimes, the people who are unable to recognize God are those blinded by their religion. The Book of Mark challenges us to make sure our religious presuppositions do not blind us to the truth and personhood of Jesus Christ, who is the Son of God.

Dear God, open my eyes to see you.
Let not religion blind me. You are the Son of God. Amen.

Easter Sunday, April 5

Peace Be With You

John 20:19-23

Why were the disciples afraid of the Jewish authorities?

The disciples had locked the doors "because they were afraid of the Jewish authorities." These were the religious leaders who had Jesus executed under the pretense of treason. Many times, the Romans would publicly execute groups of people they deemed as traitors and potential usurpers. If the Romans executed Jesus as a usurper, it was quite possible they would seek to execute his followers as well. Thus, the disciples locked the doors.

Instead of the Romans appearing, however, Jesus did, saying, "Peace be with you." This message assuaged the fears of the disciples. They need not worry about being arrested and executed. Moreover, they could have assurance of victory in Christ. Jesus' resurrection proved that not even death could defeat him. Even though he died, he was not defeated. He was raised from the dead, just as he said (Matthew 16:21). As his disciples, then, they too could walk in that victory.

That reality applied to the disciples, and it applies to us. Like the disciples, we too can fear death. It may not manifest in the form of Romans arresting and executing us, but it does manifest in various ways. And like the disciples, we can out of fear "lock the doors" of our lives. But Jesus stands in our midst, speaking peace to us as well. We need not fear death, for he has conquered it. As his disciples, we can stand victorious over death as well.

Lord, you stand in my midst speaking peace. You defeated death. As such, death will not defeat me. Amen.

Praise the Lord!

Psalm 118:1-9, 14-18

What does the psalmist mean by the phrase "God's faithful love lasts forever!"?

The first four verses in this psalm repeat the phrase "God's faithful love lasts forever" four times, once per verse. This psalm also ends with the same phrase (verse 29). The repeated phrase helps set the tone, give meaning, and provide evidence for the rest of the psalm. That is, the reason this claim is valid is because of the foregoing material in the psalm.

So what does the psalmist mean that the faithful love of the Lord endures forever? First, the love of the Lord connotes God's goodness, kindness, loyalty, and unconditional favor to God's people. Second, God's love is resolutely firm and unwavering. It does not, and will not, change. Therefore, it is better to trust in the Lord than in "any human leader."

The term "lasts forever" indicates that God's faithful love will remain in existence for all time. It implies patient suffering as well. God's steadfast love is not conditioned upon the behavior of the people. As Paul suggests elsewhere in Scripture, God's steadfast love for God's people will put up with all things and will endure all things (1 Corinthians 13:7). Thus, the psalmist boldly declares that God's unconditional favor upon God's people is resolutely firm and unwavering and will endure unto eternity. That reality is evidenced by the cross. That reality applies to God's people. That reality applies to you. Praise God, indeed!

Dear Lord, your steadfast love for me
endures unto eternity. Praise you! Amen.

Exceptional Devotion

Matthew 27:57-61

How did Joseph show devotion to Jesus after he died?

Typically, those who suffered crucifixion were left to hang on their crosses where their corpses would slowly decompose and be devoured by vultures until all that remained was sinew and bones. These remains were then thrown into a pit. In execution and burial, these dead individuals received neither honor nor dignity. By contrast, if someone were to provide a burial plot for them, it would be due to an exceptional amount of charity and respect. Joseph of Arimathea showed this type of charity and respect for Jesus.

Such an undertaking was an extravagant act of devotion. Jesus was unrelated to Joseph, thereby making him a "stranger." He had also been convicted of treason. Joseph was motivated beyond mere conventional piety and obedience to Mosaic law. Instead, he was motivated by an extreme sense of loyalty and dedication to Jesus, for he "had become a disciple of Jesus."

His example should inspire us all. How willing are we to go beyond simple piety based on conventional standards of Christian worship? Are we willing to show "exceptional devotion" to the Lord? Are we willing to go above and beyond words and move to actions and attitudes that confirm them? If so, how would that demonstrate itself in your life?

Dear Lord, help me grow in
my devotion to you. Amen.

Guard Duty

Matthew 27:62-66

If Jesus' disciples had kidnapped his body after his crucifixion, what would they have had to do?

The second-century Christian apologist Justin Martyr acknowledged that there was a rumor that Jesus' disciples had kidnapped his body and fabricated the Resurrection story (Dial. 108). Today's passage, however, offers details that make that almost impossible. Matthew 27:64 indicates that the tomb holding Jesus' body was made secure. This was done by sealing the tomb with a boulder, weighing from one to two tons. Boulders were inserted into a sloped groove at the entrance of the tomb, then sealed by a stone wall, which was used to fit the boulder into the opening of the tomb. Moreover, Pilate sent a guard of Roman soldiers to protect the tomb from tampering. Such a guard would have been well-armed and quite efficient at killing their enemies.

To fabricate the Resurrection, the disciples would have had to overcome and defeat a highly skilled, trained, and efficient Roman guard. Then, they would have had to unseal the boulder and push it up an incline. It is highly improbable, if not nigh impossible, that they would have succeeded in accomplishing such a plan.

The tomb of Jesus, being sealed by a boulder and guarded by soldiers, emphatically highlights the significant triumph of the Resurrection. Despite every human attempt to prevent the Resurrection, even the slightest hint of a fabricated one, Jesus rose from the dead.

Dear Lord, nothing can prevail against you. Victory is always
in your hands. Christ is risen indeed! Amen.

THURSDAY, APRIL 9

Jesus Defeats Death

Matthew 28:1-10

What enemy did Jesus defeat and conquer? What problem did he solve?

The problem Jesus faced, the great foe he battled, was death. This great foe is an enemy all people face. Every person who has faced death in a competition has lost. All people have died. Granted, there have been stories in the Bible where death was temporarily halted. Some people were raised from the dead (1 Kings 17:17-24; 2 Kings 4:18-37; John 11:1-44). However, they eventually succumbed to death and remained dead. No person has ever definitively defeated death in such a way that they remain alive. That is, no person other than Jesus.

When Jesus died, he did not remain dead. After he rose from the dead, he remained alive, never to face the threat of death again. He even ascended into heaven alive. In every way conceivable, Jesus conquered death. As Paul wrote, "Death has been swallowed up by a victory" (1 Corinthians 15:54). Thus, we might translate Matthew 28:6 as "He isn't here, because he's been raised, for all time, from the dead."

Part of the good news found in the gospel message is that, although Christians will eventually face death, they too will be raised similarly to the resurrection of Jesus. Christians will eventually be raised, for all time, from the dead (Revelation 21:1-4). And in that new life, they will spend eternity with God in relationship.

> Dear God, Jesus conquered death! One day, I will be raised, for all time, from the dead. Thank you. Amen.

Friday, April 10

The Power of Truth

Matthew 28:11-15

Why did the religious elites seek to suppress the truth of Jesus' resurrection?

According to Matthew 28:4, the guards at Jesus' tomb were so terrified when an angel appeared to them that they fainted. They reported this incident to the religious leaders at the time. Interestingly, these leaders were primarily concerned with hiding that truth the guards had reported.

Matthew gives no indication or explanation as to why the religious leaders went to such extremes to keep the truth hidden from the masses. However, it is highly probable that their motivation was rooted in a desire to hold on to the power and wealth they possessed. Throughout his Gospel, Matthew portrays Jesus as a consistent threat toward the power, elitism, and wealth the religious leaders possessed (Matthew 5:17–6:18; 21:12-17; 23:1-36). It seems, therefore, that to remain powerful, esteemed, and wealthy, the religious elites sought to conceal the truth.

The religious leaders in this story knew the truth because the soldiers had reported it to them. However, instead of accepting the reality of that truth, they chose to suppress it. Have you ever done that? Our walk with God will inevitably lead to truth. Do we suppress that truth? Do we ignore it? Or do we accept the reality of whatever truth God is revealing and allow it to shape us into the people God desires us to be? When God inevitably reveals truth to you, what will be your response?

Dear Lord, thank you for revealing truth to me. When this happens, give me the courage to accept it. Amen.

SATURDAY, APRIL 11

Witness at the Cross

John 19:31-37

What is the foundation of your faith as a Christian?

Despite the order to do so, Jesus' legs were not broken because he had already died. John's report that a soldier pierced Jesus' side, causing blood and water to flow out, further validates this fact. John stated that he had seen this happen, that his testimony was trustworthy, and that no matter what anyone else claimed, he was being honest about these events. He also gave a clear reason for reporting these events: "So that you also can believe."

It is likely, given the reports that Jesus still lived after the events of his crucifixion, that some might have claimed that he never died in the first place. In fact, church history is rife with people who have claimed this. In response to these claims, John boldly reported Jesus' death, which would then validate the claims of his resurrection. His eyewitness testimony is important because it corroborates the claim that Jesus was raised from the dead. And Jesus' resurrection hinges on his death.

Jesus could not be raised from the dead if he had not first died, and it is by Jesus' death and resurrection that people are saved (Hebrews 9:23-28). In fact, Paul states that the cornerstone of Christian faith is found in the Resurrection (1 Corinthians 15:14). Thus, in some ways, the Christian faith also hinges on the death of Christ as well. In other words, your faith and life as a Christian are made possible by the sacrifice Christ made on the cross, a sacrifice that killed him.

Dear Lord, you died. My faith and life as a
Christian are possible because of that. Thank you.

SUNDAY, APRIL 12

Don't Be Afraid

Revelation 1:13-18

What do these verses tell you about Jesus?

John describes Jesus as the "Human One," or "Son of Man," as many translations render it. This phrase points to his identity as fully human yet also the Messiah who ushers in the kingdom of God. Jesus is surrounded by seven golden lampstands, which symbolize the seven churches mentioned in Revelation to whom Jesus speaks. This points out how Jesus is in the midst of his church. These verses describe Jesus in majestic terms, pointing to the reality that he is God Almighty. Verse 16 describes him as being able to speak out a "sharp, two-edged sword." The sword signifies Scripture; he is the author of Scripture, and his words can pierce one's soul as a sword pierces the body. Verse 16 ends with a description of his face, which shines like the sun. This most likely is an allusion to John 1:1-9, where Jesus is described as the one who illuminates humanity with moral and Divine truth.

Jesus is also described as the one who holds "the keys of Death and the Grave." Some translations use the word "Hades" instead of "Grave." This is significant, for it reveals that Jesus has authority over hell (Hades). By rising from the dead, he defeated and conquered hell and now has authority over it. We need not fear hell, for Jesus is in control. As followers of Christ, we will not wallow in hell for all of eternity. We will experience life everlasting in relationship with God.

Dear Lord, you have conquered hell. You are in control.
I need not fear death or hell. Thank you. Amen.

MONDAY, APRIL 13

God at Work

Ezra 1:1-11

How easily can you look back and see God's hand in events and circumstances?

Psalm 22:28 states, "Because the right to rule belongs to the LORD, he rules all nations." This verse reflects one of the essential theological points of today's passage: God caused Cyrus to legislate the return of the Jewish people to their homeland. This is so significant that the author highlights it within the first verse of Ezra 1 by stating, "The LORD stirred up the spirit of Persia's king Cyrus." The author of Ezra claims that the only reason Persia had authority over all the nations of the known world was because the Lord had granted it. In fact, the author is so bold that Ezra claims Cyrus himself admitted and accepted this reality. Thus, from the beginning, the author of Ezra attributes the Israelites' return to their homeland to the Lord Almighty. The entirety of Ezra 1 is written in that context.

That reality can bring us comfort and challenge. On the one hand, we need not fear the threat of nations, their decisions, or the laws they enact. No matter who sits in authority over those nations, God is always in control. On the other hand, this realization forces us to acknowledge that our hope does not lie in any one political figure or movement, but rather in the Lord Almighty, who controls all nations. We are kingdom citizens first and foremost. Therefore, we act within our respective nations according to kingdom principles. We follow and obey God Almighty.

> Lord, you rule the nations. I am not afraid.
> I will trust and follow you. Amen.

Foundation for a New Beginning

Ezra 3:8-13

When has a gracious new beginning resulted in happiness, sadness, and regret over past actions?

When Cyrus announced that God had instructed him to legislate the return of the Israelites to their homeland and to allow them to rebuild their kingdom and Temple, there was great cause for celebration. After decades of exile, such a declaration announced that God had not forgotten them and was choosing to have mercy on Israel despite their past history of idolatry and wicked behavior. God was restoring them.

This is the reason that all of Israel praised God. However, some of the older Israelites wept at the sight of the Temple, because the restored Temple was not as glorious and grand as the original Temple Solomon had built. While the Temple restoration symbolized the restoration of Israel and the mercy of God, it was also a sober reminder of the consequences of their past sinful behavior.

This story challenges and comforts us. It can challenge us by reminding us that even though God will restore us, we still may have to bear the consequences of our actions. At the same time, God is a God of mercy. Yes, God may discipline us, but it is always for our good (Hebrews 12:10). Furthermore, God's mercy is always new. No matter how many times we mess up, we can always return to God's immeasurable and eternal grace. God is a God of restoration.

Lord, you are a God of restoration. I return now
to your grace. Please restore me. Amen.

WEDNESDAY, APRIL 15

Right Priorities

Haggai 1:1-11

When have misplaced priorities resulted in drought or neglect in other areas of your life?

Today's passage takes place during Israel's restoration after exile. Haggai explains the reason why the Israelites suffered: misplaced priorities. They had made no attempt to rebuild the Temple of God, although they had rebuilt their own homes.

Verse 8 declares the implied solution to their predicament: If a ruined Temple brought suffering to the Israelites, then a restored Temple would reverse their suffering. Given that implication, it would be easy to assume that the solution to their problem lay in rebuilding a physical structure. But that was not the case. The Temple (or lack thereof) was not at the core of their suffering. Rather, it was their priorities. God and God's house were less important than their houses and interests. The restoration of the Temple would represent the restoration of the relationship between God and the people and would remind the people that God was present with them.

The lesson here is about priorities. "Take your ways to heart," God told the people through the prophet. Remember what is most important: the covenant relationship between God and the people. You will not be satisfied until God is at the center of your lives.

God, remind me that nothing is more important
than my relationship with you. Show me what stands
in the way of that relationship, and help me to
remove those things. Amen.

Thursday, April 16

Be Strong. Don't Fear.

Haggai 2:1-9

How do outward circumstances affect your faith and your relationship with God?

One of the more interesting aspects of today's passage is that God declared that the glory of the restored Temple would be greater than the glory that filled the former Temple. That idea might have comforted the older Israelites, who wept at the sight of the restored Temple (Ezra 3:12). According to them, the former glory of Solomon's Temple was greater than that of the restored Temple. This word from God would have challenged their worldview. They would have learned that outward appearances do not always indicate the degree to which the Lord is present.

That challenge has profound implications for our lives. Often, we believe that good fortune and success are indications of God's pleasure with us and that misfortune and failure are indications of God's displeasure with us. We may tend to gauge the level of God's presence based on outward appearances and circumstances. But good times are not an indicator of God's pleasure any more than difficulties are an indicator of God's displeasure. Both are simply realities of living in the world. We must be careful not to interpret God's presence by outward appearances. Be obedient. Have faith. Follow God. Strive for these things. Regardless of the way things seem at a given moment, God is pleased when we live this way.

Lord, thank you that you are present in
my life in all seasons and all circumstances.
Help me live faithfully and obediently. Amen.

Friday, April 17

Kindness and Compassion

Zechariah 1:12-17

How do you experience God's compassion in your life?

Have you ever lost something valuable to you? Most people, when losing something valuable, seek after it with great passion and energy. They show great zeal for it. You may recall the parables Jesus told about the lost sheep and the lost coin (Luke 15). In each case, the owners dropped everything and searched relentlessly until they found what was missing, celebrating with friends that what was lost had been found. Jesus told these stories to illustrate the extremes to which God will go to seek and find us.

That type of zeal is present in this passage. Zechariah declared that the Lord had a great amount of energy and enthusiasm in pursuit of the people. Such zeal explains why the Lord declared that prosperity would return to the people and that the people would experience salvation from their foes. Thus, the Temple not only represented God's mercy on the people but also God's zeal for them.

That truth applied to the Israelites during the restoration period, and it also applies to us. God has a great amount of zeal for it. God exudes energy in seeking after us (Matthew 18:10-14). God is enthusiastic about pursuing us. God takes pleasure in seeking after us, and God goes to great lengths to seek after us. The cross is proof of the zeal the Lord has for us. Take comfort, this day, in that reality.

Lord, you pursue after me with great zeal.
You care about me passionately. Thank you. Amen.

A Courageous Stand

Ezra 4:17–5:5

When have you stood firm in the face of opposition to do what God called you to do?

Today's passage takes place within the middle of a particular subplot (Ezra 4–6). Chapter 4 recalls how certain people sent a letter to King Artaxerxes to convince him to stop the city's restoration. Their attempts worked, and the king ordered a stop to the rebuilding. In Chapter 5, we learn that in an act of sheer defiance to the king's command, the people continued the rebuilding process. Given that the king halted the process because he viewed Israel as a threat to Persian sovereignty, this defiant act would have been ruled treasonous and therefore would have resulted in the people's execution. Yet the people remained steadfast and courageous. They continued to rebuild.

Chapter 6 tells us that King Darius took the throne and then reissued the original legislation given by King Cyrus (Ezra 1:1-4). Moreover, the king exonerated the defiant Israelites and issued protection for them and the rebuilding process (6:11). Eventually, the fruition of their efforts culminated in the rebuilding of the Temple (6:13-18). Such a thing may never have occurred had the Israelites not chosen to defy a king and follow God's direction.

Their story encourages us to be strong, courageous, and faithful to what God calls us to do. Once we are certain that God has spoken and is directing our lives toward a certain direction, then we can follow God, no matter the cost.

Lord, give me the courage to follow you faithfully
and confidently, in spite of opposition. Amen.

SUNDAY, APRIL 19

Celebrations With a Purpose

Ezra 6:13-22

What do you do to mark special events and occasions?

After the Temple had been rebuilt and restored, the people "celebrated the Passover" and "also joyfully celebrated the Festival of Unleavened Bread for seven day, because the Lord had made them joyful by changing the attitude of the king of Assyria toward them so that he assisted them in the work on the house of God, the God of Israel." Both celebratory meals were important feasts. They commemorated the liberation of the Israelites at the hands of the Egyptians (Exodus 12:1–13:10). The feasts were instituted so that future generations would remember how God had delivered the people. These feasts commemorated the Lord's deliverance of the people and also reminded them of the covenant they made with God.

Each successive generation of Israelites was called to observe Passover and the Festival of Unleavened Bread. In these celebrations, the people remembered God's deed of deliverance in the past, declared God's presence and working among them in the present, and renewed their commitment to God.

Those three aspects are also present in Communion. When we partake, we remember what God accomplished for us on the cross through Jesus; we declare, seek, and experience God's presence among us; and we renew our commitment to God. The next time you partake of this holy meal, remember, declare, seek, experience, and renew.

Lord, you saved me. You are present in my life. And I renew
my commitment to you. I love you. Amen.

MONDAY, APRIL 20

God Speaks Peace

Psalm 85:1-2, 8-13

What helps keep you hopeful in times of despair?

Psalm 85 is written from three vantage points: past, present, and future. First, the psalmist recalled the past ways in which God had delivered the people. Second, the psalmist viewed his present reality and asked God to be merciful. While we don't know the historical context of this psalm, it's clear that the psalmist believed that God had brought judgment on the people and asked God to be merciful toward them.

The psalm ends with hope. In a pattern typical of many of the psalms, the psalmist declared that the redemption of the Lord will eventually transpire. In these verses, the writer declares, "God's salvation is very close to those who honor him," and the Lord gives that which is good. All these aspects reflect one underlying theme: The Lord's future salvation is near. Although the psalmist was experiencing a trying time, he or she could remain hopeful.

In essence, this was the message that John the Baptist proclaimed. He called the people to metaphorically make a way for the Lord, for salvation was at hand. This is our message as well. In this world, there will always be hardship. There will even be times we may experience God's judgment and discipline. But we need not wallow in despair or allow such a reality to depress us. For "God's salvation is close to those who honor him." Therefore, remain hopeful. Make way for the Lord, for salvation is near!

Lord, I will not wallow in despair.
Your salvation is near. Thank you. Amen.

TUESDAY, APRIL 21

Refined and Clean

Malachi 3:1-4

What would a spiritual makeover involve?

The Temple had been rebuilt and rededicated for worship in 515 BC, and that was supposed to have served as a catalyst for God's people to rededicate themselves as well, renewing their commitments to God and to each other. Instead, immorality and corruption, even within the Temple and among the priests, abounded. Malachi's prophesies, which appear as conversations between God and the people, reveal that God was paying close attention to what the people were saying and doing, and God was not pleased. The people needed a spiritual makeover, and Malachi knew that God is the only one who could purify them and make them into the people God wanted them to be: refined, cleaned, purified, and "presented as a righteous offering."

The Gospel writers identified the unnamed "my messenger" of Malachi 3:1 with John the Baptist (Matthew 11:10; Luke 7:27; Mark 1:2; Luke 1:76). In this interpretation, verses 1-4 are re-read in the light of John the Baptist and his preaching, who announced the coming salvation of Jesus Christ. Malachi announced a "messenger who will clear the path before me." John the Baptist was a messenger in the sense that he cleared a path for the coming of Jesus Christ. Jesus Christ is the messenger and the message of our salvation. Jesus cleans, purifies, and refines us, making us into the people God wants us to be.

> Lord, cleanse, purify, and refine me so that
> I am the person you want me to be. Amen.

God's Word Lasts Forever

Isaiah 40:3-8

What promises do you find hard to believe?

While God sent numerous prophets with messages of judgment and warning, God, too, sent declarations of hope and comfort through the prophets. The people of God may experience earthly hardship or divine judgment, they assured, but God is long-suffering, patient, and kind. God's mercy and restoration will eventually occur.

That concept is the essential message of Isaiah 40:3-5. The prophet describes hearing a voice telling him, "Call out!" while another voice asks, "What should I call out?" The prophet seems to respond with doubt because he saw nothing that endured; he struggled to believe the voice and prophesy because there was nothing in life that seemed to validate the previous hopeful claims. Still, though "the grass dries up" and "the flower withers, . . . our God's word will exist forever." When all else perishes and decays, God and God's promises endure.

We can trust in the enduring promises and truths of Scripture. Not only can we take comfort in these promises and truths, but we can also boldly declare them to a watching world. Take comfort from this passage and believe its promises. Whatever your present circumstances, trust the faithful promises of God to bring deliverance and salvation. In the words of the prophet, "the word of our God endures forever."

Lord, your word endures forever. Help me to
believe and trust you when my faith is weak.
And help me declare your faithfulness to
others who need this assurance. Amen.

THURSDAY, APRIL 23

Prepare the Way

Luke 1:67, 76-80

What do you need to do to prepare the way for Christ to live in and through you this day?

A prophet speaks on behalf of God, interprets the will of God, and declares the Lord's will for the people of God to the people of God. As God's prophet, John the Baptist declared the coming salvation of the Lord, grounded and rooted in Christ, and called the people to make ready their hearts to receive Christ. John the Baptist was not pointing to a concept, but rather to a person. When he told the people how to be saved, he was teaching them about the coming Messiah, about Jesus Christ. He prepared a way for the Lord.

John not only called the Israelites, but he also calls to us with the same message. The same challenge John gave the Israelites, he also gives to us. How shall we respond? How do we receive Christ into our lives every day? What do we need to do to make room for Christ? What do we need to get rid of so that Christ can fully and completely live within us? How does Christ's presence in our lives change the way we think, speak, and act?

Prepare your heart this day to receive Christ as your Messiah, your Savior, your Redeemer, your Lord, your Guide. Ask God to use you in giving "light to those who are sitting in darkness" and help guide them "on the path of peace."

God, thank you that you prepared a way for Christ.
Help me to prepare for you in my life every day.
I receive you. Amen.

Changed Hearts and Lives

Mark 1:1-8

What does baptism mean to you?

Mark's Gospel tells us that "everyone in Judea and all the people of Jerusalem went out to the Jordan River and were being baptized by John as they confessed their sins." John's baptism was symbolic of the inner changes in people's hearts and lives. The act in and of itself had no real power to cleanse or purify, and John explained why.

"I baptize you with water," John told the people, but "one stronger than I am . . . will baptize you with the Holy Spirit." Interestingly, the same word used with reference to water baptism is also used to refer to the baptism of the Holy Spirit. That is, Jesus Christ fully immerses a person in the Holy Spirit. In doing so, true cleansing occurs, true purification occurs, and true devotion occurs.

Paul reflected that concept when he stated that we "were sealed with the promised Holy Spirit because [we] believed in Christ" (Ephesians 1:13). Being immersed in the Holy Spirit proves that we are "God's children" (Romans 8:16). Being immersed in the Holy Spirit purifies and sanctifies us (1 Corinthians 6:11): "You were washed clean, you were made holy to God, and you were made right with God in the name of the Lord Jesus Christ and in the Spirit of our God." Being immersed in the Holy Spirit also empowers us to remain devoted and committed to God (Philippians 2:12-13), living out God's "good purposes."

Lord, you baptized me with the Holy Spirit. I am cleansed.
I am purified. I devote myself to you. Amen.

Saturday, April 25

John's Witness

John 1:19-28

How do you define or describe yourself?

John the Baptist was clear: "I'm not the Christ." But the priests and Levites questioning him wanted answers. "Then who are you? Are you Elijah? . . . Are you the prophet? . . . Who are you? We need to give an answer to those who sent us. What do you say about yourself?"

John was none of these people, but he knew clearly who he was and what God had called him to do. He was merely the one who was preparing the way for the Messiah. John explained that his baptism was different from the one who was to come, the one, he proclaimed, "who takes away the sin of the world!"

John was a way-maker. Once the Messiah appeared on the scene, it was time for him to exit the limelight and allow Christ to take center stage. It was time for his ministry to cease, so that the ministry of Jesus could flourish. John essentially pointed to Christ and said, "Don't look at me. Look at him."

Such humility is inspiring. We may at times want the attention of others and enjoy being in the limelight. We can all be self-centered. When our positions or careers naturally put us in the limelight, it can be easy to expect that attention all the time. John's example in this passage, however, challenges us. Will we point to Christ? In all that we do, will we turn the gazes of others toward Christ? How do we live in such a way that others see Christ, not us?

Lord, remind me of who I am and who you want me to be.
Use me to point others to you. Amen.

Way-Makers

Acts 19:1-7

Who has been like John the Baptist in your life, preparing you to receive Christ?

Somehow, John's message of repentance and baptism had reached Ephesus. Since John preached about the coming Messiah, they most likely were still waiting on the coming of the Lord's anointed one. Imagine their great joy and happiness when Paul declared, "The one in whom they were to believe. This one is Jesus."

Baptism in Jesus resulted in changed hearts and lives for these disciples. Moreover, the preaching and baptizing of John had prepared them for such a time as that.

This event reveals two important theological truths. First, baptism in Jesus results in changed hearts and lives. Second, God is always at work, even today, preparing people to receive salvation and the Holy Spirit. Even before we are aware of it, God is at work in our lives, drawing us ever closer to Christ. And since we were saved and "baptized in the name of Jesus," God has been at work in our lives, transforming our hearts and lives for God's purposes. Like John preparing the way for Christ in the lives of these disciples, certain way-makers have also come into our lives, helping us get ready to receive the good news of salvation. God has been, is, and will always be at work in our lives. And God wants to use us in preparing the way for others to receive salvation.

> Lord, thank you for bringing way-makers into
> my life and continuing to work in my life.
> Help me be a way-maker for others. Amen.

MONDAY, APRIL 27

The River of Pure Joy

Psalm 36:5-10

What is God's desire for those who love God?

Despite the evil in the world, God has given us the gift of life within God's *hesed*, God's always faithful, everlasting, all-encompassing love. The difference between the wicked and those who enjoy God's graces is that the people of God realize their dependence on God's goodness and are aware of the richness God's character adds to their lives

It's easy to wake up every morning thinking of what we need to get done and to base our lives on our successes. But this psalm reminds us that if we live that way, we are blind to God's great gifts of life and light itself that God gives us every moment we exist. And God's wishes for us go so much further than survival! God wants us to feast. In a parched land, God tells us to drink from a river of delight and a fountain of joy! God wants to protect and shelter us and overwhelm us with goodness. In this psalm, God is the indulgent parent, showering God's children with all they could want or desire. What an incredible God!

This psalm assures us that the most real and reliable thing in the universe is the love of God. It's God's *hesed*, faithfulness and righteousness that keep the world spinning and allow us to take each breath. The world is a scary and dangerous place at times, but ultimately God's love and God's will are paramount. We don't have to fear. God's love will prevail over all!

Lord, help me always to remember the great
blessings you have given me, and keep me from
doubting that your love will prevail! Amen.

TUESDAY, APRIL 28

A Place of Refuge

Psalm 46:1-11

What sustains you when you feel as though everything around you is falling apart?

Psalm 46 describes disaster. The mountains sink into the sea. Governments come crashing down. War is all over the face of the earth. Everything is desolation. But despite this horrific setting, Psalm 46 is a hymn of praise! There is one constant, one landmark that never changes. That, of course, is God, our refuge, our strength, and our help. When all is falling apart around us and all that we have relied on is gone, God remains strong, secure, and reliable.

Martin Luther used Psalm 46 as inspiration for his hymn, "A Mighty Fortress Is Our God," possibly written for his friends who were martyred. Many who have been persecuted for their faith have sung it. Even though everything else had failed them, they could face their fate with confidence, knowing that their souls were safe with the Lord.

In yesterday's and today's psalms, we read about a life-giving river. In both, it's a symbol of God's provision in the worst of circumstances. This is the same "living water" that Jesus promised the Samaritan woman in John 4. It's the very essence of life, our ultimate protection and our most profound hope and joy. Even in the midst of earth-shattering chaos, the river flows to satisfy all our thirst. When all is destroyed around us, God's kingdom is a refuge and a place of safety that triumphs over everything else.

O Lord, may I always seek your refuge when disaster strikes,
and may your living waters satisfy my needs. Amen.

WEDNESDAY, APRIL 29

God's Glorious River

Ezekiel 47:1-12

When have you seen restoration?

Ezekiel's vision was a prophecy for Israel in the midst of exile. It was a picture of hope for those who longed to return home again, but it was also a vision of a thriving world watered by the word of God. The path of the river was through land called the Arabah, dry wasteland that is only inhabited by dangerous, wild animals. God's water of life transformed it into a paradise!

What a beautiful metaphor for the transformative power of God's blessings! When have you seen someone who has been in a desolate place in their life who has found the life-giving waters of the Lord? What barren and hopeless parts of your life could be transformed by God's healing waters? God can turn lives that seem meaningless into great treasures. The dead areas of our lives and of our society can once again become teeming with hope and purpose.

And what a beautiful metaphor for how God's blessings increase! From a tiny trickle, God's love can become an unstoppable torrent! People who drink from God's life-giving waters and are transformed can then lead others to the same life-giving waters. As healing takes place, all that touches them becomes healed as well. Think about how the one life of Jesus Christ transformed the world! As people of God, we can become part of this river, allowing the current to take us places we never thought possible and being part of a mission of wholeness, justice, and mercy for all of creation.

Lord, may I be part of your glorious river
of healing and hope! Amen.

God's Desire for the People

Revelation 21:9-14

What is God's ultimate plan for creation?

The final vision in the Bible is that of the New Jerusalem, the Holy City of God, come to earth. God's dwelling place and humanity's home become one and the same; heaven comes to earth, and God's vision of a whole, just, and merciful society is finally realized. The promise of the prophecies is that the earth will be blessed, healed, and whole, and God's *hesed*—everlasting love—will be the force that rules the earth.

The description of the city is highly symbolic. It has 12 gates and foundations, 12 being the number of totality or perfection. Each gate is inscribed with the names of the 12 tribes of Israel, symbolizing the beginnings of the relationship of God with the people. Each foundation of the city has a name of one of Jesus' apostles, symbolizing the people of God who were transformed by Christ's death and resurrection. The entire city sparkles like a jewel, precious as God's people are to God. This glorious city is a symbol of utopia, Eden come again, the perfect place for the beloved people of God.

It's wonderful to know that a world of healing and *hesed* is God's ultimate desire for us. It's a vision of the kingdom of God come to earth, promised to us by Jesus Christ himself. However it comes to pass, we know this is God's desire for the people of God, and we have the firm and sure hope of God's goodness and love one day healing all of creation.

Lord, may I be comforted by the vision of your
hope for the world. Come, Lord Jesus! Amen.

MAY

CONTRIBUTOR:

Sue Mink
(May 1–May 31)

A City of Astounding Beauty

Revelation 21:15-21

Where is the most beautiful place you've ever been?

Jerusalem is often referred to as "Zion" and was God's city on the hill that was the seat of Hebrew kings. But throughout the Scriptures, Jerusalem has also been a name for a spiritual state of righteousness and relationship. Of course, God is not tied to a specific place, and so the New Jerusalem, described in today's passage, is God's heavenly kingdom, not the earthly city. The New Jerusalem is a place of indescribable beauty and unimaginable worth. This city will be the most awe-inspiring, stunning, and beautiful thing ever seen by human eyes. It will be God's glory visible to all people.

The incredible thing about this text is that the city comes to earth, meaning that God will share God's holy place with the people. Because this is God's kingdom, there will be justice and mercy, and every person will have the opportunity to live to their full potential. Sin will not have a foothold anywhere. For the first time, humanity will live as God intends: in righteousness and responding to the will of God.

And what could be more beautiful than that? Every human will have dignity, and all will join together in praising God. When every person lives with compassion and grace for one another and in gratitude and obedience to God, golden streets won't be the most beautiful part of the city. The true beauty will be in the hearts and souls of the whole and healed people of God.

O Lord, I long to see your holy city!
Come, Lord Jesus! Amen.

A City of the Presence of God

Revelation 21:22-27

How would the world need to be transformed to make it worthy to be God's home?

I found it surprising to read in John's vision that the New Jerusalem would have no temple or house of worship. They will not be necessary in the New Jerusalem because the entire city will be holy. Every inch of this huge and glorious place will be infused by the presence and power of God. The entire city will be one glorious cathedral to God's grace and glory, built not by human hands, but by the vision of God. God will not be distant but will be alive, knowable, and present in every corner of the city.

All the nations will follow the will of God. That's why there will be no more war and no more oppression. God's way will finally become the way of humanity. The New Jerusalem will be God's symbol of all that the earth was created to be. It is the culmination of creation, with a new society, a new community, and new people, all with new hearts that are attuned to God. This is our hope and our promise as Christians: that the world will one day be transformed into the world that God created it to be before sin entered. One day, God's presence will be so infused into every moment, every place, and every heart that there will be no more room for darkness, no more place for pain, and no more specter of death. Heaven and earth will be one, and our hearts and minds will be one with God.

Lord, help me to live as a worthy inhabitant now of the New Jerusalem that will be. Come, Lord Jesus! Amen.

Seeing the Face of God

Revelation 22:1-5

What would it be like to gaze on the face of God?

When Moses asked to see the face of God and God's glory, God refused. God told Moses, "You can't see my face because no one can see me and live" (Exodus 33:20). The best that Moses could do was to hide in the cleft of a rock and catch a glimpse of the back of God as God went by. It was all that a human being could withstand, yet Revelation 22:4 says that the inhabitants of the New Jerusalem will see God's face.

This is the relationship God wanted when God created humans. In Eden, God created the perfect environment for beings created in God's image. But sin entered the picture, and the relationships and the environments were soiled. But in these last chapters of Scripture, the world comes full circle. Eden is re-created, and people can, for the first time, look into the face of God.

All through his life on earth, Jesus spoke of the day when God would defeat sin and death, a day whose dawn was Easter morning. We struggle now and wait in certain hope for the dream of the New Jerusalem to arrive in full. Revelation tells us that the hope and joy of Easter will continue into eternity as God's light will never fade, the crystal river of life will flow forever, and all of God's people can shine in the light of the glory of God, gazing on God's face.

Lord, cleanse my heart so that I may be worthy
one day to see your face. Come, Lord Jesus! Amen.

God Is Our Help and Shield

Psalm 115:9-18

What is God's desire for relationship with us?

Trust is defined as confidence or faith, a sense of security and safety, physically and emotionally. When you trust someone, you don't have to worry about their reliability or their motives. Today's psalm is saying that those who follow God don't have to worry because God will be on the front lines, making good things happen for them and be protecting them from bad things.

A greater thing is that this God of protection and blessing is none other than the maker of heaven and earth! It's important to realize what this phrase means. All that is in the world was designed and created by God, the ultimate artist. Colors, emotions, tastes, perceptions of beauty, and everything else in the cosmos—all were crafted by God and then given to humanity. What we call creativity as humans is a pale shadow of the magnificence of God's work.

It's crucial to remember we are also part of this created realm. God created us in God's image, but sometimes we seem to create God in our image. However, God is not like us; God is beyond our understanding. The first half of Psalm 115 warns against idol worship, and if we reduce God to our own understanding, we are diminishing God to an idol. We were created as earthly beings to praise and serve God here while God dwells in heaven. As verse 18 reminds us, our place here and now is to praise God while we have breath in our lungs, ever grateful for God's blessings, help, and protection.

Mysterious and powerful Lord, thank you for
your help and your shield. Amen.

TUESDAY, MAY 5

God, My Help and My Rescuer

Psalm 40:11-17

How can we trust that God will save us?

Our reading for today speaks of overwhelming trouble. It's a strange turnaround when most psalms start out with trouble and then end in praise because the Lord has come to their rescue. But life isn't stuck on happy endings, is it? Just because some troubles have ended doesn't mean that more won't come later. We're never safe from bad things happening, and even if we've been delivered by God, there's always something new around the bend. We are never in a place where we don't need God's help.

It's precisely because God helped the psalmist in the past that he feels confident to call on God now. The call of anguish is also a call of trust, made in certainty that God will hear, will care, and will do something about it. The cry of pain is a cry of faith that believes that God is there despite suffering.

The psalmist knows the character of God. Verse 11 mentions God's mercy, *hesed* (or steadfast love), and righteousness. It's because of God's character that we can cry out in trust and confidence when the world turns against us, too. We know God's history with God's people. We also know that God is merciful, loving, and righteous. Armed with this knowledge, we can cry out in our pain, not concerned that we affront our Lord with our need but secure that God hears, cares, and is pleased to save.

Lord, may I have the confidence of the psalmist, trusting in
your mercy, *hesed*, and righteousness. Amen.

A Big Fish

Jonah 1:4-17

How do people respond when God asks them to do something they don't want to do?

When, after casting lots, the sailors found out that Jonah was the cause of the storm, he offered to throw himself overboard to stop the storm. That sounds altruistic of him, until we realize that all he had to do was to obey God at that point. He would rather have died by his own methods than obey God, risk going to Nineveh, and fall into hostile Assyrian hands.

We know what follows. Jonah was thrown into the sea, but a great fish swallowed him and then spat him out on Nineveh's shore. God didn't let him get away with running away. Jonah was successful despite himself, and Nineveh repented. God used an unwilling "servant" to achieve God's goals even though Jonah fought God every step of the way.

Jonah didn't obey God and didn't trust in God's protection. He chose his own course to save himself and condemn the people of Nineveh. But God set up guardrails to keep him on track despite himself. God's goodness and protection prevailed and saved not only Jonah but the inhabitants of Nineveh.

When God gives us clear direction, we can trust God's provision for us as we obey. Our tasks may be difficult or even terrifying, but God's protection and grace surround us in our obedience.

Lord, give me the courage to do the
things you ask of me. Amen.

THURSDAY, MAY 7
A Safe Place

Revelation 12:1-6, 13-16

How do people keep themselves safe from harm?

In Revelation 12, the woman in labor is a sign of hope and life. Even though she was vulnerable in the midst of labor, she didn't capitulate to the dragon, but stood firm until she gave birth, then fled to God's protection. She symbolizes the struggle to bring the kingdom of God to earth, as evil, the seven-headed dragon, lay in wait to destroy it. Before the dragon could kill her and her newborn, she was rescued, cared for, and nourished by God. She was in a completely vulnerable state but found safety with God.

Ultimately, like the woman, we need to rely on God for safety. There's nothing we as humans can do to completely protect ourselves from harm. In the end, the very things we may rely on for self-protection, such as stockpiling wealth or segregating ourselves from others, can begin to destroy our integrity and draw us away from God's protection. Only as the people of God do we have the sure promise of eternal life and eternal safety.

In the end, what will keep us safe is boldly following the way of Christ. It may seem dangerous to those watching and holding fast to their possessions. It may seem foolish to choose the right instead of the cautious way. But if we trust in God and call ourselves people of God, then we can trust in the promise of light, love, and life eternal for those who follow in the footsteps of Jesus Christ. Our true safety is with him.

Lord, may I trust always in your
protection of my soul. Amen.

FRIDAY, MAY 8

Lessons From Birds and Lilies

Matthew 6:25-34

What are the treasures people value in their lives?

Jesus wasn't saying we should be like birds or flowers; rather, we should learn from them. Jesus was telling his disciples to consider and study the world that God has created, where seemingly inconsequential birds and flowers are so lavishly cared for. And then trust.

Reevaluating the treasures we are accumulating in our lives is one of the things we can learn from the birds and lilies. Are your treasures things you lock up and hide from others? Are they things you are afraid of losing and need to protect? Or do you collect treasures of a life well-lived: a sense of purpose and worth, being loved and having loved well, of integrity and of living a life that is pleasing to God? These are the investments that are secure.

This passage is a call to reorient ourselves. It asks us to reassess what is important in life and base our lives around those things. Such riches that will lessen anxiety instead of increasing it. We're enfolded into God's provision, designed to be happiest when we pursue the riches of God's kingdom.

The checkbook may still not balance, and yes, that is a concern. But knowing that you are a beloved child of the Creator of the universe holds solace. And to know that there's a place for you in God's glorious kingdom is a wonderful comfort indeed.

Lord, help me to orient myself to seeking your treasures and not being anxious about the treasures of the world. Amen.

SATURDAY, MAY 9

Cain and Abel

Genesis 4:1-9

What does it mean to be your brother's keeper?

When God saw that Cain was jealous, God responded by telling Cain that sin was lurking at his door. This is the human condition: our anger, jealousy, greed, and selfishness. The second half of that verse reads, "But you must rule over it." In most translations, the Hebrew verb *timshel* is rendered "you must" but it is also possible to translate it as "you may" (master sin). In other words, God has given humanity agency over sin. We have the choice to deal with the sin by conquering it or by succumbing to it.

Of course, Cain did not master it. He gave in to sin and murdered his brother. Cain violated the bond of brotherhood and sisterhood that God has created among all of humanity. By murdering Abel, he cut himself off from the very earth. (In Hebrew, the word for earth, *adamah*, is firmly linked with the word for humanity, *adam*.)

When we hurt our brothers and sisters, we are giving power to the sin that crouches at our door and destroying the bond that God created among all of humanity. God gave us as a gift to one another. We are more than our brother's (and sister's) keepers. We are joined in heart and soul, flesh and blood. First John 2:9 reads, "The one who claims to be in the light while hating a brother or sister is in the darkness even now." God designed the world so that our bond with one another is both our joy and our responsibility. We are one another's brothers and sisters because we are all children of our Lord.

Lord, help me to master sin so that I may cherish my
brothers and sisters. Amen.

SUNDAY, MOTHER'S DAY, MAY 10

God's Care for Cain

Genesis 3:21; 4:10-16

How does God respond to our sin?

God gave Cain a way forward. God put a mark on his forehead that reminded him that he was his brother's murderer, but it also protected him from any harm. It was a punishment and a sign of mercy. God would watch out for the sinner, for the murderer. Cain was given a chance to succeed after all.

And this is how we, as sinners, live today. We are all marked by sin. We all have the scars of disobedience and willful behavior marked on our souls and psyches, and we can't escape it. Humanity's sin has seeped into the soil and pollutes the earth with war, oppression, and discrimination against our brothers and sisters. But our relationship with God is defined by grace, so despite our failure to fight off the sin that lurks at our doors, we are held in the palm of God's hand, protected and cared for. Broken and exiled from Eden, we are still God's beloved, and we still have the promise of eternal life before us.

God created us for Eden but equips us for the sin-filled world. Eden didn't require clothing, but when Adam and Eve left, God sewed skins together for them. I can't imagine God's sorrow as God prepared them for life tainted by sin. Cain was marked by murder and mercy. Our journey back to Eden, the kingdom of God, is a journey of shamed and broken people, shepherded by grace and mercy.

Gracious God, forgive me for my sins
as I rest in your mercy. Amen.

Monday, May 11

Meat in the Wilderness

Numbers 11:4-9, 21-23

How do people tell the difference between what they want and what they need?

What do we want that isn't what we need? Our houses are crammed with things we thought we wanted, to the point where many have outside storage to accommodate everything. Maybe it's not material goods we think we need, but social prestige, a fat bank account, or the perfect job. Our lives become crowded with stuff, stressed with worry, and empty of time with those we love because we're chasing the things we think we want instead of the things we need.

The Hebrew people complained that manna was not enough. They rejected the nourishment that God sent and went out to look for something different. They wanted meat. God sent huge flocks of quail, more meat than they could eat. But those who ran out of the camp—the place of God—to harvest the meat sickened and died. The place of true nourishment was within God's realm.

This passage is a call to reassess our lives and consider what sustains us and makes us happy. What are you chasing that could be destroying the life that God has given you? Are those the things that help you to grow strong in your spiritual life, build your relationships, and become a person of God? Can you realign your wants to be the desires of God for your life? That's where the true nourishment is, because in the end, the desires of God for your life are the things that you need.

Lord, realign my desires to be your desires for me,
because that is where I will find abundant life. Amen.

Tuesday, May 12

God's Lavish Gifts

Psalm 105:37-43

What gifts from God are particularly wonderful?

So often, God gives us more than we need, and today's psalm praises our abundant blessings. God doesn't withhold the opportunity for us to enjoy things. In fact, God gives us the riches of the world in incredible profusion; the failure of poverty is because of human unwillingness and inability to share that bounty. The earth's rich soil gives us crops, the oceans teem with fish, and animals provide meat. There are over 2,000 varieties of fruit alone in the world! We certainly don't need that many different things to eat, but God lovingly crafted each one, with its own specific tastes, only to delight us. We have sunshine and rain, trees for shade and shelter, a stunning variety of animals for domestication and to enjoy their exquisiteness and stunning natural beauty. We have the love of family and friends and the joy of companionship. God's gifts are gloriously lavish.

God made these things for us to enjoy. This psalm tells us how God cared for the Hebrew people, giving them shelter from the desert sun, light at night, and water, plus the manna and the quail. God gave them all those things in love for their comfort and sustenance because they were God's people.

Psalm 105 is a joyful thanksgiving for all these gifts from God. God gives us the blessing and the challenge to use these gifts wisely. We should use what God has given us in God's great generosity and love and share it with care and compassion for others.

Lord, may I see your love in your gifts that surround me every day. Amen.

Wednesday, May 13

Slavery or the Wilderness?

Exodus 16:2-8

Does following God take you into uncomfortable places?

Moses had led the Israelites from oppression and captivity and brought them out into the desert. But the wilderness was scary and unfamiliar. They didn't have food or water. As horrible as Egypt had been, they knew what would happen to them there, and that's where they felt secure. They grumbled and complained, asking to return to the reliability of slavery.

When we claim the freedom of the salvation of Jesus Christ, it is a risk-taking adventure. It means going out into the figurative wilderness away from comfortable living to challenge ourselves, not only in our personal growth in faith but in loving our neighbor as ourselves. It means recognizing and then challenging systems of oppression and discrimination as Christ did. It means living as Jesus Christ, a life that often "bucks the system" and can feel like being in the wilderness. It's understandable that at times, we would want to go back to the comforts of Egypt, a place where we don't have to worry about the call of holiness.

But God hears our grumbling and, in grace and mercy, gives us nourishment in the desert. When we become followers of Christ, we may be in unfamiliar territory, but we are never alone. God gave the Hebrew people the manna in the desert so that they would know that God was with them and caring for them. Through amazing miracles and everyday blessings, God walks with us on our Christian journey.

Lord, thank you for my freedom in you, and help me
to trust your provisions for me. Amen.

Unexpected Answers to Prayer

Exodus 16:9-15

When has God answered your prayers in ways you did not anticipate?

The word in Hebrew for "manna," *man hu*, literally means, "What is this stuff?" It was something completely new. When the Hebrews grumbled about getting food, they certainly did not ask for manna. God's provision for them was tasty, plentiful, and nutritious, but it wasn't what they'd thought they'd get. Their response was not grateful praise, but a confused question to one another, "What is this stuff?"

How often does this happen when we pray for God to help us with a need? We may have the solution in mind and inform God what to do, but God has solutions we haven't considered. When God answers our prayers in unexpected ways, our response is often to ask, "God, what is this stuff?"

But when God answers our prayers, it's exactly what we need. Moses told the people that the manna was the bread that the Lord had given them to eat. Think how perfect it was! Usual bread is a high-labor food. The manna came ready-to-eat on the desert floor. Grain would be heavy and difficult to carry across the desert. The manna appeared every day and couldn't even be gathered in excess. It was the perfect food for their time in the wilderness.

We need to trust God to answer our prayers in the best possible way. We may respond, "What is this stuff?" But God's provisions are exactly what we need.

Lord, open my eyes to your unexpected
answers to prayer. Amen.

FRIDAY, MAY 15

Gathering Manna

Exodus 16:16-21

Why do people keep more than they need of something?

The story of manna in Exodus confronts our desire to hoard and have more than we need. God told the people to gather as much manna as they needed for that day, and that day only. Every morning when they woke up, there was more bread. Every evening when they went to bed, the bread was used up or spoiled. If they tried to gather more than they needed and hoard it, "it became infested with worms" and was worthless.

Hoarding any of God's gifts lessens their worth. Talents and skills unused are wasted. Unused goods take up space and aren't enjoyed. Even money can often be used in more beneficial ways than saving it. God has given all to us, and it is our responsibility to see that the things we're given are used in the most productive ways.

This passage also teaches us to trust in God's provision. Every night the Hebrew people went to bed with no food in their camp, but woke every morning to find that once again, God had provided for them. They wandered in the desert for 40 years, and as long as they needed manna, God sent it. It was daily care that became quite routine, but God's care often comes in routine ways. Through this care, we can see God's love for us and the need for us to use God's gifts wisely.

Lord, may I trust in your care enough
to live with an open hand to others. Amen.

The Sabbath Rest

Exodus 16:22-30

Why did God give us the sabbath?

While the Hebrew people were in Egypt as slaves, they didn't have a day of rest. Sabbath was something new to them, even though it had been decreed by God since creation. Teaching them about sabbath was a way of God reclaiming them as God's people, bringing them into the way of life that God had intended for them.

In today's world, where time is money, the idea of an entire day of rest can seem unrealistic. Sabbath rest is something that seems outdated and impractical. But when we think about taking sabbath, this passage is an important insight into God's provision. Sabbath was not a burden to the Hebrew people because God gave them extra manna the day before. They could rest assured that their needs would be met. In fact, if they went out on the sabbath to gather manna, they would find none. If they tried to work, it would be ineffective.

We can always do more. But God's call to sabbath tells us that filling our lives with work and things we must do isn't the way we were created to live. The provision of manna teaches us about trusting God with our needs. The provision of the sabbath manna teaches us to trust God with our time. In both instances, the result is not less, but more: more of the riches in this life that count. It's the riches of relationship with God and others, and of freedom from the slavery of anxiety and fear.

Lord, help me to value rest in my life and teach me
to adjust my life to accommodate it. Amen.

Sunday, May 17

Bread From Heaven

John 6:26-35

When have you failed to recognize a miracle?

The crowd asked Jesus for a sign like the manna from heaven that the Hebrew people had gotten in the desert. Manna was not only a symbol of God's loving provision for the people, but it grew to become a metaphor of God's wisdom, or the Torah. So when Jesus responded that he was the bread of life, he was saying that he was sent to them by their loving Father in heaven to feed them through God's grace and wisdom. They had not understood his miracle of physical feeding, but there was another miracle standing right in front of them: the miracle of spiritual salvation.

But like the Hebrews in the desert who saw the manna and grumbled, "What is this stuff?" the people around Jesus didn't understand the blessing God had given them. They didn't understand that God's great gifts were there for the taking, asking Jesus what works they had to do to earn God's favor. The only thing Jesus required was that they recognize the miracle that was before them and then believe in him.

Like the manna in the desert, Jesus was like nothing the people had ever seen before. He was a new and unexpected answer to their prayers for salvation, perfectly suited to humanity's needs. And like the manna, Jesus answers prayers in new and unexpected ways.

Lord, may my eyes always be open to your miracles in this world, especially the grace and love of Jesus Christ. Amen.

Praying for Spiritual Maturity

Colossians 1:9-14

How should you pray for your church?

Paul didn't know the Colossians. He had only heard of their conversion through Epaphras and was concerned that their faith would be polluted by false teachers. Paul's prayer was for a knowledge of God that results in spiritual maturity.

Paul began by praying for the Colossians to have knowledge of God's will. Without an understanding of God's desires, it's difficult to live a life that is pleasing to God. The ability to discern between our desires, opinions, and prejudices and the will of God is a great gift to any congregation. Next, Paul prayed that they would be strengthened by God. They would need the power of God to be patient and endure in the faith. The next part of the prayer is praise for God's great gifts. In this passage, every believer has been lifted out of darkness into God's kingdom of light!

It's a gift to pray for others. But prayer can and should go beyond requests for physical health, comfort, and happiness. Prayers to know the mind of God and the strength to live a life of God build us up as people of faith who can work toward the kingdom of God on earth. By possessing this knowledge and the will to live out the demands it entails, we can take our places beside the saints and angels in Christ's kingdom of light.

Lord, may all those who follow you discern
your will and be strengthened in your work. Amen.

TUESDAY, MAY 19

Liberated by Christ's Blood

1 Peter 1:17-23

What is the consequence of salvation?

The epistle of 1 Peter starts with the joys of salvation through Christ. But in this passage, Peter tells us there are responsibilities, too. We can't claim salvation and then live consequence-free, even though we are forgiven. If we claim Jesus Christ, we are then called to pursue holiness.

Salvation is incredibly costly, not in terms of the things humans think are valuable, like silver or gold, but because it was bought by the blood of Jesus Christ. There couldn't be a higher price! And so our responsibility when we accept this salvation is high indeed. The first responsibility that Peter lists as a recipient of Christ's salvation is to love one another. This is not a casual friendship, but a deep, sincere affection for fellow believers. One of the most important consequences of our salvation is becoming part of a community of believers who are responsible for one another's physical and spiritual needs. That's because, as God's children, we're all in this together; not only in this life on earth, but for all eternity.

Becoming a Christian is not an exercise in consequence-free living where our sins are forgiven and we can go on as we were. Instead, it's a transformation from a life of irresponsibility to one of obedience to the Word of God and commitment to our fellow believers. Our salvation was bought at an incredible price. Our calling then is to live a life of holiness befitting Christ's sacrifice for us.

> Lord, may I embrace the responsibilities
> of holy living in obedience to you. Amen.

God Made Us Righteous

1 Corinthians 1:26-31

How racially, economically, and socially integrated are most churches today?

Most commentators believe that in this passage, Paul was writing to those who had become pretentious in the church. Paul's words to them here reminded them of the entire history of God interacting with humanity. God often chose the least and the last for special blessings. Jacob, Joseph, and David were not the oldest sons. Many of the disciples came from humble origins. Even Jesus himself was born to peasants and slept his first night on earth in an animal's feeding trough. One's background, education level, employment, or status mean nothing to God. For those in the church to elevate themselves over others because of any of those things is against the very heart of Christ's teachings.

If a Christian is to boast about anything, it's what God has done for them, Paul wrote, because nothing else matters. Their praise should go not to inconsequential things—wealth, prestige, fame—but to God and how God has changed them.

These are difficult words for today's churches, which tend to be highly stratified. How many churches today are racially, socially, and economically mixed? Even if the Corinthians had difficulties in seeing everyone as equal, at least they worshiped together! This passage is a call for the church to open its doors to all, mindful of the gifts and blessings that every person called of God has to offer. Together, let us boast of what God has done for us!

Lord, may I see others the way you see them,
not as the world would see them. Amen.

Pride in the Lord

2 Corinthians 12:1-6

What parts of spiritual life do people take pride in?

For the Corinthians, the church was strongly at odds with the culture. Corinthian culture was concerned with status, social appearance, and reputation. Before today's passage, Paul spoke about boasting only in Jesus Christ. Calling himself weak and foolish, he reiterated that he himself was nothing to boast about, a direct contradiction to Corinthian culture, where self-promotion was commended and accepted. Instead, he told a story about a man he knew 14 years ago. Every commentator states, and certainly his readers knew, that he was talking about himself.

Paul related this story in the third person, partially because he had just condemned self-praise, and he didn't want to sound boastful. He worked hard to walk the tightrope between humility and making himself credible. He told this story to relate how close his relationship was with God and that, as a person who experienced such mystical insights, he was qualified to teach them.

Yet Paul didn't want to be judged by visions or mystical experiences. He refused to gain credibility the same way the Corinthians did. What was important was the way he lived his life. That's where his authority came from, and that's how they would know that he was a man of faith. If he wanted to play the game of boasting, he could out-boast them all. But Paul's point was that visions, spiritual gifts, or anything else that one could brag about are inconsequential when it comes to the way one lives their day-to-day life.

Lord, keep me focused on how I live for you. Amen.

Stephen Sees Paradise

Acts 7:54-60

How could the vision of Jesus transform someone's life?

As he faced the furious crowd, Stephen had a vision. He saw Jesus standing at the right hand of God, the place of testimony, in defense of Stephen in heaven. It was Stephen's welcome into the company of his Savior and his last testimony to those on earth. Like Abraham, who saw God, and then Peter and later Paul, Stephen's witness was blessed and affirmed by his vision of Jesus. His last moments were bathed in the certainty of faith and knowledge of salvation.

This is why he was able to pray for his murderers as he died. Like Jesus on the cross, his last thoughts were for the souls of those who killed him. By crying out to God for their forgiveness, he underscored his own innocence and demonstrated his righteousness.

His cries of joy at seeing Jesus Christ and his calls for his executioners' forgiveness made a profound effect on one of those present. Saul, later known as Paul, was holding the cloaks of those who stoned Stephen. Soon, Paul had his own vision of Jesus, but Stephen's vision and prayers must have impressed Paul enough to make him think. Certainly, God heard Stephen's prayers for forgiveness, and Paul became Jesus' greatest apostle, responsible for the salvation of great areas of the ancient world. The God of second chances worked through the prayers of a martyr to save an accessory to murder who then witnessed to much of the world.

Lord, comfort me with the certain
knowledge of my salvation. Amen.

SATURDAY, MAY 23

An Eternal Home

2 Corinthians 5:1-10

What will it be like to have a heavenly body?

According to Paul in this passage, we're all living in tents. He compared our physical bodies to fragile and unreliable tents that will ultimately fail us all. Happily, we're promised a heavenly dwelling, a new body that will be eternally reliable. We don't know what these heavenly bodies will be like. But because of the promise of eternal life, when we die, our physical body will be covered over by our resurrection body, and all that is mortal will be swallowed up in life. We'll have nothing to fear, and we will be more alive than ever before in a new kind of body, which Paul called a heavenly dwelling.

However, the physical body isn't something to be hated, even if it's fragile and pales in comparison to what is to come. Rather, the physical body is our place of action, the place where we can do things to help bring about the kingdom of God on earth. Our physical bodies are where we labor for God before we rest. In so doing, we can stand before Jesus at judgment, knowing that we've spent our time on earth striving to do the work of God.

And so, even though our bodies can be slow and painful and limiting, every moment within them is precious. Each moment we live on earth, we can be doing God's work, affecting other lives, and changing the nature of the world. It's what we were put on earth to do. And when this body finally wears out, we will step into our new home, a heavenly dwelling that will surround us with life, love, and glory.

Lord, guide me to use my time on earth to your glory,
so that I may rest in your glory in heaven. Amen.

Pentecost Sunday, May 24

The Spirit Comes to Jesus' Followers

Acts 2:1-13

How is the Holy Spirit evident in the world?

Often, we think of the Holy Spirit quietly visiting individuals during times of contemplation and prayer. Sometimes that happens, but Pentecost was an event that blasted all the senses; a rushing sound, the sight and presumably heat of flames, and the strange ability to suddenly speak multiple languages. There was nothing subtle about it! It was a miraculous demonstration that the good news of the gospel is open to all people, and that God can and will enable everyone to be part of it. It also demonstrated how God would enable Jesus' followers to spread the good news of the gospel. It was an explosive birth of God's church.

Imagine yourself among those crowds. Galileans, known to be poor in learning other dialects, entered the street proclaiming God in many different languages. It must have been disconcerting to the crowds. The best way they found to explain what they saw was that the disciples were drunk. The power of God bursting through heaven's barriers could only be explained away by new wine.

The Holy Spirit isn't of this world. It doesn't make sense. It can even look foolish. But it's the power that breaks down barriers, that inflames the hearts of believers, and draws people into the saving grace of Jesus Christ. It's the hope of creation, and the strength of those who obey the call of Christ throughout the world.

Lord, fill me with your Spirit, so that I may
proclaim your Church in word and deed. Amen.

MONDAY, MAY 25

Jesus Forgave the Dying Thief

Luke 23:32-33, 39-43

How could a person die surrounded by what could save them?

When Jesus began his ministry, he said that he had come to "preach good news to the poor, to proclaim release to the prisoners . . . and to liberate the oppressed" (Luke 4:18). In Jesus' last moments on earth, he did exactly that for one of the most desolate people on earth. While Jesus was being ridiculed and hanging in agony, he was still doing the work of salvation. He promised the criminal a place in paradise.

All that can be given to us as well. There are many alive today who ridicule the idea of salvation and eternal life, rejecting the saving grace of Jesus. Like the taunting criminal on the cross, the path to eternal life is right before them, but they will die because of their cynicism. There are others who recognize their sins. At that moment, on the cross, Jesus was also broken and bleeding, suffering not for his own sins, as the other criminals, but for the salvation of humanity. The second criminal saw his sacrifice and claimed his part. To those who call for Christ, the gates of heaven swing open. Paradise awaits!

The great irony of humanity is that so many forfeit eternal life while it is so freely offered to us. To leave this world without the salvation of Jesus Christ is like dying in the desert just steps away from fresh water. May we instead all drink deeply of Jesus' saving grace!

*Jesus, remember me when you
come into your kingdom. Amen.*

Call on the Lord and Be Saved

Joel 2:28-32

How can we be sure our prayers for deliverance will continue to be answered?

In the passage before today's text from Joel, Israel had been devastated by a swarm of locusts. The people prayed for deliverance, and God destroyed the locusts and promised rich harvests. In today's passage, Joel promises that these prayers for Israel's deliverance will continue long after the harvests are brought into the fold. They will continue after all who prayed for them have died. God will continue to deliver Israel right up until the end of the world.

This passage is about the end times. It talks about the final salvation of God's people. Joel wrote that God's Spirit will be poured out on all the people. Peter quoted these words to explain the presence of God's Holy Spirit at Pentecost. The power and presence of God's Spirit has woven itself throughout the history of God and God's people.

During the last days, our world will be turned upside down, and all that we've known about the earth will change. But as terrifying as this sounds, Joel reminded the people of Israel that this is a time of salvation and deliverance. They can count on this again and again and again until the end of the earth. When we call on the Lord for help, God is never done with the task of saving us until the world itself is done. God's relationship with God's people runs through all of history, and we can rest in God's holy power, confident that all who have called on the name of the Lord will be saved.

O Lord, thank you for your promise of salvation
that follows your people through all the ages. Amen.

Wednesday, May 27

Living Within the Family of God

Romans 8:12-17

What does it mean to be part of the family of God?

One of my friends lived on the streets of Washington, DC, for 18 years as an addict. During that time, he lost all connection with his family. When he got clean and off the streets, his happiest moment was being reunited with them. They joyfully took him in and loved him as if he had never left them. He became part of a family once again.

We are part of the family of the people of God, but there are things that estrange us, too. Paul spoke of being obligated to the world, that a worldly focus will ultimately harm us. Instead, our obligations are to live by the strength and guidance of the Holy Spirit.

As children of God, we are heirs of God. Paul spoke of adoption, a concept that especially related to Roman life. The Romans often adopted even adults into their families. For those who were adopted, it meant giving up their previous family for a better life and future. But for Christians, adoption into the family of God means that salvation and eternal life are now our inheritance. It also means, however, that we give up our place as people of the world, so things won't always be easy. The world stands in opposition to those things that it does not understand. But to be part of the family of God is a gift well worth the challenges. And to look forward to eternal life within our holy family is a gift like none other.

Father, thank you for my place and
my inheritance within the family of God. Amen.

Thursday, May 28

Called to Be God's People

1 Corinthians 1:1-9

What are the attributes of a strong and healthy church?

Because Christians are sanctified and dedicated to Jesus Christ, we are not part of the culture of the world. Christians simply don't act like other people. Our standards are dictated by God, not society. And because we are united with all who call to Jesus, we are a worldwide family of God.

Paul thanked God for the knowledge, testimony, and spiritual gifts of the Corinthian Christians. However, while they were blessings, they were misused and misunderstood by the Corinthians. They equated wisdom and knowledge of Jesus Christ with spoken eloquence, believing that those who spoke in tongues or had visions were treasured by God over others. Love, Paul told them, is the greatest gift of all. Christianity is not only following Jesus' teachings but living in relationship with him and the Holy Spirit. There's work involved, and they needed to depend on their relationship with Jesus to stay holy and strong in the faith.

Our transformation from people of the world to people of God is entirely a gift of grace and has nothing to do with social status, personal history, or ethnicity. We are defined by love for one another and the world, not by eloquent preaching or charismatic experiences. We are to be in an alliance with God that results in grace for the world and a personal increase in holiness. And we are to be ever thankful for the transformative power of the salvation of Jesus Christ.

Lord, help me to be defined by love, in partnership with you,
and ever thankful for your salvation. Amen.

Friday, May 29

God Wants All to Be Saved

1 Timothy 2:1-7; John 3:16

Who could be turned away from the salvation of Jesus Christ?

In his first letter to Timothy, Paul encouraged his readers to pray for all people so that they might all be brought into the family of God. That's God's strongest desire: to have every person God created aligned with Christ and the Holy Spirit. After all, if God would seek out Paul, the "biggest sinner of all," then certainly salvation is open to everyone.

How do we know that God wants everyone to be brought into the family of God? It's because God gave Jesus Christ to the world. In John 3:16, the word used for "world" (*kosmos*) can be translated to mean those who would be excluded from any exclusive club: those who are not already believers or righteous people. *Kosmos* refers to the broken people, the rebels, the people on the outside who are often rejected by others. The door is not closed to anyone for any reason. God welcomes all to claim Christ and eternal life.

Those of us who claim membership in the family of God are to welcome all, because only by Christ's grace are we welcome. It's the wonderful and incredible news of the gospel because it means that we and everyone else can dare to claim salvation. It also means that every person, even those we might be uncomfortable letting "into the club," can belong to the family of God, too. As family members, our call is to welcome all with open arms and open hearts.

Lord, thank you for being my mediator for
salvation. May I welcome all with the same
love with which you welcome me! Amen.

Saturday, May 30

The Lord's Spirit Placed on Them

Numbers 11:24-29

Where are some unexpected places God can be found?

The Spirit of God has a way of slipping out through the cracks. It doesn't stay where we say it "belongs": in churches, in Bible studies, or in Sunday schools. It seeps out onto the streets, into everyday events, and common interactions.

Moses took 70 elders out into the desert. The Spirit of God fell on all of them, and they began to prophesy. But a bit of that Spirit seeped back into the camp, falling on two men, Eldad and Medad, who also began to prophesy. This was concerning to those in the camp because they were in the "wrong place" to catch God's Spirit. They weren't supposed to get this power! It was God let out of the box. Moses wasn't concerned. He encouraged the men in the camp. The power and presence of God should be promoted wherever it's found! It was no reflection against Moses that God's Spirit leaked out of the meeting in the desert. Instead, Moses wished that everyone were filled with the Spirit of God.

That's how the power of God works. It's not controlled by human rules or boundaries and doesn't pay attention to whether someone is "qualified." As followers of Jesus, we need to be open to the Spirit wherever we might see it. We need to keep our eyes and ears open to the surprising places we see God at work. And we need to be willing to be vessels of the Spirit ourselves, boldly speaking God's word when our hearts are touched by the power of the Holy Spirit.

Lord, open my eyes to see you in unexpected places,
and my heart to accept your power. Amen

SUNDAY, MAY 31

Peter, Filled With the Spirit, Preaches

Acts 2:14-21

How did Joel's prophecy relate to Pentecost?

While Joel's prophecy spoke of end times, it also spoke of the workings of the Holy Spirit throughout history, like a thread that is woven throughout the story of humanity. Joel spoke of a cosmic shift to a new relationship of the earth with heaven, a relationship made known by the presence of the Spirit. The alignment of heaven and earth changed with the birth, death, and resurrection of Jesus Christ, and we are now living between the dawn of the kingdom of God and the victory of Jesus' return. Many, including Peter, anticipated the end times during their lifetime, but prophecy can be tricky! We're still waiting for that glorious day of the kingdom of heaven coming to earth to reign.

Peter quoted Joel to the crowds, reminding them of the unbroken line of faith from earlier times. While this outpouring of the Holy Spirit was something new, they had been told about this before. Still, it took them by surprise.

When Peter called the crowds to listen, he used an unusual term that literally means "let me place the word of God in your ears." When the Spirit speaks to us, it is God in our ears, our hearts, and our minds, transforming us into new people, the people of God. The Spirit may come in surprising places and unexpected times, but as God's people, we have been assured of salvation, and that "everyone who calls on the name of the Lord will be saved."

Lord, may your word be in my ears
and your Spirit be in my heart. Amen.

JUNE

CONTRIBUTORS:

Clara Welch
(June 1–June 28)

Sue Mink
(June 29–June 30)

The Original Passover Celebration

Deuteronomy 16:1-8

How are the elements of bread and juice meaningful religious symbols for you?

Originally, Passover and the Festival of Unleavened Bread were separate observances. Exodus 12:1-13 provides a description of the first Passover meal eaten on the last night of Israel's bondage under the Egyptian pharaoh. The Festival of Unleavened Bread was celebrated by the Israelites after settling in the Promised Land to remind them that their ancestors "fled Egypt in a great hurry" (Deuteronomy 16:3).

In this text from Deuteronomy, the writer has combined these two observances into one. This writer emphasized that the combined observance will take place "at the location the Lord selects for his name to reside" (verse 2). Scholars believe Deuteronomy was written during the time of King Josiah. At that time, the Lord's chosen place was Jerusalem.

The blood of the sacrificial lambs smeared on the doorposts saved the lives of Israel's firstborn on the night of their escape from Egypt. Jesus became the final sacrificial lamb when he died on the cross, "so that everyone who believes in him won't perish but will have eternal life" (John 3:16). In our observance of Holy Communion, we remember God's providence and faithfulness as we partake of the bread and cup.

> Loving Christ, thank you for giving us the
> tangible symbols of the bread and cup to
> remind us of your saving love. Amen.

Triumphal Entry Into Jerusalem

Mark 11:1-10

Do you speak of Jesus with a question mark or an exclamation point?

The people who spread cloaks and branches before Jesus did not ask questions. They shouted confident exclamations of praise and declared that Jesus was "the one who comes in the name of the Lord!" In him they saw "the coming kingdom of our ancestor David!" (verse 9). But the people did not have an accurate understanding of what it meant for Jesus to come "in the name of the Lord." They did not comprehend the nature of "the coming kingdom."

As we grow in our faith, it is good to ask questions and voice our praise. When we read a biblical text, it can be helpful to ask, What does this Scripture passage tell me about Jesus Christ? What is God calling me to do through this Scripture passage? How does this passage of Scripture assure me of God's love, forgiveness, and mercy?

When we carefully seek answers to our questions, we will come to a better understanding of who God is, the nature of God's kingdom, and our place as followers of Christ. When the people shouted "Hosanna!" (verse 9) to Jesus, they were placing their hope in an earthly political government and thus selling themselves short of what God desired for them. When we shout "Hosanna," we do so with the secure hope of eternal life in God's heavenly kingdom.

Saving God, I offer you my questions and my praise. Amen.

WEDNESDAY JUNE 3

Preparation for the Passover Meal

Mark 14:12-16

How do you prepare for Jesus' presence in your life?

Jesus' disciples asked, "Where do you want us to prepare for you to eat the Passover meal?" (Mark 14:12). Mark reports that the disciples "found everything just as he had told them, and they prepared the Passover meal" (verse 16). We have two possible explanations of how Jesus knew the disciples would be met by "a man carrying a water jar" (verse 13): omniscience or previous arrangement. Either of these will satisfy us. However, these first-century disciples would have wondered, "Why is a man carrying a water jar?" In their culture, this was the work of women. But the disciples did not question Jesus' instructions. They accepted on faith that they would find things as Jesus described. They were willing to follow his directions.

The disciples asked Jesus a specific question, "Where do you want us to prepare for you to eat the Passover meal?" (verse 12). We, too, may find ourselves asking specific questions as we seek to live in the presence of Christ. We may ask for guidance in deciding about a service opportunity in our church or community. We may ask God to open our hearts to receive God's Word as we study the Bible. We may ask for help in forgiving someone who has wronged us.

When we listen with prayer and patience, we will hear Christ's answers to our requests.

Holy God, thank you for inviting me to live in your presence.
Open my ears to hear your word for me. Amen.

The Heart-Centered New Covenant

Jeremiah 31:31-34

How are God's instructions engraved on your heart?

Sometimes when something is broken, that is the end of it. Sometimes, however, something good grows out of the brokenness, and restoration occurs. God said through Jeremiah, "The time is coming, . . . when I will make a new covenant with the people of Israel and Judah. It won't be like the covenant I made with their ancestors. . . . They broke that covenant" (Jeremiah 31:31-32). The covenant Jeremiah had in mind here was made at Mt. Sinai, when God gave the Law to Moses. The new covenant will not be written on stone tablets, as the Ten Commandments were. Instead, it will be engraved on the people's "hearts" (verse 33). Under the new covenant, a person's motivation to love and honor God will come from within.

God never turned away from the divine promise, "I will be their God, and they will be my people" (verse 33). Even though the Israelites broke the first covenant, God did not turn away. God promised a new covenant and restored the relationship through forgiveness for "wrongdoing" and the promise to "never again remember their sins" (verse 34).

Have you opened your heart to God's love? Does your motivation to live in relationship with God come from external influences or from within your heart? How has the assurance of God's forgiveness drawn you closer to God?

> Loving God, open my heart to receive your forgiveness.
> Hold my hand, and always walk alongside me. Amen.

FRIDAY, JUNE 5

The Lord's Supper Shared With Disciples

Luke 22:14-23

How are the bread and cup symbols for you of your covenant relationship with God?

During his last meal with his disciples, Jesus announced, "This cup is the new covenant by my blood, which is poured out for you" (Luke 22:20). In Jesus, the promise of the new covenant and a new way of living in relationship with God became a present reality.

On this occasion, there was still a sense of anticipation, a sense of the "not-yet." As the meal began, Jesus said, "I won't eat it until it is fulfilled in God's kingdom" (verse 16), and "I won't drink from the fruit of the vine until God's kingdom has come" (verse 18). These were still future events, but Jesus knew that his betrayer had already set the chain of events in motion. Before the meal, Judas had "discussed with the chief priests and the officers of the temple guard how he could hand Jesus over to them" (verse 4).

At this point in the Gospel story, the disciples did not fully understand how this new covenant relationship with God would impact their lives. It is a relationship they would respond to from their hearts (Jeremiah 31:33) as they accepted the gifts of forgiveness, salvation, and new life made possible by Christ's sacrifice and resurrection.

Holy God, thank you for the promise of
salvation through Christ. Open my heart to
receive and respond to your love for me. Amen.

SATURDAY, JUNE 6

Clean Feet, Clean Hearts

John 13:2-7

How do Jesus' acts of service inspire you to serve others?

According to the Gospel of Luke, during this last supper, "an argument broke out among the disciples over which one of them should be regarded as the greatest" (Luke 22:24). After such an argument, it is doubtful that any of them would have volunteered to do a servant's task and wash the feet of the others. Peter was surprised, then, that Jesus, the one he addressed as "Lord," was doing this task. Was he also ashamed that he had not offered to wash his Lord's feet instead?

Peter resisted—at first. Jesus assured him, "You don't understand . . . now, but you will understand later" (verse 7). Understanding came over time for Peter, as he listened to Jesus' teaching after dinner (Chapters 13–17), after he denied Jesus three times (Chapter 18), after the Crucifixion and the Resurrection, and on the seashore one morning at breakfast (Chapter 21).

Jesus wants us to accept his gift of sacrificial love and serve others in his name. We may feel unworthy or inadequate at first, but as Jesus offers to wash our feet, he also sees into our hearts and promises that we "will understand later." Perhaps you can even hear Jesus saying, "You will thank me later." As we grow in faith and experience the joy of Christian service, we do!

Holy God, thank you for Jesus, who helps
me understand your amazing love for me. Amen.

SUNDAY, JUNE 7

This New Covenant

Mark 14:17-24; Hebrews 8:6-7, 10-12

How have you experienced the fulfillment of God's promises made possible by the new covenant?

The author of Hebrews quoted Jeremiah's promise of a new covenant (Hebrews 8:8-12) and then explained why a new covenant is necessary: "If the first covenant had been without fault, it wouldn't have made sense to expect a second" (verse 7). The fault of the first covenant was that it did not provide a permanent solution with regard to the sin of the people "because it's impossible for the blood of bulls and goats to take away sins" (Hebrews 10:4).

John the Baptist called Jesus "the Lamb of God who takes away the sin of the world!" (John 1:29). Jesus provides "a better covenant . . . with better promises" (Hebrews 8:6). Jesus became the sacrifice that took away all the sin of all the people, once and for all.

God promises to "be lenient toward [our] unjust actions" and not to "remember [our] sins anymore" (Hebrews 8:12). This is a liberating promise. We may sometimes feel as if we have reached a dead-end and have no hope, but with God, we always have hope. God does forgive our wrongdoing and does not remember our sins. This is a gift of freedom and allows us the opportunity to embrace the new life God offers us, over and over again!

Holy and forgiving God, thank you for writing
your law of love on my heart. Thank you for new
opportunities and new beginnings. Amen.

MONDAY, JUNE 8

Turmoil at the Last Supper

Mark 14:26-31

What helps you remain faithful through hardship?

Peter was sure his faithfulness would not falter. He declared, "Even if everyone else stumbles, I won't" (Mark 14:29). Jesus continued speaking and predicted that Peter would deny him three times "on this very night" (verse 30). Yet Peter insisted, "If I must die alongside you, I won't deny you," and the other disciples "said the same thing" (verse 31).

Even though you probably know the rest of the story, pretend for a moment that you don't. Imagine how Peter might have felt during this conversation. Was he hurt or surprised that Jesus believed he would deny him? What was his tone of voice and his body language?

Imagine Jesus saying to you, "You will . . . falter in your faithfulness to me" (verse 27). How do you respond? We noted in yesterday's reading that God is always offering us new opportunities to be faithful. God remains with us when we stumble and surrounds us with forgiveness and grace. God offers us the strength and direction we need to face all of life's circumstances.

Loving God, thank you for remaining with me and
loving me, even when I falter in my faith. Help me
grow stronger in my faith each day. Amen.

Tuesday, June 9

Jesus Prays, the Disciples Sleep

Mark 14:32-42

How do you stay alert and fulfill God's will for you?

Imagine Peter telling a close friend about his experiences that night. Perhaps Peter's story went something like this: "It was a difficult night for me. First, Jesus predicted that I would deny him, not once but three times. I insisted that I would not deny him, but he was so sure. Jesus even told me when it would happen, before the rooster crows twice. I had no idea what rooster he was talking about!

"At supper, he shared a cup with us, calling it his 'blood of the covenant, which is poured out for many.' I did not realize at the time the suffering he would endure for that to happen. Then we went to Gethsemane on the Mount of Olives. As Jesus prayed, he asked God to spare him the 'cup of suffering.' But even as he prayed that he might be spared the suffering, it was much more important to him that he do God's will. He prayed, 'Not what I want but what you want.'

"That night, when Jesus was feeling such despair, all he asked me to do was stay near him and remain alert. But did I? No! I fell asleep! I still remember Jesus asking me, 'Couldn't you stay alert for one hour?' He said, 'The spirit is eager, but the flesh is weak.' That is certainly true. He had to wake me up three times! I did not have time to tell him I was sorry. At that moment, Jesus said that his betrayer had come. No, it was not my best night."

Loving God, thank you for forgiving me when I falter.
Help me stay alert and be faithful. Amen.

Wednesday, June 10

Jesus Betrayed and Arrested

Mark 14:43-50

In what ways are you a courageous disciple?

Earlier that evening, Jesus quoted a prophecy from Zechariah 13:7 (Mark 14:27). The prophecy was fulfilled as the mob came at him with swords and his disciples ran away (verse 50).

The mob was "sent by the chief priests, legal experts, and elders" (verse 43), the very ones who should have known better! They were experts when it came to the content of the Law and the Prophets. The ones who were responsible for providing religious leadership to the Jews did not see in Jesus the king they were expecting. Instead of accepting Jesus as the fulfillment of God's promise and encouraging the community of Jews to do the same, they arrested and condemned him.

Judas shared supper with Jesus that evening, as one of the chosen 12. Now, he betrayed Jesus with a sign of friendship, a kiss.

On that fateful night, the chief priests, legal experts, and elders knew what was happening, and with cowardice, they sent others to do their dirty work and make the arrest. The disciples, who had agreed with Peter that they would "die alongside" (verse 31) Jesus, did not understand what was happening, and they ran away. Yet in spite of all the things so many did wrong, Jesus accepted arrest and death on a cross for the salvation of them all.

Holy Lord, give me the courage to follow you. Amen.

THURSDAY, JUNE 11

Jesus Crucified

Mark 15:16-24

What feelings do you have as you read this Scripture?

Jesus was a prisoner sentenced to crucifixion with no legal protection from harsh treatment. The soldiers "called together the whole company" (verse 16). They mocked Jesus according to the charge against him; they dressed him in royal purple and placed "a crown of thorns" (verse 17) on his head. Do you wonder about the depth of their cruelty and the apparent delight they took in inflicting pain on this person they did not know? How would they have reacted if they had known Jesus had already predicted their behavior: "They will ridicule him, spit on him, torture him, and kill him" (10:34).

Golgotha, the sight of the Crucifixion, was outside the city walls. The "wine mixed with myrrh" (verse 23) would have served as a pain-reliever or a sedative, but Jesus refused to drink it. The soldiers likely had no idea they were fulfilling prophecy when they drew lots for Jesus' clothes. Psalm 22:18 says, "They divvy up my garments among themselves; they cast lots for my clothes."

Jesus remained strong throughout this ordeal. There is no indication that he wavered in his resolve to fulfill God's will. What strength did he draw from his intimate prayer with his "Abba, Father" (14:36) in Gethsemane? His amazing love for God and humankind was deeper than any pain the Jewish leaders and Roman soldiers inflicted on him.

Holy God, grant me strength to remain faithful,
even in times of adversity and suffering. Amen.

Seeing and Believing?

Mark 15:27-32

What would you have said if you had been walking by the cross at the time of the Crucifixion?

People voiced their contempt for Jesus as he suffered on the cross. One group, simply identified as "people walking by," taunted him saying, "You were going to destroy the temple and rebuild it in three days, were you?" (verse 29). At Jesus' trial, the "testimonies didn't agree even on this point" (Mark 14:59). It is disturbing that these passersby were comfortable with basing their hatred on false testimony.

A second group was made up of "the chief priests . . . together with the legal experts" (15:31). They joined the passersby in challenging Jesus to "come down from the cross" (verse 32). It is somewhat amusing that they said, "Then we'll see and believe" (verse 32). They knew the prophecies. They had many opportunities to see and believe that Jesus is the fulfillment of those prophecies as they witnessed Jesus' miracles of healing. For them, seeing was not believing.

Through the ages, people have continued to insult Jesus and to request miracles, saying, "Then we'll see and believe." Paul wrote, "You are saved by God's grace because of your faith" (Ephesians 2:8). The author of Hebrews writes, "Now faith is the assurance of things hoped for, the conviction of things not seen" (Hebrews 11:1, NRSV).

> Loving God, thank you for your gifts
> of grace and salvation. Amen.

Saturday, June 13

Faithful Women

Mark 15:40-47

How do you show your love for Jesus through actions?

Since Jesus died late in the day Friday, there was not enough time to prepare his body with spices before the sabbath began at sundown. Two of the women who witnessed the Crucifixion, "Mary Magdalene and Mary the mother of Joses" (Mark 15:47), followed Joseph to see where he buried Jesus. They planned to return after the sabbath to anoint his body. The women dared to come to the Crucifixion, although they watched from a distance. We can imagine their deep grief as they heard the insults and watched their friend suffer and die. They showed their love for Jesus by being present.

At the time of Jesus' arrest, his disciples became frightened "and ran away" (14:50). Peter denied that he even knew Jesus. In contrast, Joseph of Arimathea showed great courage when he approached Pilate and asked for Jesus' body. It was risky to admit allegiance to a man Pilate had just crucified. Members of the Sanhedrin would not be pleased that a Jewish leader was acting in support of Jesus.

Sometimes God calls us to serve in ways that are outside our comfort zone. How have you experienced God's strength and presence when you needed courage to follow in faith?

Ever-present God, grant me
courage to live faithfully. Amen.

SUNDAY, JUNE 14

Jesus' Blood

Mark 15:6-15, 25-26, 33-39

What signs of hope do you see in the Crucifixion story?

Two phrases caught my attention in this reading: "At daybreak" (Mark 15:1) and "During the festival" (verse 6). The word "daybreak" calls to mind the beautiful colors of a sunrise splashed across the sky and God's gift of new opportunities in a new day. The Passover Festival was a time to remember God's faithfulness in the past and to trust God's continuing faithfulness into the future.

The symbolism and meaning of daybreak and the Passover Festival were completely lost on the chief priests. Religious leaders accused Jesus of blasphemy when he claimed to be "the Christ, the Son of the blessed one" (Mark 14:61). They did not want to accept that this Jesus was the promised son of David.

Mark noted that "the whole earth was dark" (verse 33). This darkness is associated with the end times and the return of the Son of Man "with great power and splendor" (13:24-27). The curtain in the sanctuary, noted in Mark 15:38, separated the people from God's presence. As Jesus died, that curtain "was torn in two from top to bottom" (verse 38). Jesus quoted Psalm 22:1, "My God, my God, why have you left me?" (Mark 15:34). But Jesus knew God had not deserted him. This psalm also proclaims, "Generations to come will be told about my Lord. . . . [and] what God has done" (Psalm 22:30-31).

Holy God, thank you that
you do not forsake us. Amen.

MONDAY, JUNE 15

The People Promise to Obey

Exodus 24:3-8

How do you fulfill God's call to obedience?

After God gave Moses God's instructions for the people (Chapters 20–23), "Moses came and told the people all the Lord's words and all the case laws" (24:3). The phrase, "the Lord's words," indicates the Ten Commandments written on the two stone tablets. The people promised obedience multiple times while at Mount Sinai.

Moses led the people in a ritual to affirm their promise of obedience. He took the blood from the animals that were sacrificed and threw half of it "against the altar" (verse 7), which represented God's presence. After the people promised obedience for the third time, Moses threw the other half of the blood "over the people," saying, "This is the blood of the covenant that the Lord now makes with you" (verse 8).

The Israelites broke their promise of obedience many times over and suffered the consequences, but God remained faithful to the "most precious possession" (19:5). Generations later, Jesus said, "This is my blood of the covenant" (Mark 14:24). With his blood, Jesus made the final atoning sacrifice, not only for Israel but for all humankind, including us.

> Faithful God, thank you for remaining faithful,
> even when I falter. Thank you for the gift
> of salvation through Jesus Christ. Amen.

The Atoning Sin Sacrifice

Leviticus 16:11-19

How have you experienced forgiveness and reconciliation with God?

God instructed, "This will be a permanent rule for you: On the tenth day of the seventh month, you must deny yourselves . . . On that day reconciliation will be made for you in order to cleanse you. You will be clean before the Lord from all your sins" (Leviticus 16:29-30). Aaron was the first priest of Israel. On the Day of Reconciliation, God instructed Aaron to make a purification offering for the "reconciliation for himself and his household." He was then allowed to go "inside the inner curtain," a privilege only granted a priest. If a person looked at "the cover," or mercy seat, located "inside the inner curtain," he would die, because God was "present in the cloud above the cover" (verse 2). Aaron was instructed to make a "cloud of incense" to conceal the cover from his sight.

We saw in yesterday's reading from Exodus 24 that the blood of sacrifice was the sign of the covenant between God and the people at Mount Sinai (Exodus 24:8). Here the blood of sacrifice is a sign of reconciliation between God and the people, necessary because of the people's "rebellious sins, as well as for all their other sins" (Leviticus 16:16). Again, we are reminded of Jesus' offering of his blood as the final sacrifice for the reconciliation of all humankind.

Loving God, thank you for your forgiveness
and your enduring faithfulness. Amen.

Wednesday, June 17
Redeemed and Purified

Titus 2:11-15

In what ways does God's gift of redemption motivate you to eagerly live a godly life?

We live in an in-between time, between the first appearance and the promised second appearance of Christ. In this letter to Titus, Paul gives instructions about the way we are called to live in this in-between time as "we wait for the blessed hope and the glorious appearance of our great God and Savior, Jesus Christ." We live in Christ's new covenant by eagerly doing "good actions" and living "godly lives right now." We also look forward to "the blessed hope and the glorious appearance of our great God and savior Jesus Christ," the second appearance of "the grace of God."

We have the exciting privilege of living in this in-between time. We can know the joy and peace of God's salvation. We can rely on our hope in Christ to see us through challenging times. The instruction is easy to remember: "Live sensible, ethical, and godly lives right now."

Are you eager to do good actions? Are you eager to live a godly life and share the good news of Christ right now?

God of grace, thank you for sending Jesus to show
what it means to live a godly life. Thank you for
the gifts of hope and salvation through Christ. Amen.

Entering the Sanctuary by Jesus' Blood

Hebrews 10:19-25

How do you spark love and good deeds as you enter God's presence?

The author of Hebrews wrote, "We can enter the holy of holies" (Hebrews 10:19). In our reading for June 16, we saw that originally only a priest could go "inside the inner curtain" (Leviticus 16:12); and even the priest had to take precautions when he entered. When Jesus died, this curtain that separated God from humankind "was torn in two from top to bottom" (Matthew 27:51; also Luke 23:45). The barrier between God's presence and humankind is gone. Now it is possible for all of us to draw near to God without fear of death.

As followers of Christ, we are called to "hold on to the confession of our hope without wavering." In other words, we hold on to our faith in Christ with "confidence." We "draw near with a genuine heart with the certainty that our faith gives us." Our understanding of God's gift of reconciliation is enhanced when we make connections between ancient Israelite rituals and Christ's sacrifice.

How do you draw near to God and accept the gift of reconciliation? The author of Hebrews calls us to continue "meeting together with other believers" and to "encourage each other."

Holy God, thank you for removing the barriers
and calling me into close fellowship with you. Amen.

FRIDAY, JUNE 19

The Time Has Come

Hebrews 9:1-10

In what ways does your experience of worship feel superficial, and in what ways does it feel genuine?

The author of Hebrews began his sermon with the words, "In the past" (Hebrews 1:1), and immediately contrasted this with "these final days" (1:2). He reminds us that previously "God spoke through the prophets" (1:1), but now God has spoken "through a Son" (1:2). The author described two tents: "the holy place" and "the holy of holies." The suggestion of two tents is not historically accurate. When the Tabernacle was constructed in the time of Moses, it consisted of only one tent, with a curtain separating these two holy spaces. God instructed Moses, "The veil will separate for you the holy from the holiest space" (Exodus 26:33). The illustration of two tents in the context of Hebrews may be interpreted to be symbolic of the old and new covenants.

The sacrificial system described in the Old Testament provided a means for reconciliation between God and the chosen people. It did not, however, provide a way to "perfect the conscience;" in other words, to remove or to take away sin. The ancient "regulations" and rituals were "superficial" and "imposed until the time of the new order." We will consider the significance of this new order as we continue our study of Hebrews 9 in the next two days.

God of new beginnings, let me turn away from the
superficial and embrace the new life you offer me. Amen.

Christ, the Final Sacrifice for Sin

Hebrews 9:23-28

How do you express gratitude for Christ's sacrifice?

The author of Hebrews wrote that "the earthly holy place . . . is a copy of the true holy place," which is heaven. The holy place in the Tabernacle, and later in the Temple, was "made by human hands." It is interesting that the holy place itself needed "to be cleansed" before it could serve as a place for the cleansing of the people. The priest Aaron was instructed to sprinkle blood to "make reconciliation for the inner holy area because of the pollution of the Israelites and . . . their rebellious sins" (Leviticus 16:16).

When Jesus Christ offered himself as the sacrifice for the sins of humankind, he bypassed the holy place on earth and entered "into heaven itself." Under the law of Moses, the high priest offered the sacrifice in the Holy of Holies every year. With Jesus' sacrifice, animal sacrifice ended. Jesus' blood has the power to cleanse the sins of all humankind for all time, and additional sacrifices are not necessary. Jesus died once and, in so doing, removed our sin.

Sin is serious and creates a barrier between us and our Creator. Humankind is powerless to remove that sin. Only God, through the sacrifice of God's Son, can accomplish this. How do you respond to this wonderful gift of grace?

Holy God, thank you for removing my sin, which
created a barrier between your presence and me. Amen.

Christ, Mediator of the New Covenant

Hebrews 9:11-22

What does it mean to you to live within the new covenant?

The author of Hebrews stated that "Christ has appeared as the high priest." Christ's qualifications for this role surpass those of the other high priests. Christ is called and appointed, but as a son, he has a closer relationship with God than even the angels (1:4). He offered "his own blood. . . . as a sacrifice without any flaw," a sacrifice with the power to completely wash away the people's sin. His sacrifice was offered only once, but it secures "our deliverance for all time."

We live under the new covenant, and we have "the promise of the eternal inheritance." Or as the apostle Paul put it, "We have been made righteous through his faithfulness combined with our faith," and we live with "the hope of God's glory" (Romans 5:1-2).

Since Christ's sacrifice secured our deliverance for all time, we are free from the rules and regulations of the sacrificial system under the old covenant. We are free to embrace God's enduring gift of forgiveness and promise of eternal life.

How do you express your gratitude for this gift and promise? How do you share Christ's amazing love and mercy with others?

Forgiving Lord, thank you for your enduring gift
of salvation. Open my heart to ways I may
share your love with others. Amen.

MONDAY, JUNE 22

Christ, the Source of Life

1 John 5:6-12

How do you witness to the truth of Jesus Christ?

The author of 1 John wrote, "The Spirit, the water, and the blood" testify to the life God offers us through Jesus Christ. What images come to mind when you think of water? A glacial lake, a waterfall, an ocean wave, a glass of cold water, a sprinkler watering the lawn? Water is refreshing and cleansing and necessary for good health. At the beginning of his ministry, Jesus was baptized in the Jordan River. The water of baptism is a symbol for us that we belong to Christ.

What images come to mind when you hear the word blood? I admit I turn my head away when the lab technician is drawing blood! Blood, like water, is necessary for our health and life. Jesus ended his earthly ministry by shedding his blood on the cross. His was cleansing blood with the power to take away the sin of all humankind.

Before his death, Jesus promised, "I will ask the Father, and he will send another Companion, who will be with you forever. This Companion is the Spirit of Truth" (John 14:16-17). First John 5:6 says, "The Spirit is the truth." Note that verse 11 is in the present tense: "God gave eternal life to us, and this life is in his Son." Eternal life in God's presence is not only a future promise; it is a present reality. When we live "in his Son," we know God's abiding love, gracious forgiveness, and constant presence here on earth.

Holy Spirit, live within me so that I may
witness to the truth of Christ. Amen.

TUESDAY, JUNE 23

Pursue Unity in the Church

1 Peter 3:8-12

How do you chase after peace and seek to live in unity with others?

What does it mean to "chase after" peace? "Chase" is a word that calls us to action. I imagine one friend chasing after another following an argument, asking forgiveness, offering forgiveness, restoring peace to the relationship. I see a person kneeling in prayer, crying out to God for peace.

When we want something, we are willing to chase after it and give the time and energy necessary to obtain it. In this text, Peter encourages us to "be of one mind" and "have unity of spirit" (NRSV). Thankfully, he did not mean to be of one opinion. Congregations would never be able to attain this, at least not on every issue! Peter calls us to be like Jesus in our relationships with others: to love one another and to treat one another with sympathy and compassion. When others are evil and insulting toward us, we are called to "give blessing in return."

My father-in-law and I did not agree on every issue, but we enjoyed a great relationship. We were of one mind in that we cared about one another, and we wanted unity within our family. Interestingly, as we put differences aside, we discovered many ways that we were alike. We reaped the blessings of peace and friendship.

God of peace, grant me courage and direction
as I chase after peace and seek to live in
unity with Christ and his followers. Amen.

All Peoples United in Christ

Ephesians 2:11-22

How do you experience unity within the body of Christ?

Imagine the challenges that Jewish and Gentile believers faced as they worked to accept their unity in Christ. After all, the Jews understood themselves to be God's chosen and covenant people, marked with the physical sign of circumcision. The Gentiles, on the other hand, were "strangers to the covenants of God's promise." Historically, a "barrier of hatred" separated these two groups.

Paul pointed out that Jesus "canceled the detailed rules of the Law so that he could create one new person out of the two groups, making peace." In his letter to the Ephesians, Paul assured the Gentiles that in Christ, the divisive barriers have been broken down. Jews and Gentiles alike are "God's people . . . God's household." Paul wrote that God's people are the temple, "built on the foundation of the apostles and prophets with Jesus Christ himself as the cornerstone." The church is not a stationary place but a growing and living body in Christ. Paul wrote, "God is building you into a place where God lives through the Spirit."

As followers of Christ, we are called to break down walls of division. We are called to proclaim the good news that God's love and salvation are for all people. How is God calling your church to work toward reconciliation with all people within your community and throughout the world?

God of unity, help me break down barriers of hatred and
work toward unity among your people. Amen.

THURSDAY, JUNE 25

Christ, the Image of God

Colossians 1:15-20

If you wrote a hymn about Christ, what key points would you include?

Paul included a "Hymn about Christ's work" (the CEB title) in his letter to the church in Colossae to help the early church understand the nature and ministry of Christ. As you read this passage, you may think of texts in Hebrews and the Gospel of John.

"Image" and "creation" in Colossians 1:15 remind us of the Creation story in Genesis 1. Genesis 1:27 says, "God created humanity in God's own image" (italics added), meaning humans are created in God's likeness. The Son, however, "is the image of the invisible God" (Colossians 1:15, italics added), not a likeness. The author of Hebrews wrote, "The Son is . . . the imprint of God's being" (Hebrews 1:3). This hymn from Colossians proclaims that the Son "is first over all creation." This is not to say that the Son is the first created, for we have seen that "he existed before" Creation.

The hymn closes with a testament to the saving power of Christ. Just as God created the world through the Son, God offers salvation and the peace of reconciliation through the Son.

God of reconciliation, thank you for your Son. Show me
how I may share the good news of Christ. Amen.

Paul's Ministry in the Congregation

Colossians 1:24-29

In what ways have you suffered for the sake of Christ?

The phrase "completing what is missing from Christ's sufferings" does not mean that Christ's atoning sacrifice was incomplete. Christ's suffering and sacrifice of himself on the cross were sufficient to pay the penalty for the sin of all humankind. The phrase means that sharing in Christ's sufferings is necessary to complete God's mission for us in bringing about the Kingdom of Heaven here on earth.

Christians are willing to suffer various forms of persecution from nonbelievers and opponents of Christ in order for Christ's church to grow. Paul was happy to suffer for the sake of the church, which is the body of Christ. As the body of Christ in the twenty-first century, we are called to share in the process of completing Christ's ministry and growing the church. Like Paul and the first-century church, we are not immune to suffering.

Our suffering may be financial as we generously share our resources with others. It may be physical as we live and serve in poverty-stricken areas as a member of a short-term mission team or a longer-term missionary. It may be emotional as we endure criticism from opponents or sit with others who are suffering illness or loss. But we, like Paul, are happy to share in Christ's suffering when we see the church grow and more people come to know the Savior.

Holy God, grant me strength and courage to endure
suffering for the sake of Christ and the church. Amen.

Saturday, June 27

Maintain Your Union With Christ

Colossians 2:16-23

What rules impede your union with Christ?

The churches in Laodicea (Colossians 4:16) and Colossae were struggling against the temptation to revert to following the Jewish law. Paul wrote, "Don't let anyone judge you about eating or drinking." Jews advocated the observance of food regulations required under the Law. Paul encouraged believers to resist the temptation to follow any of these practices. Jesus abolished the food laws, teaching that "nothing outside of a person can enter and contaminate a person in God's sight" (Mark 7:15).

Paul also encouraged the young congregations to ignore judgment related to "a festival, a new moon observance, or sabbaths." These had become legalistic rituals, not expressions of sincere worship. God criticized insincere worship through the prophets (Amos 5:21, 23-24). Jesus, in his conversation with the Samaritan woman, spoke of a time when worship would no longer be subject to regulations (John 4:21-23). Christians offer devoted worship to God and God alone.

Paul was not criticizing visions that are from God. He met Jesus in a vision on the road to Damascus. Paul was criticizing people who claim special knowledge from visions and "become unjustifiably arrogant by their selfish way of thinking." True believers practice humility.

> Faithful God, help me resist the way the world thinks
> and acts and worship you with a sincere heart. Amen.

United With Christ and One Another

Colossians 2:1-15

What worldly temptations threaten your unity with Christ and other believers?

Paul knew the churches were being deceived into believing that it would be better to follow "human traditions and the way the world thinks and acts" than to follow Christ. Some scholars suggest Paul was writing against the influence of gnostic philosophy, which claimed to have secret knowledge that was revealed to only a select group. Paul reminded his readers of "the secret plan of God," which is the reconciliation of all people through Christ. God's plan is not a secret for believers; it has been revealed in Jesus Christ. We are called to share this secret with those who do not yet know Christ. Reconciliation is available to everyone who opens his or her heart and life to Christ.

The unity of the church today is threatened by worldly influences just as it was in Paul's day. First-century Christians exhibited courageous faith as they remained united in Christ and supported the work of the Church. We are called to continue the work of spreading the good news of salvation and reconciliation through Christ.

Paul prayed that the hearts of believers "would be encouraged and united together in love." We can follow Paul's example and pray for the encouragement and unity of all Christians around the world.

God of unity and reconciliation, grant me strength and wisdom to remain faithful in prayer and love. Amen.

MONDAY, JUNE 29

A Few Will Be Spared

Ezekiel 6:1-10

How could a God of love destroy God's people?

The Judeans worshiped other deities and idols, even while aware of their history with the Lord. They knew of the covenants God had made, but their faith had become casual and unimportant. They no longer recognized God's power and glory and were careless and apathetic toward their Creator and Lord. God destroyed them so that they would "know that I am the Lord." Their idols would not save them. They had denied their God and minimized God's power, so it was necessary for God to reassert divine authority.

I struggled with these verses until I put them in another perspective I like to paint, but sometimes my paintings are not as I'd hoped. There's nothing else for me to do but paint out that area of the picture and start again. The entire painting would fail if I didn't. God, as the Creator of the Cosmos, works with humanity to "paint a picture" of the Kingdom of God on earth. But sometimes, we humans mess up the picture so badly that the only thing to do is paint it over and start again. That "painting over" can be bold and brutal, like in today's Scripture, or it can be a sudden, swift turn in our lives that is painful but ultimately productive. In the end, the destruction is an act of love for the world, even if it's devastating. It makes room for the holy. God's desolation becomes a place of glory once again.

Lord, keep your vision for holy living in my heart, so that my
actions will never displease you. Amen.

A Few Will Return

Isaiah 10:20-27

When have you witnessed restoration after brokenness?

God promised the Hebrew people that there would be a "remnant" who would remain after the Assyrians attacked. Destruction was decreed, but there would be survivors who would rebuild. A new shoot would grow out of the ashes.

The ancient Hebrews were the only ones who held the covenant as the chosen people of God. For God, the survival of the people was important because if the history of the Hebrew people ended on earth, so would the history of God's relationship with those God had chosen since the time of Abraham. Once the Hebrew people realized the great worth of their unique relationship with God and learned to cherish it, God allowed the remnant to grow and prosper again. God's anger against the people ended. Hope came back from the ashes because God is a God of restoration and new beginnings.

The Hebrew people were never a lost cause. The spark that had begun with Abraham would be fanned into flames again, and the people of Israel would grow in faith and in power. Just as our faith is sometimes challenged and nearly quenched by tragedies in our lives, God is there to blow on the embers, bringing life back to places of devastation and hope back to times we feel our faith is only a remnant, too.

Lord, bring hope to those places where
your presence is held within a remnant.
May your love grow and flourish there. Amen.

JULY

CONTRIBUTORS:

Sue Mink
(July 1–July 26)

Randy Cross
(July 27–July 31)

The Remaining Sheep

Jeremiah 23:1-8

How important is leadership in a nation's righteousness?

God promised a new chapter in the rule of Israel. There would be no more kings from the line of Jehoiachin, but God would find a new descendant of David who would rule in wisdom, justice, and righteousness. This king would be named "The LORD is our righteousness," and his wisdom would allow the people of Israel to live in safety and peace.

This passage is sometimes used during Advent. Certainly, the greatest king, who rules in wisdom, justice, and righteousness, is Jesus Christ. But while we can read this with the promise of Jesus to come, God was also promising the people of Israel an end to the Exile. This passage not only promised the Israelites that their nation would be re-established, but also that the greatest of all kings would come. It's a passage of hope for times past, for the future, and for our future, too, when Jesus Christ will return to reign over the world in wisdom, justice, and righteousness.

This renewal of the people and of the leaders was promised to be so great that it would overshadow the Exodus out of Egypt. The people would have a new story to tell that eclipsed all that had come before. The story of Jesus Christ is the greatest story ever told, and we can look to the future with hope with all who have suffered under oppressive leaders throughout history and look to the day when we will be ruled by the greatest shepherd of all.

Lord, grant me the discernment to see your
path, the wisdom to choose it, and the strength
to walk it as I go about my day. Amen.

Gather Us Back Together

Psalm 106:39-48

Why have the people of God survived for centuries?

Psalm 106 is a chilling recitation of the sins of Israel against God. They distrusted God's providence on the shores of the Red Sea. God saved them, but they rebelled and fought against God's love again and again. They built a golden calf to worship. They grumbled. They worshiped Baal and other idols. They polluted their land with the blood of innocents. They even sacrificed their children to other deities. Their disobedience to God cost them dearly and tore at the heart of God.

It was only because God persevered with them and continued to love them that their story continued. Their hope was not in their own ability to turn to obedience but entirely in the character of God. God's steadfast and unending love saved them and gave them a future.

Without God's care, Israel would have destroyed itself. But God's grace kept the story alive, as God keeps the story alive today. Despite the failings of the church and her people to love all and to devote themselves to responding to God's grace with grace to others, God's steadfast and unfailing love continues to heal and nurture. As the people of God, the only appropriate response for us, the broken, disobedient, and headstrong, is to call out in thanks and praise to our Lord of grace. It is because of God's grace that we can claim a heritage in the story of God's people, claim a place in the family of God, and claim an inheritance in heaven.

Praise to the God of Creation for life-giving
and sustaining grace! Amen.

FRIDAY, JULY 3

The Returnees

Ezra 2:1-2, 64-70

How important is the heritage of the family of God?

Imagine how the Israelites felt when the Babylonian king told them that they could return to Judah from exile! They left as soon as they got permission. After 70 years of exile, their trek across the desert to Judah was a joyful return to a home they'd never seen before. They were reclaiming their history, their heritage, and their roots as the people of God in their Promised Land.

The first thing they did when they entered their homeland was to collect freewill offerings to rebuild the Temple. The amounts of gold and silver that the Book of Ezra recorded as being donated are extraordinary for a returning group of exiles! Rebuilding the Temple, the focal point of their faith, was their highest priority. God's great grace preserved them and brought them home again. It was of the highest importance that they responded in gratitude with praise and a restoration of their heritage of faith.

The Hebrew people's great joy was centered in their ability to reclaim their place in the family of God. It was a place they had taken for granted and then lost, but their return marked a new appreciation for their history and heritage with the Lord. As people of God, we have a story that goes through the ages and a story that tells of our relationship with our faith and our salvation. Both are precious, to be cherished above all else in our lives. May we never stop celebrating our place in the family of God!

Lord, thank you for protecting my place in the family
of God with your all-encompassing grace. Amen.

SATURDAY, JULY 4

Ezra's Prayer

Ezra 9:5-15

What is our response when we face the sins of society?

Ezra spoke of the tension between judgment and grace, and God's willingness to heal a broken people again and again. Ezra's prayers were not only repentant for the current sins of the people, but for a long history of disobedience that went back many generations. Yet God preserved a remnant, protected them, gave them a place of refuge and protection, and allowed them to rebuild the Temple. Verse 8 says that God has given "us a stake in his holy place."

So after all this grace and mercy, how could the people go on sinning? This is why Ezra was so ashamed before God. He counted himself among the sinners; as their faith leader, he could not claim innocence. He realized that while sin was the responsibility of the individual, it was also a reflection on their society. The final part of his prayer was a heartfelt plea for God to show them what they should do. How should they rectify the sins of their times?

Ezra's response to God is a lesson even for today. While circumstances have changed, people are still embroiled in sin and disobedience. Ezra realized that as members of society, we are responsible for combating society's sins. He also recognized the great gift of God's grace and the people's unworthiness to receive it. So he asked God what they should do to please God. While many things have changed, the heart of Ezra's prayer is still a prayer for today.

Lord, as a sinner, I thank you for your miraculous
grace and ask for your guidance. Amen.

Sunday, July 5

Sunday, July 5

Restoration for All People

Zephaniah 3:9-20

How does God feel when people repent?

This song that called the people back to the Lord reached far beyond the borders of Israel, Judah, or Babylonia. Verse 10 says that the call goes "beyond the rivers of Cush," which is sometimes translated as "Ethiopia." The region probably also includes modern-day Sudan. At the time, it was at the edge of the known world, so this passage called to all known people to be part of God's covenant. So even though the oracle of Zephaniah celebrated the homecoming of the Israelites, it was not a celebration of restoration but a cry of joy for an entirely new order. All people belong to the Lord, and all people can join the family of God. It was a celebration of all the known people of the world joining together to praise the Lord!

Read the final oracle, verses 14-20, once more. God's joy is bursting from these verses. Despite the failings of humanity, again and again, and despite the profound pain that God feels when we sin, God waits and welcomes those who return to God. God is a God of justice, but it is justice that responds with mercy when people turn back in repentance. It's also a mercy that joyfully takes in those who see God for the first time, looking to the future of each person instead of what might have been in their past. Every door is open. Every possibility is achievable. "Watch what I am about to do!" God cries to the broken people. "I will restore your fortunes before your very eyes!"

Lord, may I join with all people of the earth in celebrating
the new things you have made in each of us! Amen.

Understanding the Lord

Deuteronomy 29:1-6

How does God teach us to trust in God's care?

In his moving last speech, Moses pleaded with the Hebrew people to see the power and the love of God and to obey the covenant. They had left Egypt with nothing, and God had provided. Now, standing with the panorama of the Promised Land below him, he begged them to follow the Lord. But they did not have "insight to understand, eyes to see, or ears to hear." None of God's provisions had caused them to trust and depend on God.

God's provision for the Hebrew people in the wilderness was not a unique experience. Many similarities exist between the time Moses stood on a rock looking over the Promised Land and spoke to his people and when the prophets of the time of the Babylonian exile called for a recommitment to God as they reentered the Promised Land. But the important point of the story is that caring for disobedient, undeserving people with lavish love is not a strange, one-time thing, but is simply the character of God.

By trusting God's provision and by hearing and believing the good news of God's everlasting love, we will understand our relationship with the Creator. The care of the Lord in times of wilderness is how God reveals the divine character to us and how we learn to rely on God with confidence. God's great desire is for all people to stand on the edge of the land of hope, knowing that it is by God alone that they have journeyed so far, and proclaim, "You are the Lord my God!"

> Lord, may I have eyes to see, ears to hear, and
> a heart to understand your love for me. Amen.

Tuesday, July 7

The Lesson of the Rechabite Family

Jeremiah 35:1-14

What excuses do Christians use for not obeying God?

We might think of the Rechabites as the Amish of Jeremiah's time. They chose to live simple lives, rejecting a modern lifestyle in response to a call they heard from God. They rejected agriculture, living as nomads. As they did not grow grapes or grain, they did not drink alcohol, specifically wine.

Strangely, this passage begins with God telling Jeremiah to invite a Rechabite family to the Temple to drink wine. They arrived at the Temple but predictably refused the offered wine. The point of God's command was to show the Hebrew people a group that was committed to obeying the difficult rules of their ancestors and dedicating themselves to purity and obedience. This was in direct contrast to the Hebrews' accommodations to their society and putting aside the commands of God when it was inconvenient or unpopular. The Rechabites proved that it was possible to listen to the word of God and choose a life of obedience.

At the time of Jeremiah, people who claimed to be people of God were ignoring the Word of God and the word of God's prophets because they were disturbing and challenging. Listening to God is the first part of obedience, and while obedience can look strange to outsiders, a life of listening and responding to the words of God is a life of faith and discipleship.

Lord, may obedience to you
come first in my life. Amen.

Great in the Lord's Eyes

Luke 1:11-16

What is the job of a prophet?

I'm sure that Zechariah was overjoyed to hear that he would have a son. But the last prophet to come to Israel had been Malachi, about 400 years earlier. The announcement of a new prophet was also the announcement of a new age, and John's job would be to call people into God's future. Gabriel told Zechariah that John would be the herald of great joy, but it was also unavoidable that his son John's life would not be easy. Announcing change never is.

Zechariah's first reaction to Gabriel's announcement was fear, but Gabriel assured him that his proper response was joy. Our initial response to change is often fear, too. That's one of the reasons we don't always want to follow prophets. But Gabriel told Zechariah, in effect, "Don't be afraid; this is great news! You will have a son, which is a personal joy, but your son will usher in a time when all people can rejoice. Trust me. Obey God. Others will obey, too, and turn back to God, awaiting this new thing that will happen."

That's how we can recognize a prophet. They point back to God and to obeying the call for justice and mercy. They bring the people to the heart of God's desires for them, to love God and to love their neighbors. A prophet prepares people for new ways that God will work in the world. And there was never a more profound and powerful way that God touched the world than through God's Son, Jesus Christ, the new way that John announced to God's people.

Lord, open me to the words of your prophets so that I may
be ready for all the ways you touch the world. Amen.

Thursday, July 9

Chosen for Royal Service

Daniel 1:1-7

How can the culture around people affect their faith?

The Babylonian king chose high-status, attractive, intelligent young Hebrew men to train them to serve the king. This was a propaganda move to enlist the Hebrew people's most admired and talented into positions of importance, thus appeasing the Hebrew people and lulling them into acceptance. These young men were to be trained in language and literature, living lives of luxury and eating the king's diet. The most likely up-and-coming leaders of the Hebrew people would be made so comfortable in Babylon that they wouldn't want to leave.

The Book of Daniel introduces the four young men of this story who were chosen for this assimilation with their Jewish names, but they were also given Babylonian names. This was also a way of lessening their Hebrew identity. The goal was to erase as much of their previous life as possible.

Becoming Babylonian meant turning their backs on God's ways. But even when there's no obvious attempt to erase identities, it can be challenging at times to protect our own integrity and character from the pressures of society. It's seductive to make choices to blend in or that lead to a comfortable lifestyle rather than to safeguard a life devoted to God's desires. These young Jewish men were under tremendous pressure to turn from the ways of God, but protecting our identity as people of God means safeguarding the most important part of ourselves.

Lord, help me to protect my identity
as a person of God. Amen.

Faithfulness, Even in Diet

Daniel 1:8-17

What would you risk to save your culture and identity?

When Daniel was told to eat from the king's table in Babylon, much of the food offered to him did not adhere to Jewish dietary law. For him to take this food would be "polluting" his body. What's more, Daniel would be participating in the domination of his people.

Daniel's refusal to eat the king's food was a dangerous move. God softened the heart of Ashpenaz, the palace master, and while he sympathized with Daniel, he was afraid for his life if Daniel sickened after eating inferior food. So, Daniel made a deal with him. Let the four men eat only vegetables and drink water for ten days. If their health suffered after that time, they would do what Ashpenaz asked of them. After the ten days, they looked healthier than those who ate the king's rich food and so were allowed to continue the restricted diet. God not only made them healthy but also sharpened their minds and gave Daniel the ability to interpret dreams and visions.

God's priority was to save a remnant of the Hebrew people who would continue beyond the Exile. Despite the dangers, Daniel and his friends trusted in God's protection as they fought to save their faith, identity, and culture. Even in the midst of defeat and exile, even in the house of a foreign king, even in a place of wealth and power, these young men held fast to their faith in God, turning down food fit for a king because they served the King of all creation.

Lord, may I be bold for you, even when my surroundings
ask me to compromise my beliefs. Amen.

SATURDAY, JULY 11

In the King's Service

Daniel 1:18-21

How should we negotiate the demands of society with the requirements of faith?

We can think of Daniel and his friends as being in a sort of internship. For three years, they were to learn the ways of the Babylonians, including language, culture, and literature. After that time, the king would assess their knowledge and choose the young men who had progressed the most to be in direct service to the king. But Daniel and his friends had chosen a diet that could have affected their vigor and health. God was with Daniel and his friends, however, and they remained strong and healthy and were chosen for this honor. It is unlikely that the king knew their eating habits. But it is important to note that they were successful within the Babylonian structure without sacrificing their integrity.

This is ultimately a story about trusting God in a place where the world would say it simply makes sense not to. Daniel and his friends risked angering the king by refusing his food, and risked their health by eating a diet that may not have been the best for their physical condition. But by eating the king's diet, they would have had to compromise their faith and give up part of their identity. Standing firm in our convictions is the mark of a devoted servant of God, and embracing integrity demonstrates that our souls do not have a price. For Christians today, what could be more valuable than the price already paid for our salvation, the blood of Jesus Christ?

> Lord, enable me to stand strong when
> the world questions my integrity. Amen.

For God's Glory

1 Corinthians 10:23-31

Can a community unite when dealing with divisive issues?

Most Corinthian social events involved a nod to a deity. Food was ceremoniously sacrificed to a god and then eaten by the attendees. It created a dilemma for those who were concerned about eating sacrificial food. It was also a problem for those who had been invited to an event. Should they refuse the invitation? Should they attend but not eat?

Paul's response was that since these pagan deities were not real, then it wasn't a sin to eat food that had been offered to them with one strong exception. If a Christian was present who was weaker in the faith, in other words, someone who would have been negatively influenced if sacrificial food was eaten, then Paul advised against eating it. The well-being of these Christian brothers and sisters was more important than anyone's right to eat the food.

To reduce complex situations to cut-and-dried answers is impractical and divisive. Paul realized that and instead asked the Corinthians to turn outward and consider how their behavior was affecting others. Paul respected a range of beliefs on this issue, but not when it came to damaging one's relationship to God and turning focus away from Christ. In a society awash with individual interpretations and arguments about the Christian faith, Paul's words remind us that difficult conflicts do not have to be divisive when people approach one another in love and concern for community.

> Lord, may my focus be on you and how
> my behavior affects your people. Amen.

MONDAY, JULY 13

No Gods Before Me

Exodus 20:1-6

How do the first two commandments shape how we live for God?

At first glance, the first two commandments in today's Scripture passage sound easy. If we're Christian, there is no other deity we worship, and we certainly don't have idols. But if we dig a little deeper into these verses, we realize that the issue is about our priorities.

The first commandment, "You must have no other gods before me," clearly speaks of God's priority in our lives. We can pursue many things for happiness, security, and love, and they are not necessarily bad. But this is the God who created the heavens and earth, and breathed life into creation. Anything else that we give our loyalties to is less than God. If something else is more important to us than God, we're settling for second best at best.

Closely related is the command against idols. Idols or images diminish God to something that we can categorize or grasp with our imaginations. Anything that humans do to make God more manageable or convenient is making God into an idol that can be controlled. To accept God as an uncontrollable, mysterious power that is the ruling force in our lives is to become completely vulnerable to God. It goes far beyond claiming God as our Lord. It means allowing God to claim us as servants, giving God our full obedience, and allowing God to use us in the formation of God's kingdom on earth.

O Lord, may I submit to you completely, allowing
you to shape my life and my heart. Amen.

Taste and See How Good God Is

Psalm 34:1-10

What is the source of peace in a difficult world?

The psalmist who wrote Psalm 34 was no stranger to pain and even terror. This psalm is a powerful testimony to the peace in the storm we can find in God's arms. It was not written from the sidelines but by "this suffering person" who called to the Lord from the depths of his troubles and was heard (verse 6). Watched over by God's angel, the psalmist felt the peace of the Lord and could even praise God with a shining face from a place that was once filled with fear.

How does this happen? It is because of the realization that nothing, not even death, can separate us from the love of God. When everything else in life falls away, those who have been powerful no longer have the power, those who have been wealthy find that wealth is irrelevant, and those who have been respected only have pity. But those who have found the grace of God have a place where they can rest in peace and in joy. The psalmist cried out to others to join with him in this security. Once he had found God's grace, he devoted himself to calling others to find it, too, and to praise God for the peace that they could find.

This psalm calls us to do the "work of the living" while we have time still on this earth, finding that place of peace where nothing else but the love and grace of God is relevant, and we can confidently rest in God's arms as we do God's work in the world.

> Lord, help me to find your peace in the
> midst of a world of trouble. Amen.

Wednesday, July 15

The Flame Won't Burn You

Isaiah 43:1-7

How does God demonstrate love for us?

In this passage, God showed unique love for the people of Israel. God saved them from Egypt and again saved them from Babylon. God called to all the Hebrew people in all the corners of the world to return so that God could watch and protect them with an everlasting love.

In these verses, we see that God is an active, invested, and empowered participant in the human story. Creation was not a one-time event, but is ongoing with every birth, every spring flower, and every act of salvation. God's hand is powerful and working in the world, calling out and protecting God's people with everlasting, never-ending love, to heal their brokenness. God creates, nurtures, and loves the people who were "created for my glory." In other words, nothing is more precious to God than those people who demonstrate God's holiness and make it real in the world.

Think of what wonderful words these were for the exiles in Babylon! When these words were written, the people were broken and contrite, eager yet frightened to reconnect with God. God's response was, "I created you. I love you. I will keep you safe, and am calling you back to me." As we confront sin, we have the assurance of the same words from God. The Lord of Love, our Creator, wants us back within the divine arms of love, where we can grow strong in God's care and then demonstrate God's holiness and glory to the rest of the waiting world.

Lord, thank you for your everlasting love and protection.
May I be a demonstration of your glory! Amen.

Thursday, July 16

A Plot Against the Faithful

Daniel 3:1-12

What things do people believe deserve honor?

This passage in Daniel tells of a statue commissioned by King Nebuchadnezzar. This one was a stile, or tall pillar, nine-feet-wide and 90-feet-high, made of gold. The king had it placed in Dura, which is thought to have been along important trade routes. While we don't know which deity it symbolized, if indeed it did symbolize a deity, it seems obvious that it was also a testament to the wealth and power of the Babylonians. Greek records show that this stile was erected the same year that the Temple in Jerusalem was leveled. The Babylonians destroyed a place of worship and built a false one in its stead.

King Nebuchadnezzar commanded that everyone gather to worship the statue. The call was for everyone: all peoples, languages, and nations. But the Chaldean officials brought to the king's attention that Shadrach, Meshach, and Abednego—three Jews supervised by Daniel—had not worshiped King Nebuchadnezzar's new statue.

Shadrach, Meshach, and Abednego risked everything to stay true to the Lord. It is worth examining what things we might venerate that would displace the worship due to God. Everything else in the world—nations, authorities, powers, and dynasties—ultimately will fall. Only God is worthy of our praise.

Lord, examine my heart and show me those things that displace the honor I should give only to you. Amen.

Friday, July 17

Faithful No Matter What

Daniel 3:13-18

Where do martyrs get the courage to stand up for their faith in the face of death?

In Daniel 3:13-18, we have a glimpse into the mind of a martyr. There's a sense of victory in this passage, even if we didn't know that the three young men would be saved. The king's goal was to destroy their faith and compromise their obedience to God. But in facing death, they won. Amid all his trappings of wealth and power, the king was unable to change their dedication to God.

Knowing that we serve a God of love, there's a comfort in knowing that even if we suffer for God, then that suffering is honored by the Lord and that our story does not end with the end of our lives. The loss of life is a far less serious matter than turning away from the everlasting love of the Lord.

Shadrach, Meshach, and Abednego stood before the greatest symbol of human power on earth, the king of Babylon, and stated with confidence that there was a greater power yet: the power of the Lord God of Israel. The powers of evil cannot stand against the final glory of God, even if that vindication would wait until God's final victory.

We don't know how God will comfort and protect us, and it won't always be the way we would choose. But there is no doubt that even in the worst moments, the power of God in the lives of those who love God is greater than all the power of the earth.

Lord, give me the unbending strength of my convictions
for your peace, justice, and love. Amen.

Inside the Furnace

Daniel 3:19-25

How has God given comfort in the worst times of your life?

It's not surprising that King Nebuchadnezzar responded with intense rage when Shadrach, Meshach, and Abednego told him that they would not deny the Lord, even at the threat of death. And so he had the furnace set to burn as hot as it could and bound the three young men. The passage describes their clothing, so that when they were pulled unburned from the fire, the circumstances were even more remarkable because cloth would burn first. The passage stressed that the men were bound, a powerful symbol of the king's dominance and authority. And then they were thrown into the fire, a fire so hot that it killed the soldiers tasked with their murders. But God sent an angel to step into the fire with them and, before the power of the earth, demonstrated the power of the heavens.

God did not keep Shadrach, Meshach, and Abednego from being thrown into the fire, but God was with them when they needed God the most. There is a lot of suffering in the world, but as Psalm 23:4 states, "Even when I walk through the darkest valley, I fear no danger because you are with me. Your rod and your staff—they protect me." We will be bruised and battered from life. That's a given. But through it all, we have the presence of the Lord walking beside us, offering us salvation. We don't need to fear. The Lord God will be with us.

Lord, may I trust that you will be with me
in the flames, whatever the outcome. Amen.

Nebuchadnezzar Praises God

Daniel 3:26-30

What miracles have you seen God work in the world?

When Shadrach, Meshach, and Abednego walked through the furnace unharmed, it was a miracle that could not be explained away. God was powerfully, unmistakably present. Nebuchadnezzar, who had been furious at the suggestion that there was something greater than his power and his gods, was now entirely convinced. "May the God of Shadrach, Meshach, and Abednego be praised!" he cried out. "There is no other god who can rescue like this!"

Nebuchadnezzar acknowledged the Lord's power and reality and allowed the Hebrew people to worship their God. He harshly commanded that the God of the Hebrew people be shown respect. He integrated God into the Babylonian religious structure and permitted the Hebrew people to practice their religion. It was a big step forward from executing those who would not worship his statue. Nebuchadnezzar's change of heart was a miracle, too.

The evidence of God is everywhere. When we're open to the work of God in the world, all God's miracles, big and small, become detectable every day, all around us. And as we see these miracles, may we shout with joy for the Lord, who can create the stars, save God's children from the furnace, and change the heart of a king.

Lord of miracles, open my eyes
to all your work in the world. Amen.

God's Laws Are Wonderful

Psalm 119:129-136

How do we know how to live effectively in the world?

The topic of Psalm 119 is the Torah, or Law. In fact, the word *torah*, or a word with a similar meaning, is in every verse but four in the entire psalm. The overall effect speaks of the overwhelming importance of God's commands for a fruitful and happy life.

Psalm 119's definition of *torah* recognizes three sources of God's commands. The first is what we would normally think of: the taught commands by oral or written tradition. The second is nature and the innate working of the world. The third is the word of God we glean through inspiration and personal experience. Therefore, the psalmist's definition of God's commands is open to divine revelations and new insights.

As we grow in our faith, our discernment and grasp of God's Word grow, too. Verse 136 tells of the tragedy of rejecting the Word of God. The secret to all of life is held in the law of the Lord, yet people turn away! Despite our science, technology, and innovation, human knowledge has limits. We come up against the mystery that is the Lord. To live our lives richly as servants of our Creator, we need to accept that our lives depend on the grace of God. As God's servants and disciples of Jesus Christ, it only makes sense to pick up the instruction manual and listen to the Creator.

Lord, may my ears be open to all the ways that
you speak to me. Let your precepts mold me to be
your wise and obedient servant. Amen.

TUESDAY, JULY 21

You Alone Are God

Nehemiah 9:1-8

Why is it important to consider God's character when we confess our sins?

When the Hebrew people were finally able to leave Babylon and return to Israel, they rebuilt the city walls of Jerusalem, then rededicated the city and themselves to the Lord. As part of this rededication, Ezra read all the commandments of God before all the people. After he read the Law out loud to everyone, they offered a prayer to the Lord. Nehemiah 9 is the text of this prayer.

The prayer begins with praise to God and acknowledgment of God's works as the Creator of the cosmos. Next, the prayer speaks of Abraham. This is a God who intimately interacts with God's people! God, the Creator of the universe, made promises to an old man with no heirs and kept them. The knowledge that God always keeps God's promises is terrifying and encouraging.

When the Hebrew people prayed this prayer to God, they made sure that they knew exactly who it was that they had wronged. Because they started their prayer examining God's character, they realized the severity of their sins and grasped how important it was that they repent. When we confess our sins to God, it's equally important that we take time to consider just who it is that we have wronged and to confess with sorrow and humility to the Lord of all creation, the one who keeps all promises.

Lord of all creation, I humbly
confess my sins to you. Amen.

The Exodus

Nehemiah 9:9-17

What attributes of God allow us to trust God?

Nehemiah told the gathered Hebrews that, when they were enslaved in Egypt, God saw their suffering. They were not invisible. God had the compassion and power to help them and was aware of all their needs and fulfilled them.

As Nehemiah and the people prayed, they knew that God saw them and had the power to help them while they were in Babylon, too. Their story was the same: God had not changed, and they could trust God's promises. This is why Nehemiah told the Exodus story in such detail. God has a history of salvation. There was historical proof of God's character, mercy, and grace. Despite the bone-trembling thought that they were addressing the Creator and Designer of the cosmos, they could trust that in their prayers, they were coming to a place of love.

The Exodus story has always been a story of hope for people who are struggling and suffering. Throughout history, people have heard how God rescued the Hebrew people from slavery in Egypt. They knew that God does not turn away from suffering and that God is powerful enough to change any circumstance. People wrestling with the effects of sin can also turn to this story as an illustration of how God transforms lives. It doesn't matter in what form of slavery people find themselves, be it tyranny, oppression, abuse, or addiction. We worship a God of compassion and power.

Lord God, see me in my need!
I trust in your power to save. Amen.

Thursday, July 23

God Did Not Abandon Them

Nehemiah 9:18-25

What has saved humanity from destruction?

God showered the Hebrew people with everything they needed as they traversed the wilderness. But they felt entitled to God's grace and created an idol to worship and thank for those things God had given them. We can shake our heads in sorrow over the Hebrew peoples' blindness, but this is the story of humanity, our story, not just the story of Israel. How often do we forget about God's provisions for us?

The wondrous thing is that despite the Hebrew peoples' disloyalty, God refused to abandon them. It seems entirely reasonable that God would leave them to die after their faithlessness. God remained steadfast, giving God's "good spirit to teach them." God's patience and compassion for them was astounding, as they continue to be today.

This is the character of our Lord God, and this is the only reason that humanity has not only survived but has also flourished through the centuries. Despite the blindness of the human race to God's grace, despite our disloyalty time and time again, and despite our refusal to follow God's commands, God has been ready to forgive, slow to anger, and abounding in steadfast love. God uses compassion to turn people back to God. If we worshiped a god of anger and retribution, the human race would be long gone. As the character of humanity points itself toward destruction, the character of God steps in with mercy, grace, and salvation.

Almighty Lord, open my eyes to the sins of
my people and help me to follow your ways. Amen.

Arrogant and Rebellious People

Nehemiah 9:26-31

Can a community be responsible for sin?

What we do affects other people. As much as we speak of personal responsibility, we also bear corporate responsibility for how our actions affect others. The stain of sin spreads through all people, changing the community. It's an attitude of disobedience to God that permeates society. While individual sin condemns each of us, it doesn't stop with the individual, but can alter the hearts of the people.

This is what happened to the Hebrews after they settled in the Promised Land. Despite God's gracious provisions, they "turned their back on [God's] Instruction." In Nehemiah's prayer, they finally confronted the corporate effects of sin head-on. It was their ancestors who had built the golden calf and had murdered the prophets, but those experiences created them and their hearts. They claimed their shameful heritage of sin and acknowledged how it had shaped them as a people.

God stands at the ready to transform and forgive. Despite what seems like a never-ending cycle, God continues in the work of salvation, not just for each one of us, but for our homes, our communities, and our nations. Like the people praying with Nehemiah, we need to face our responsibility not only for our individual but also for our corporate sin and repent, so we are individuals, communities, and nations striving to do the will of our Creator and Lord.

> Lord, open my eyes not only to my individual but also to corporate sin and help my community to heal. Amen.

Commitment to Follow the Instruction

Nehemiah 9:32-38

What hope does humanity have to break the cycle of sin?

After Nehemiah recounted the centuries of sin of the Hebrew people, it must have seemed quite hopeless to them. They could see how they had failed, again and again. They wanted to change, but how could they get rid of that shovel that had dug them into such a deep hole? When they looked back on their history with God, they had to admit that they deserved their fate. None of them had served God, and now they were fated to serve their foreign oppressors.

So how could they stop this cycle? This heartfelt prayer to God was the first step. Through this prayer, they saw that if they were to serve a holy God, they must be holy, too.

This prayer also spoke again and again of God's great compassion. It spoke of God's character of mercy and forgiveness. This was the same God who forgave their forefathers in the wilderness, and they could trust that they could start once again with a new beginning.

God is equipped for every circumstance. If those who love God remain dedicated to God, then God can help them overcome their inadequacy. God delights in equipping the weak. Although we humans are unable to conquer sin, we worship the Creator of the universe, who is equipped with unlimited power and means. By relying on the Lord God, we can, like the Hebrew people that day, recommit ourselves to love, loyalty, and dependence on our Creator and step into a new relationship with God.

Lord, my sin is before me. But you are a Lord of mercy, and
I ask you to guide me in faithful service to you. Amen.

Give Thanks to the Lord

Psalm 136:1-2, 10-16, 23-26

What is the defining characteristic of God's relationship with humanity?

"God's faithful love lasts forever." Every line in Psalm 136 ends with these words. The Hebrew word for "faithful love" is *hesed*. It's the most repeated word in the Old Testament and probably the most important concept in the entire Bible.

Psalm 136 recounts human history, and at every point, God's *hesed* was the reason that the world and life within it continued. *Hesed* is a love that molds us to holiness. We are not able to completely understand it. *Hesed* is eternal and unchangeable. *Hesed* is sacrificial. *Hesed* is what enabled God to send Jesus for us. *Hesed* is the reason for grace, mercy, and forgiveness. It is the love that God has for us. *Hesed* is the guidance of God toward the final victory against sin and death. It's humankind's hope for salvation.

But *hesed* is a demanding love. It calls us to join with God in holy righteousness. It calls us to do better. *Hesed* can be harsh, because while it loves each person, it is dedicated to molding each person into the best that person can be for God, which means that it does not abide sin.

Our truest potential as God's creations can only be realized by the guidance of God's *hesed*. And so, as people being shaped into holy beings, our only possible response is to cry out in thanks and praise for the *hesed* of God. It has been the foundation of our past relationship with our Creator and the hope for our future. God's *hesed* endures forever!

Lord God of heaven, I give thanks to you for your *hesed*!
Mold me into your holy servant. Amen.

Monday, July 27

Living the Righteous Life

Psalm 112:1-10

What does it mean to you to live a righteous life?

When we read today's Scripture, the idea of living a righteous life is pretty encouraging! Over and over, the psalmist declares the benefits and strengths of living this way. Why would anyone not live righteously?

Of course, we know that answer already. To live righteously means that we give up as much as possible, living our lives just for ourselves or making choices simply for what benefits us. God's righteousness is always seen in relationship with God's people. As righteous people, we are called to act the same way. Our choices in life must be made to help the world become a better world, and such that the people around us may become more blessed and just and live fuller lives. Our joy comes in what we may give and, frankly, how well we can live as we have been created: in the image of God and God's righteousness.

We must guard against envy or jealousy or even feeling disgruntled when we are about the work of living in righteousness. Others will have an easier way, it seems, with lots of benefits. Even with what the psalmist says, living as God wants us to live takes a lot of work and effort because our goal is to make sure our neighbor is loved and able to live in justice.

Will you claim the power and work of living as a righteous person today?

O God of justice and love, grant me the privilege of living a righteous life before you this day. Amen.

TUESDAY, JULY 28

Looking for the Lost One

Luke 15:1-7

What's the best word you can find to describe God?

Jesus' story about the lost sheep is much more about the searching shepherd. It's the action of the shepherd that captures our attention. To leave 99 well-behaved, stay-put-even-when-the-gate-is-open sheep and go after the one who got away says much about the individual. The shepherd sounds like God, doesn't he? God is not at all concerned with "risk management," absorbing some loss so long as most of the profit is found. No! If we get lost, God will come and find us. God will bring us home where it is safe and loving once again, and when it happens, a great celebration will follow.

Today's question asks what word best describes God. With today's Scripture, it sure seems to be the word "searcher" or, better yet, "Savior." God goes the extra mile, recovers us, and carries us to joy.

If that is such a marvelous truth about God, why would we grumble when someone who doesn't act or look like us is brought home by the caring Shepherd? So many times, in otherwise nice churches, the "strange sheep" who come feel rejected and leave because of the cold welcome of the other "sheep." How could we do that? How could God's children ever act in a way that was other than complete joy when someone is "found"? When we are invited—even commanded—to love our neighbor, there is no condition placed on that love.

Dear Good Shepherd, thank you for your love. Help me
learn to love others as you have loved me. Amen.

WEDNESDAY, JULY 29

The Right Call

Mark 2:13-17

What is God calling you to do?

There they were going about their normal business, and Jesus said simply, "Follow me." The call was irresistible, and Levi, like the others, "got up and followed him."

The Pharisees were angry that Jesus would actually want to eat with sinners and tax collectors, but Jesus' response to their criticism was that he had come into this world not to call the people who never need to change, who aren't broken and hurting and feeling as though they are worthless. Jesus doesn't call the people who feel they have no need for Jesus, but instead calls sinners. Jesus calls the ones who don't have their lives all in place. Jesus calls the "messy" people who need to know and claim God's love for their lives. The fact is, Jesus came to call us. Jesus can look into our hearts and see the many ways in which we have failed or have cut ourselves off from others, and in that calling, Jesus can restore our lives, our dignity, and our purpose for living.

So if today, you are feeling a little "messy" yourself or think that your life doesn't have meaning and purpose, listen for the call. Listen to the way in which Jesus Christ offers you life by calling you into a new life, allowing you to put aside all the mess and the bad past and to start anew as a follower of the one who saves us.

What is the best way to respond to Jesus' call to you today?

God of Grace, let me hear and respond
to the call of your Son this day. Amen.

Thursday, July 30

Making Amends

Numbers 5:5-10

How can you best say you are sorry?

In the wilderness, all the Israelites had was God and one another. As God's people, there was no room for keeping grudges or allowing for ongoing feuds or bickering. Therefore, the Lord gave Moses a way of dealing with rifts in relationships. If you had done something against someone else, God's people believed that you not only sinned against another person, but you had sinned against God. As we read today's Scripture, we find the important way in which someone could "make it up" to another person and to God. A gift was required, payback larger than the sin, and then a sacrifice of an animal. It was much more than just saying you were sorry. The work of atoning for the sin was important to show once again that you did love your neighbor.

Receiving the gift and restoring the relationship were mandatory. The one who was offended couldn't say, "I don't accept this! I don't forgive you!" No, when the Law was followed and the paying back and sacrificing were done, no one was allowed to keep a grudge.

Imagine if we were able to do that today. Instead, it seems that when someone offends, it is held against him or her forever! Have we forgotten how to forgive or forgotten what it means to be restored to another person? If someone says and means they are sorry, do we continue to hold it against him or her forever? Who needs forgiveness from you today? How can you best say you are sorry or say that you forgive?

> Loving God, teach me how to not keep a grudge
> but instead live as your forgiving child. Amen.

Friday, July 31

Making the Gift

Deuteronomy 15:7-11

How generous are you?

Isn't it interesting that we are told that the "poor persons will never disappear from this earth"? The reasons behind poverty are complex, but the presence of poor people among us gives us opportunities to help and respond to their needs. The poor can help us become better neighbors because they teach us how to show love in tangible ways.

As we make offerings, like the Israelites, to care for those in need, we are blessed. I believe the blessing is not something God adds to our life, but the blessing is found in the realization that all that we have is also a gift of God, and that when we use those gifts to care for others, they become even more precious. We are not giving away what we "own," but instead what God has entrusted to our care.

As I offer gifts to others in need, I am reminded how much I am in need of God's care and how I am to bless the world with God's love. When I forget that, however, then I begin more to live out of fear of running out of my resources. I get stingy because I want enough set in reserve so that I won't have to be one of the poor. I begin to think only about me and my needs instead of God and what God intends for me. Instead of blessing, I come under the sin of setting myself apart from God's will for my life and this world.

When we are generous, we reflect our place as a child of God. How can you live out the joy of being generous today?

Holy God, accept my offerings,
as I care for the world. Amen.

AUGUST

CONTRIBUTORS:

Randy Cross
(August 1–August 31)

SATURDAY, AUGUST 1

God's Grace Given to You

Ephesians 2:1-10

What is your witness of what God has done in your life?

In today's reading, we are transported in our understanding from being students to being those who have received the grace of God through Jesus Christ. When we lived doing whatever felt good or what we wanted to do, the writer says we were like dead persons, disobedient to God's will and following a destructive power. However, the good news for all time is that God came to you and me, "brought us life," and saved us from death because God loves us. The salvation that is ours is ours not because we participated in a self-help program or followed the rules and did the right thing.

Salvation is God's gift. The writer says, "We are God's accomplishment!" What a powerful and life-changing realization to know that, more than just living a good life, God has brought us actual eternal life in Christ. Our response to this wonderful, gracious gift is that we offer our lives in return. The best way to do that is to follow Jesus' example and teaching. Following the teachings doesn't bring us salvation but instead is the way for us to be thankful for the gift beyond our imagination.

Can you see how salvation is so much more than following commandments or teachings? Can you feel in your heart the gratitude for what God did? Who do you know today who needs to hear that good news? What neighbor needs to hear that loving story from your life?

Gracious God, put someone in my path today
who needs to hear of your love! Amen.

SUNDAY, AUGUST 2

Zaccheus, Come Down!

Luke 19:1-10

Do you grumble when Jesus spends time with sinners?

Jesus utterly transformed Zaccheus's life, and indeed the life of the town, when he accepted and blessed the tax collector with his presence. No condemnation, no wagging of a finger, just an invitation to the man to climb down, be part of the community, and receive Jesus' gift.

The response? A restoration of all that had been stolen, a gift to care for the poor, and a pronouncement by Jesus that "salvation has come to this household." I'm sure Zaccheus felt as though he had been given life and a way to turn around and leave what he had been doing for so long.

That's the point of the story. Jesus was not at all concerned about appeasing the grumblers in the crowd. Instead, his care was to find perhaps the worst, most abhorrent person in the community, redeem his life, and bring him back to the neighborhood to save the lost.

We search to find Jesus in all of the "nice" places where people are well-behaved and don't have time for the rascals or the crooks, but we may not find Jesus there. Instead, if we want to follow Jesus, we need to stand at the foot of a sycamore tree, invite the worst person to come down, and find forgiveness and acceptance as well. That's our calling as we care for our neighbors, even those we would consider to be the worst ones!

How will you find ways to offer that grace to others in this world in the name of Jesus?

> Forgiving God, forgive me for failing to join you
> in loving the last, the least, and the lost. Amen.

Monday, August 3

Why Do Such a Thing?

Jeremiah 2:4-13

What would it be like to forsake God?

Why can't you remember who you are? Through the prophet Jeremiah, God lamented that the people had forgotten what God had done for them, what they had experienced. Israel was a mess because the people had decided to go their way, forget God, and even change the God they worshiped for a bunch of idols. The saddest thing God said was that they had forsaken living water and had dug wells for themselves that couldn't even hold water.

How does it happen that we can wander so far from that which gives us life, focus, and inspiration? An addiction, a problem with alcohol, gambling, pornography, and an affair—we face possibilities every day of doing what is destructive in life instead of what is life-giving. Why someone chooses to change paths is heartbreaking and dangerous. Yet it happens due to anxiety, loss, mid-life crisis, or some other force that pushes or seduces us to turn from God.

Prayer, the vital link we have with God, is a core resource for remembering who we are and whose we are. Bible study, worship, and holy conversation with others who have the same struggles as we do also help us to stay at least closer to the path when we begin to veer off. The reason these are called spiritual disciplines is because these are exercises to keep our hearts in shape, our spirits connected, and our minds on Jesus.

Do you need to remember who you are today? Do you know someone who needs that reminder?

God who loves me, keep me always close to you. Amen.

Neighborly Love?

Luke 9:51-56; Acts 8:25

What is your reaction when people treat you poorly?

Jesus had to go to Jerusalem, but the Samaritans had no respect for Jerusalem and the rituals of the Jews; they worshiped on a different mountain. It was a grudge well-preserved between the two peoples, and when they heard that Jesus was coming, they simply "refused to welcome him." They refused to extend the simplest of neighborly expressions. It was rude. Even worse, it broke down the condition of living with civility.

The worst part of this incident was the suggestion of the disciples to Jesus: "Do you want us to call fire down from heaven to consume them?" A bit of an overreaction! And of course, Jesus' response was to speak sternly to them. They just never seemed to get what Jesus was all about.

We have to get along with one another, whether we want to or not. Frankly, in the Christian faith, there is no room for violence or horrible wishes for harm to someone. We abuse and dishonor the name "follower of Christ" when we even consider reacting badly to someone who has treated us badly. It just can't be part of our lives anymore. Instead, when faced with the reality that someone has mistreated us, it appears that Jesus wants us to simply go to another village and not hold the sins of others against them. We learn that later, the disciples even preached "the good news to many Samaritan villages."

How will you treat an ill-mannered world today?

God of Love, help me to forgive and
to give love in return. Amen.

WEDNESDAY, AUGUST 5

Can I Get a Witness?

John 5:31-40

Who speaks the truth about you?

As Jesus responded to the Jewish leaders who criticized him, he said, "If I testify about myself, my testimony isn't true." However, he had John's testimony, the Scriptures, and even the acts of healing that testified to his power and his relationship with God.

What are the different kinds of testimony you could claim to tell the world who you are? Likely, there are people who might vouch for your character. You might also show written documents such as your credit score, your grades, and achievements. Most importantly, we must think soberly and humbly about what we have done that testifies to the people we are. The things we have done, great and small, that have led to a more loving, more holy, more just, and more joyful world certainly will end up sounding across the world like bells in a church. Not only is doing good works the core of our lives, but those works also reflect our relationship with God and our calling as children of God.

It's important that we commit to live solely for God's pleasure and purposes. Next, however, is the critical work of intention. What do we intend to do, how do we intend to live today so that the world will know God's love and know that we are followers of the living Christ? Our lives are a testimony to what God has done for us. What does your life tell others about Jesus?

Hear my prayer, O God. Let me serve
you with my whole heart. Amen.

Thursday, August 6

In This Together

Romans 1:8-14

How can you share in faith with others?

To be able to visit the church of Gentile Christians in the center of the Roman Empire was an exciting dream for Paul! Notice, however, that it was far more than a matter of sightseeing in Rome and shaking a lot of hands. Paul wanted to join his faith with theirs, to see how they could strengthen one another. Paul wanted to go home to a place he'd never been before to grow God's church among them all.

Do you ever have a longing to greet other Christians with such passion and hope? When I visited South Korea and met with other church members, I was overwhelmed by their sense of joy and excitement in meeting us! They took our faith connection more seriously than I had ever witnessed.

I wonder what would happen if we acted that way truthfully and honestly whenever we encountered others in the faith. Imagine how differently we might approach each day and each opportunity to see another Christian if we were to do so with unmasked joy and celebration! That should be how we view one another. Each time we find another person who follows Jesus, it's like we, too, come home to a place we have never experienced, yet one where we are embraced in our mutual love of Christ.

How could you change the way you meet other Christians? What would be a meaningful way of letting them know how special they are, since they follow the same Lord that you do? Would joy arise between you?

Loving God, give me the chance today to
welcome my family in your Son's name! Amen.

FRIDAY, AUGUST 7

The Best Water!

John 4:4-14

How do you quench your thirst?

Everybody gets thirsty. We all know that feeling! But imagine taking in a drink of something that would end your dryness of spirit, your thirst for something that is more than just getting by, or your desire to be hydrated by the very water of life. Deep within each of us is a desire for that drink of water. Within each of our hearts, we sometimes feel the desert of life in which nothing seems to grow, or we only see sand or miles of asphalt. We grow weary and dry, and we look for something to give us life again.

This is what it means to be filled with God's forgiving and sustaining love for you. God will fill you today and do so with a sweet and satisfying long drink. All you need to do is ask, "Fill my cup, Lord." And Jesus will fill you and give you rest and strength to fill others with the same sweet love.

Where do we find living water? We only have to ask God to satisfy our thirst and bring us to a new life, a new joy, and a new hope. Then drink of that spring of never-ending life offered just for us.

Makes you thirsty, doesn't it? That's good because our desire to receive God's blessing also makes us open to sharing that blessing with others. Others are as thirsty as you. Why not offer the drink to them today?

Who do you know who needs a drink of that living water today? Name that person and choose to share your gift with them.

God of Life, quench the thirst of my
soul through your love for me. Amen.

Saturday, August 8

The Best Way to Worship

John 4:15-26

In how many different places have you worshiped?

In Jesus' conversation with the woman at the well, they spoke about differences in worship between the Samaritans and the Jews, most specifically, the difference in where worship should happen. Jesus told her, and tells us, that the "where" is far less of an issue than the "what," that "true worshippers will worship in spirit and in truth."

That's an interesting phrase. I believe it means that for all of us, as we come before God, the most critical thing is that we are intentional about what we do. It's not a matter of going through the motions or saying the right words. "In spirit and in truth" means that our spirits seek to commune with the Holy Spirit. The way that happens is for us to let go of all pretenses or acts and come in truth with open hearts. How that happens, of course, is through the grace of Jesus, who opens the way to worship.

How can you best come to God in your worship experiences? Maybe it is a particular kind of music that opens your hearts to deep truth. Maybe a written ritual becomes the avenue to an open heart. Or maybe it needs to be spontaneous, silent, or noisy. The "how" must always follow the "what" of worshiping in spirit and truth. When we start there, however, we come to express our devotion to God as true and spiritual indeed. Think of the most special worship you have experienced in the past. What would bring you to that state of mind and heart?

My God, open my heart to worship you with
all I am today, tomorrow, and every day. Amen.

Sunday, August 9

Believe It When You See It

John 4:27-42

How did you come to believe in Jesus Christ?

We want to tell people when we experience something great. Often, when we do that, others will want to check out what we told them. That's what happened with the woman at the well. She was so overwhelmed by Jesus' words that she had to tell her village (where she most likely was not respected). Even as Samaritans, they needed to hear what this Jewish rabbi had to say. Could he be the Christ? They did hear it, and sure enough, they saw and believed and came to know that "this one is truly the savior of the world."

How do you share the powerful and important news about Jesus with the people you know? Can you recall a time when someone invited you into a new experience with God? It was so important for the Samaritan woman that she risked being further rejected by those in her town to tell them what was so significant. I would think that we who follow Jesus would also take even a small risk to invite others to come and meet this one who knows us so well and who is the Savior of the world.

If you already know that Jesus Christ is your Savior, why not share that good news with someone? Jesus told his disciples that the field is ripe for the harvest. What he meant was that this is the time to turn the face of the world to the face of God. This is our task and our joyful, hopeful work as children of God. Can you find yourself in that holy work?

Dear Lord, I love to tell the story
of Jesus and his love. Amen.

Use Your Head, Use Your Heart

Leviticus 19:9-18

How do you treat those persons who need your care?

It's a simple concept: Be generous with the stuff you own. Leave some behind for others. Act in a way that shows who you are, as someone who was freed from slavery yourself. Love your neighbor and expand your understanding of neighbor far beyond the ones who live next door to you. Why do that? It's simple: "I am the Lord," God says.

The power of today's Scripture is not the "what," but the "who." The Israelites, and we, are commanded to act with generosity, kindness, and justice, not simply to the people we know and love, but to strangers and others who may not love us back. What we do is not a reaction to the world. In everything we do, the claim on our lives as children of God is to love others, first and always.

When we love and act this way, we don't lose anything. Like the wheat on the edge of the field, it's never something we will miss. To know that we help our world do better by telling the truth and making a way for those who have trouble making their own way is a mark of our character as children of God. It's who we are because it's who God is.

When we realize someone needs us and then act toward them in ways that meet their needs, we are listening to the deepest whisper we will ever hear. God says to do this simply because. Who is waiting for your kindness today?

Dear God, open my eyes that I may
see how to love more fully. Amen.

Tuesday, August 11

Summing Up the Commandments

Romans 13:8-10

How do you "fulfill the law"?

The first part of the Ten Commandments describes how we should act toward God. The second part instructed the Israelites, and us, in how to live with one another. Jesus repeated the summary of the commandments, especially the second half, when he quoted Leviticus 19:18: "*You must love your neighbor as you love yourself*" (Matthew 22:39).

It's all wrapped up in love. It's more than just the mushy, can't-wait-to-see-you feelings. It is the root behavior that moves us to avoid doing anything that would harm another person physically, emotionally, or relationally. Paul was clear: "Love doesn't do anything wrong to a neighbor; therefore, love is what fulfills the Law."

We need guidelines for knowing right from wrong, but even more, we need hearts that are focused on Jesus so that what we do is not a mere obedience to a set of rules but a desire to please him with every action and reaction. To love is to respond to our Lord. This is something we probably won't do automatically. We have to learn to love, to respond in love, and to act without needing to have our own way. We must learn how to do good, and the way that happens is when we commit ourselves to staying connected to God in prayer and in realizing that every action we do in our lives is an act of worship.

What waits for you today so that you may show God that you are "fulfilling the law" in love?

Loving God, teach me to imitate you
through my actions. Amen.

WEDNESDAY, AUGUST 12

A Neighborly Attitude

Romans 15:1-7

How can you best live as a neighbor?

Paul makes it clear in today's reading that it is a privilege and a calling for each of us to "please our neighbors for their good" for no other reason than it builds up that neighbor and gives them a more blessed and stronger life. When we act that way, it's as if we are acting in the very footsteps of Jesus, and we do so "for God's glory."

Does it feel that way to you? When you care for people for no other reason than they need the care, do you have a sense that Jesus is looking over your shoulder, giving a nod of approval? Or does it feel like a duty, grudgingly done, that impedes on your freedom to do whatever you want?

Paul writes about the possibility of "hope through endurance" and "encouragement of the scriptures." What he means is that as we suffer or when we are called on to do difficult things for the sake of another, we can endure it and be encouraged to do so with the attitude that this is what Jesus has done for us and what he wants us to do for others. It is part of being a Christian. We love. We get to care about more than just our lives. We have the example and the gift of Jesus acting that way toward us first, taking on our burdens, so that we might take on the burdens of our neighbors.

Who has cared for you that you can identify as living out Christ's example? Where have you or where might you now act that way toward your neighbor?

Lord, let me have the privilege of caring
for my neighbor this day. Amen.

Thursday, August 13

The Single Statement

Galatians 5:4-15

How do you stay focused on what is important?

Today's Scripture is part of Paul's letter to a group of distracted Galatians. They were caught between the new life offered in Christ and the rules and conditions of following the Jewish law. Paul scolded them, asking who was distracting them and confusing them about what the true path should be. It was quite a tongue-lashing!

Then we get to verse 13: "You were called to freedom . . . but serve each other in love." Paul kept it focused by telling them that the single statement of loving neighbor as self completes the Law and gives us the clear, straight path to following Christ. However, even this truth wouldn't keep them completely on the path. In verse 15, he recognizes their tendency and ability to destroy the community!

Still, we are handed the "single statement" for our lives. How often do we decide to chase after other things, ignore the truth, or put layers and layers of other things on top of it? "Love your neighbor" is not a hard concept to grasp, yet it is a tremendously profound practice to learn to do well and consistently. The only thing that will keep us on track is recalling it, stating it, writing it, praying for God's help to do it, and then doing it!

Let's not be distracted Christians. Let your life be one of focus, clarity, and honest, heartfelt action of loving in the example of Jesus Christ, who never let himself get distracted.

How can you stay focused on and attentive to this single statement?

Lord, forgive me, and focus
my heart to follow you. Amen.

FRIDAY, AUGUST 14

Treated Well

Acts 27:39–28:2, 10

When was a time when you were treated extremely well?

Sometimes it feels as if we all experience being tossed in the ocean, swimming for shore, and unsure what we will find there, just like Paul. Will we even make it to shore, and if we do, are we going to be set upon by cruel people? Or will they instead make a nice warm fire and honor us for being nothing other than persons who need that care?

In this world, it is easy to be mean, withholding love when it should be shared. In so many places, we discover harsh hearts, silent judgment, and hostility instead of hospitality. What a joy it is, then, to find a place where kindness is the hallmark. The fact is, of course, that there is no good reason why kindness can't be the way we all live. I've often used the phrase "Be kind when you can, and be just, when you must." In 90 percent of our dealings with others and others' dealing with us, welcome, openness, and the ability to give without having to take can and should be the behavior choice. How sad that we might instead always expect the worst, or even worse, that we would prepare to share the worst we can offer when we are the host!

The truth is, kindness is intentional. We must decide on that way of acting, of opening our lives to others, or accepting the openness that others offer to us. In that intentional work, we then take on the image of Christ and fill the atmosphere with love and hope instead of suspicion and fear. Which choice will you make? How will you prepare to receive a shipwrecked guest into your life?

Kind God, teach me to follow your ways. Amen.

Saturday, August 15

The Perfect Rule

Luke 10:25-28

What rules do you live by?

As Christians, we believe righteousness comes as a gift of God through the grace of Jesus Christ. For the followers of the Law, however, it came from obedience to the Law. In Jesus' exchange with a legal expert, though, the answer to keeping the Law is boiled down to two simple rules: Love God with everything you have and are, and love your neighbor the way you love yourself.

What God offers us through Jesus is far more than keeping a rule or even a dozen rules. It calls us to a way of life, even more than a behavior. It is an invitation to arrange all that we are and do around the principles of loving God and loving others. Eternal life means I throw all that I am, all my energy and dreams, to loving God and the people around me with every word, action, and intention I hold. That's all!

So many of us work so hard to accomplish things that don't matter and then somehow ignore or diminish this key work of our lives. Imagine waking up each morning and stating out loud, "Today, I will love God with all that I am and love the people around me the way I would love to be loved." How different would our lives unfold each day? What things would I choose to do first, and what other things would I never take up? I suppose that means yelling at bad drivers, too, doesn't it? Harder than I thought, and yet, follower of Christ, there is no better way to act out of gratitude for the gracious gift given in love by God to us, than to love with all we are in return! Can that be your life today?

God, help me start my day the right way! Amen.

A Beautiful Day in the Neighborhood

Luke 10:29-37

How do you decide who will be your neighbor?

The tricky thing about the question, "And who is my neighbor?" is that it can't be answered. It can't work in the kingdom of God, because it appears to ask, "What is the limit of people I have to care about? Where can I draw the line so that there are persons who will not be my neighbor?" Jesus explained that it doesn't work that way. In his story, he took someone who would have been despised, a Samaritan, and made him the hero. The Samaritan drew no line, but only responded to need. My neighbor, then, is anyone who needs me, and I become the neighbor not when someone accepts me, but when I show mercy and love.

Neighbor appears to always be in the first person: who will I care for? This understanding of neighbor is precisely how God acts toward us! God says, "Who will I love? Who will I show mercy to?" And the answer is God-sized. "I will so love the world that I will even give my Son, so that all will know my love that has no end, and no boundaries!"

We don't choose who is in and who is out of our neighborhood. Following the example that God has given us, we love until we die, and then love

Who needs you? Who must be loved? Just as we are never beyond God's love, so no one is beyond ours, and no one deserves less than our greatest love toward them. Our answer to it all becomes our guiding question: Won't you be my neighbor?

> Fill my heart with your never-ending love,
> O God, and let me serve you. Amen.

A Prayer Worth Praying

Psalm 17:1-7

What is the most sincere prayer you can offer to God?

The writer of Psalm 17 is bold enough to request that God listen to him and to focus on his cry. He's not just asking for some kind of fluff here. He is asking to be delivered from the forces in this world who would attack and try to destroy the way that he is living. Examine my heart, he says. You know, God, if I am telling the truth, and I am! Just let me take refuge in you and save me from those who would bring me to ruin.

Life sometimes seems to reach out and either grab our ankles and pull us down or take a club and knock us off our balance. We all have bad times, and granted, some of those are by our own actions. However, it is God's nature to save and to keep us from being destroyed, and the best and finest prayer we can offer at that time is to pray for God to listen and to show that holy love that comes to bring us strength to make it through the horrible times.

Prayer is the spoken substance of our life with God. It is the conversation of our relationship. Sometimes the prayers we offer express the joy and delight in life—birth, love, even accomplishments. And those times also exist when we simply need help. The key ingredient of it all, of course, is honesty. Search my heart, God. Know that I am telling the truth, and if I have deceived myself, help me see the light and continue to trust in you.

What do you need to pray to God today? How can you speak from your heart to the One who will hear you?

Listen to my heart, O God,
and bring me to new life in you. Amen.

TUESDAY, AUGUST 18

A Wise Choice

1 Kings 3:16-27

How do you make wise decisions?

Wisdom is an elusive gift. Wisdom is not intelligence, nor is it trained reasoning, although both are important. Instead, wisdom is the ability to discern the best path. Wisdom is not a tool we use; it is a mindset or a bearing we have been given through our experiences, or better, as a gift of God. In Solomon's case, wisdom helped call out and illuminate the true mother's love, and then the good decision could follow.

Where does wisdom come forward in your life? Usually, it is when we are able to ask the best questions. Smart and quick-witted people can always find questions to ask, but the wise person asks the best one, the one that brings the deepest and most important answer. Wisdom takes time, too, because it takes time to discover where the most important element of any situation is found.

Above all, wisdom exists to uncover love. As the key to any good discernment, where we find the highest love and the deepest love is usually where we discover the wisest decision and the truest path to take. To ask, "Where will love be found in this case?" takes us on the best first steps in a solid and meaningful direction.

What decision do you need to make right now that would best be made as you are guided by wisdom? Where might you see the love?

O God, direct my path to the
highest love I might discover. Amen.

WEDNESDAY, AUGUST 19

Everyone Was Healed

Acts 5:12-16

Where have you seen healing happen in your life?

Jesus often asked in his ministry, "Do you want to be healed?" People went to him asking for healing, and others took those to Jesus who needed to be healed. That also happened with the apostles. The apostles performed "many signs and wonders," and large numbers of people came to witness and believe in the power of the Spirit flowing through these followers of Jesus.

We've had times in our faith history when the Holy Spirit was active in strengthening, emboldening, and even healing persons. Times of revival and awakening among the followers of Christ produced unbelievable acts of proof that the power was there. How diabolical, then, when some persons seeking power and fame have used willing and unknowing persons to manufacture untrue "healings." The result has been to diminish the overall hope and belief that healing indeed can and will occur by the Spirit's power and not by some sham or fakery.

Two questions: When have you experienced or witnessed healing yourself or that of someone you know? Where do you hope that healing might occur, so much that you would pray to God for that gift to come?

Again, healing is a side result of the Spirit's power, so perhaps our best prayer might be, "Come, Holy Spirit!" Where might you offer that prayer? Who do you trust might be able to receive that power in his or her life and be the vessel for the healing of others?

O God, please restore and
heal our lives this day. Amen.

Do You Believe?

Matthew 9:27-31

Where would you ask Jesus for healing?

We need to be like the blind men in today's text. To be blind in Jesus' time was to be forced into a lifetime of begging from people walking by while you sat in the dirt. When they heard about Jesus and heard he was coming past, they knew it was their chance. Maybe they had been talking about it together, building up each other's faith. However it happened, they cried out, and Jesus answered, and asked them simply, "Do you believe I can do this?" Their response, "Yes, Lord," changed everything, because they believed.

Perhaps the most humorous part of the story was that Jesus told them not to tell anyone about the miracle, so their response was to "spread the word about him throughout that whole region." I expect Jesus told them not to because his desire was not to be known as a healer but to be about proclaiming the Kingdom. But their belief brought new life to them! Imagine what it would have meant to be healed of that affliction. Their lives were changed forever! They had to tell.

Where in your life is there brokenness or disease? What is holding you back from experiencing the powerful life of faith and abundance in Christ? What is unresolved, or crippling, or such an impediment that you are helpless and need your Savior? Your belief and trust make all the difference in the world. How will you bring your request to your Lord today?

God of Power, help me to trust and
believe in you for my life's healing. Amen.

Friday, August 21

A New Look

Galatians 3:23-29

What personal qualities do you have that are most important to you?

Each of us has things with which we identify and that identify us, creating our particular and unique personality. They may be what we were born with, like being left-handed, or what we have grown to love, like particular areas of the country, or particular skills, or any number of other things. There is nothing wrong with having identifiable traits or passions, but today's Scripture seems to set all of that aside for the sake of informing us about how much alike we all are. "You are all God's children," Paul told the Galatians.

Followers of Jesus Christ are to set aside all of the normal divisions and distinctions, even those things that for millennia have placed us into different camps, different statuses, and different privileges. By the love and grace of Jesus Christ, all of those convenient camps have vanished, and the work of showing how different I am from you now ends. "You are all one in Christ Jesus," Paul stressed. The very love of Jesus has removed what separates us, and the unity of our lives with one another in Christ becomes the greatest, most significant distinction we can hold.

When you think about the things that are distinctive about you, are you able to put at the head of the list the fact that you belong to Jesus? And what does that relationship say about you and about how you live and act and respond in this world? What does it say about how you will love?

Thank you, God, for claiming me through Jesus.
Let me live for you. Amen.

Tough Love

Mark 7:24-29

How have you tested whether someone was sincere in what they were saying?

Jesus knew the tendency of persons to manipulate simply to get what they want. So when the Gentile woman came to him, did he sense that a liar had come to use him? Had she heard about his power but cared not at all about who he is? I like to think that's the case, and that instead of reading that Jesus was someone who would mistreat a poor, helpless mother, he was testing in the most difficult way possible. It was there that she expressed her humility in only asking for crumbs from the table, as it were. Jesus' response was, "Good answer!" and he healed the daughter.

This healing event highlights a love that would not be manipulated and exploited. If the woman were a fake, she most likely would have just turned around and left, but instead, she gave even of her dignity for the healing of her child. Jesus saw that love and offered grace, even to someone outside of the Jewish faith.

Sometimes we need to challenge and test before extending our love in circumstances where it would only be manipulated. We also need to be ready to share our love when it indeed appears that another honestly needs it. Take this story and learn how to test for truth and to offer love generously. Can you think of experiences when taking this approach to love was necessary? Can you be this aware and ready to follow Jesus' example?

Dear God, help me to be wise and
generous when it comes to love. Amen.

SUNDAY, AUGUST 23

Never Let Go

Matthew 15:21-28

How persistent are you when it comes to prayer?

You might be scratching your head after reading today's Scripture since it is almost exactly like yesterday's, which we read from Mark's Gospel. Same story, told a little differently. While yesterday we spoke of examining for the truth, today we look at the work of persistence.

Jesus was confronted by a Canaanite woman whose daughter needed to be freed from a demon. This woman did not give up! "Show me mercy, Son of David," she pleaded. "Lord, help me," she implored, kneeling before him. And even when Jesus responded, "It is not good to take the children's bread and toss it to dogs," she responded by asking only for the crumbs. She wouldn't give up. But why? Because what she needed was more important than any status, slander, or abuse. She wanted her daughter to be healed, and this Jesus was the one to do it. Finally, he did, and praised her "great faith."

Why do we give up so easily in our prayer and in our hope that God will intervene on our behalf? Why do we believe we don't deserve or simply will never receive what we dream and long for? Where is our persistent trust that God is working out God's purpose today?

Our task and our calling are not to evaluate the difficulty before us. Our task is to pray. Our calling is to believe and never give up the hope that is ours in Christ.

For what will you be persistent in prayer today?

God of Hope, grant me the ability
never to stop praying to you. Amen.

The Best Gift

1 Corinthians 13:1-13

What would it be like for you never to know love?

First Corinthians 13 is an outstanding and powerful chapter in our Scripture because it is so clear in describing the core of all of our relationships and our relationship with God. If such love didn't exist, then I wonder what would be so distinct about our Christian faith. It explains Jesus, in that highest love possible. It explains what binds us together. It offers us the insight into the perfect eternal life to come, and it encourages us to use the gift God has placed so fully in our hands.

Now comes the challenge. How can we receive such a gift and not use it constantly? Knowing that we could never wear it out, and indeed, the more we use it, the finer and stronger it becomes, why would we ever hesitate to employ it in every conversation, every interaction, and every way we touch this world? Yet we do just that. So often we leave this finest gift in the closet as we wish instead to win over loving. We eke it out, as though we will use it up, or we save it only for those who we think "deserve it."

That's just wrong-headed. I challenge you, instead of acting like the world acts, to act instead as a child of God. Let the "best gift" flow through you to a world in need. Let it permeate everything you do, feel, and say. Let it become the hallmark of your life so that anyone who sees you will not see you, but Christ living in you. That's our challenge and our hope as we follow Jesus. Where is your love needed today?

God of love, teach me how to use the gift. Amen.

Tuesday, August 25

Living the Low Life

Isaiah 65:1-5

Why do you sin?

Sometimes I am just a wonderful person. I love and share and forgive and seek justice and offer compassion and do all of the things that would, frankly, have me declared a saint. Other times, however, I am self-centered, self-important, petty, punitive, and determined to withhold my love. I won't tell you what I could have been declared during those times.

In today's Scripture, God speaks and describes the "other times" for Israel. Israel was acting and living horribly, even worse, they rejected God and said, "Keep away from me!" We might say they were "wicked," not just because they did evil things but because they made the intentional choice to live apart from God. God would finally judge Israel, exile them, and let them have time to come to understand what it means to be alone. But what about us? How do we learn not to sin?

Just as yesterday's reading painted a picture of what it means to live in love, today we see the lack of love and the inability to give ourselves away for the sake of the world. We learn how not to sin when we are ready to learn how to love and love alone. It's a long journey and not all forward either. We fall back into our selfish lives and need to be rescued repeatedly. But God is patient, and as we strive for lives that are more loving, God lifts us up and helps us move in that direction. As we love, we begin to set the sin down by the side of the road, since being with God is always better.

Will you allow love to move you beyond sin today?

Forgive me, God, and save me to love. Amen.

WEDNESDAY, AUGUST 26
A Wonderful Future

Zechariah 9:9-12

What does God have in store for you?

As we read the Bible, we discover and come to cherish the story of Creation and God's presence from the beginning of all that is, the story of Israel, and the promise and presence of Jesus Christ. However, as important as this history and these stories are for our faith, it is also critical that we embrace what is yet to be. It's crucial that we understand and claim the hope of a future that is in God's hands when we believe a new reign will replace the challenge and trial of today's living. Hope is our compass, no matter what we are going through right now. We live and walk in faith as we read and reread the words, "Look, your king will come to you!"

When we hear and receive that truth, we can be bold in our faith, acting and living and loving boldly before others. We have the power to encourage and paint the picture of the future for those persons who may not feel the same optimism or have received the good news like we have. It's not my future. It's our future, a future that God controls and promises. That's why when someone dies, we can have comfort and joy in envisioning them in heaven, with the cloud of witnesses all around. A future of joy, of hope, provides for a bold trust and love today so that we begin to change the world today through our hope for tomorrow!

What do you dare to do, knowing what you know of the future? What things might you be able to risk, knowing that no matter what happens, God holds tomorrow?

> Thank you for bringing the future to us, dear God,
> and may we discover the joy that it brings us. Amen.

Thursday, August 27

A Joyful Experience

Luke 10:17-24

What was one of your happiest moments?

Luke's Gospel describes a particular moment in Jesus' life when he expressed unrestrained joy. Upon receiving word of his 72 followers returning from their first mission trip, the Scripture says, "At that very moment, Jesus overflowed with joy from the Holy Spirit." Throughout the Gospels, we find Jesus described in many ways: determined, thoughtful, sad, forgiving, and even enraged at money changers. Rarely, however, do the Gospel writers say that he was filled with joy. This must have been a wonderful moment for Jesus. It's as if he had glimpsed the Kingdom coming, praised his heavenly Father, and rejoiced in the relationship he has as part of the Trinity. It's a fantastic moment in Jesus' ministry, as everything seems to be what it should be.

I believe joy is our best response to love. Beyond just feeling happy about something, joy is an unfettered feeling of gladness, and carries with it "rejoicing," which means speaking of joy. The words that try to define it fall short, as it is one of the greatest gifts that we could feel this way!

So, several questions to ponder today: What brings you joy in your life? Not satisfaction or pleasure, but joy that is unfettered and carries you to a different level of responding to love? Second, how do you bring joy to another person? What can you do in your life to unleash the feelings in that other person's heart, to act out of gratitude for the love they have received?

O God, I thank you for times of joy.
Help me take that gift to others. Amen.

Real Authority

Mark 1:21-28

What authority do you respect?

It's interesting that the word *authority* arises from the same root as the word *author*, meaning someone or something that is original, who doesn't simply do what everyone else does. When we witness someone who acts with integrity and inhabits a place in this world that is not like everyone else, we are impressed. We listen, we consider, and we often agree, because what is offered to us seems authentic and honest. True authority arises from within people who are open, genuine, truthful, fair, wise, and respected, among other things.

So it was with Jesus as he taught in the synagogue. People were amazed that he taught them "with authority." He brought wisdom and inner clarity. On top of that, he also brought power to silence demons. Everyone was amazed that this new rabbi could perform such miraculous acts of healing and authoritative power.

Jesus' authority, of course, was not something he learned. It is an innate part of who he is as the Son of God. That's what scared the demon and overwhelmed the people. When they saw him, experienced him, they looked into the face of God.

As followers of Jesus, we need to be open and ready to speak, act, and teach as Jesus empowers us to do as well. We all have opportunities to tell the truth about Jesus. So what authority do you have? What power does the Holy Spirit express through your life? Are you ready to proclaim Jesus with authority?

I thank you, God, for the gift
of Jesus in my life. Amen.

SATURDAY, AUGUST 29
An Incredible Sight

Mark 5:1-13

What is the most remarkable thing you have ever seen?

Today's Scripture offers us remarkable images. The first image is of a madman roaming the tombs. No one could restrain him, and he would howl night and day. The second image is of the demons talking with Jesus, telling him their name is Legion. (A Roman legion at that time had around 5,000 soldiers.) The third image is of the demons negotiating with Jesus to allow them to go into a herd of swine (an unclean animal for the Jews). When Jesus allowed it, about 2,000 pigs rushed over a cliff and drowned in a lake. The final remarkable image is of the townspeople coming to see what had happened. They found Jesus, and the no-longer possessed man was dressed and completely sane.

Each of these images should create in our minds the sense of power this story contains. Simply by the words of Jesus, the spiritual world obeyed, resulting in healing and sanity for a person Jesus had never met before.

As we read this story and others like it in the Bible, it's easy to be amazed at the remarkable images it holds. Beyond the Scripture, I believe God offers us remarkable images of spiritual power and God's rule and actions in our world today. We just make the mistake of not recognizing them. It's critical to keep our spiritual eyes open so that we can experience and share what we have seen and heard of God's love and power in our world. That way, others can experience the remarkable presence of God in their lives, too.

Open my eyes, Lord. I want
to see you in my world! Amen.

SUNDAY, AUGUST **30**

Tell the Story

Mark 5:14-20

What is your story of the grace of Jesus Christ?

The man possessed by an evil spirit in the region of the Gerasenes certainly had a story to tell, didn't he? After his healing/exorcism, the townspeople "pleaded with Jesus to leave their region," probably because they only saw the power Jesus had and didn't understand the salvation he brought. The man, however, "pleaded with Jesus to let him come along as one of his disciples." Jesus had other ideas. He told the man to go home to his own people, and by his very presence and his story, he could share the mercy of God. It was quite the story, and "everyone was amazed."

We need to ask ourselves, "What has God done for me? What story or stories can I tell about how my life has been changed or refocused by the love and grace of God through Jesus?" Granted, some of us are better storytellers than others. But do your children or grandchildren or other relatives know about your life of faith? Does your spouse know? Is there an experience you need to remember that you may have long forgotten?

When we share our stories, we open the door for others to come to faith or renew their faith. It's important that our faith stories not disappear. As we retell our "God Stories," we reclaim them for our memories and have the chance once again to praise and thank God for what has happened in our lives.

Who will you tell your story to, even today?

I love to tell the story,
dear God, of Jesus and his love.

MONDAY, AUGUST 31

Needing a Savior

Psalm 7:1-10

When have you felt fear and the need to be rescued?

How many times have you felt an enemy of some sort attempting to drag you off, trample you into the ground, or even simply lay your reputation in the dirt? By nature, human beings eventually end up in conflict with one another. When I am being set upon, thrust into conflict, or forced to defend myself, I try to turn to someone who can pull me out of the mess, or at least protect me while I have to stand in the struggle. Whether that was finding refuge behind Mom when big brother wanted to do me harm or turning to God when the world wants to hurt us, we all need a savior.

The psalmist prayed for God to act, asking God to get angry, to stand up, even to wake up! This kind of prayer comes when two things are certain: one, I believe God is truly strong enough to save me from the horrible future that awaits me; and two, that God is willing to be on my side in the battle and to save me and all who are "righteous."

Of course, that doesn't mean that I am right or righteous all the time! Verse 10 promises that God will "save those whose heart is right." Perhaps the most important work we can do is to make sure that our heart is indeed "right," that we don't delude ourselves into thinking that we can do whatever we want to, and that it's always okay. The privilege of calling on God to save me must include my willingness to live each day closer and closer to the God who will protect me and bring me life.

Help me this day, O Lord, to find
my life and hope in you. Amen.

SEPTEMBER

CONTRIBUTORS:

Randy Cross
(September 1–September 27)

Gary Thompson
(September 28–September 30)

Taking Sides

Acts 7:59–8:3

When have you been on the wrong side of a conflict?

After the murder of Stephen, the persecution of the early church began, with Saul leading the way. In what sense could that ever be right? Yet the wrong was powerful, and the energy and effort to destroy the church quickly spread. It was a terrible time to be right.

This is not unusual in our world. We tend to spend more time pushing our power to show that we are right than allowing the truth of who we are and perhaps even the rightness of our convictions to be our witness. The sad fact of our humanity is that we like to be right, and if we are not right, we like to make sure that no one opposes us in our wrong.

Can you think of a time when you have experienced that? Can you recall a time when you were wrong but had the power to silence or push aside someone who spoke the truth? The problem is that even if we know deep down that we are wrong, we think that if we shout loudly enough or act powerfully enough, that will make it right.

A wise friend once told me that when I am positive that I am in the right, then that is the time for me to go into the chapel and pray. You see, our "rightness" must not simply arise out of our judgment or mindset. It must be given as a gift from God.

How will you live your "right" life today? What role will prayer and honest listening to God play in directing your decisions?

O God, forgive me, and guide
my thoughts and decisions. Amen.

WEDNESDAY, SEPTEMBER 2

Consumed With Evil

Acts 9:1-6; 22:4-5; 26:9-11

Where have you experienced evil in your life?

During the time he was known as Saul, this person gave himself over to evil. He sought out the followers of Christ, imprisoned them, tortured them, and threatened them with murder until or unless they denied the Son of God. Why? Because their testimony called Jesus the Messiah, the Son of God, which was unacceptable to the first-century Jewish faith. However, the "evil" did not come in a difference of opinion. It came with actions that were intended to wipe out a difference of faith.

Now this is tricky, because we as Christians talk about Jesus being the one way, one truth, one life to God. The difference between our faith and Saul's is that we believe and trust in that truth, but we don't feel compelled to destroy someone who holds a different belief. Our task is to share the good news of Christ, not to kill off all who do not believe as we do! Our calling is to invite others to know Christ as we do, and to do so in love, not evil, and in good news, not in threats of murder. It is in the sharing of the love of God in Jesus Christ that we find the power of the gospel and the hope of life.

Who do you know in your life who needs something other than judgment? Who needs to be reassured of Christ's love for them? Instead of seeking to imprison them in any way, how can you free them to become joyful followers of Christ themselves?

Grant me the gift of good news, gracious God,
and let me share it with the world! Amen.

Thursday, September 3

Transformation

Acts 9:7-9; 26:12-18

When have you experienced something that turned your life around for the better?

I think Saul wins first prize with a turnaround event for his life! Can you imagine a bright light, a voice that speaks directly to you, and then a time of blindness? Saul was heading to Damascus to arrest Christians, and he ended up after encountering the living Christ.

I guess there are times when God says, "That's enough." We get stopped in our tracks, unable to move forward with life as usual, maybe even recognizing our blindness. In that moment, a transformation begins. It might be painful and unwanted at first, but as we begin to change, we recognize that we, too, might be led by God's hand to a new way of life. Life can become deeper, more focused, and more hopeful than going it alone with our big ideas.

Have you prayed, or are you praying now, for that to happen? Or are you right now unaware of how you might need to change? Do you desperately need God to take you by the hand, put you on a new path, and give you a new perspective or a new life? Frankly, I think that should be our daily prayer, that God would indeed take charge and transform our lives into those formed by God's hand and love.

May we take on that approach to living! It will be then that we will hear the voice of Christ calling to us, inviting us to get up and do his will.

Take my hand, O God, and lead me
to a new life by your grace. Amen.

FRIDAY, SEPTEMBER 4
Available for God's Work

Acts 9:10-20; 22:12-16

How do you live available and obedient to God's call?

Ananias, the Scripture says, was a faithful disciple of Jesus, living in Damascus, when the Lord spoke to him and gave him the mission to restore Saul's sight. As is usually the case, we don't hear Ananias say, "Right! I'm on it!" Instead, we hear a great deal of hemming and hawing based on the fear of horrible reports the Christians have heard about Saul, true reports that were scary and life-threatening. But the Lord still said, "Go!" Isn't it interesting that God never negotiates when we are to be on a mission God sets before us?

Ananias was faithful and did what God commanded, probably with shaking knees, but as a result, not only was Saul's life transformed, but we expect Ananias's was as well.

I don't know if any of us is ready to take on a mission from God when God steps into our normal lives and tells us that something critically important requires our availability. God also doesn't try to convince us. God knows our hearts, and over and over again throughout history, God has depended on people who have depended on God to bring love and hope to this world.

I hope that when God calls us, even with knees shaking, unsure of ourselves, we will answer the call, the invitation to be faithful, and share God's good news with another person. Are you ready to do that? Are you prepared to be not necessarily able but available for God to use you in this world to bring holy love?

I may not be ready, O Lord, but use me anyway.
I am your servant. Amen.

Saturday, September 5

The Appearance of Christ

1 Corinthians 15:1-11

Where have you seen Christ?

In today's Scripture, Paul gives his testimony of the resurrection of Jesus Christ. He recounts Christ's death, burial, and rising on the third day, and then lists those to whom Jesus appeared in his resurrected state. Hundreds witnessed the resurrected Christ. Then, Paul says, "and last of all he appeared to me," recalling his experience on the road to Damascus.

I wish I would have or could have seen the living Christ. To see Jesus face-to-face would be such a holy and wonderful thing, but I expect that's only going to happen after I have left this earth. Still, I have seen Christ with eyes that look beyond what is physical to see the heart and soul of others;. I have encountered Jesus in many different places and events and people. Through worship and mission and teaching and learning, Jesus has appeared in many ways to strengthen my faith and my love for this world in Christ's name.

What about you? Where do you believe you have experienced Christ? As you spend time with other followers of Jesus, as you hear their stories, can you also see Christ in your midst? How will you share what you have experienced of the grace of Jesus Christ, as though he were right beside you? Who needs to hear that good news and see Christ for themselves?.

Let me present you to the world, dear Jesus,
and may others see you in me. Amen.

SUNDAY, SEPTEMBER 6

What's in a Name?

Romans 1:1-6

What title do you give yourself as a follower of Jesus?

Titles, whether earned, inherited, or conferred, are used to identify us in one way or another. They also help to distinguish us from one another. And then we come to Paul, once known as Saul, of Tarsus. In Romans 1, Paul identified himself by a title I'm sure he cherished: "From Paul, a slave of Jesus Christ, called to be an apostle."

He was a slave of Jesus. A slave in this case was a lifelong servant, cared for, given position, and in return offering loyal and faithful obedience to a master. Paul didn't call himself Jesus' friend, his brother, or anything of the sort. His life was committed to serving Christ as faithfully as possible. Paul was an apostle not by his ideas or actions but because he was called by Jesus' command. An apostle is under the authority of the one who sends him or her. Paul was sent by Jesus and obeyed him.

What difference did it make that Paul had these titles? The purpose was that they identified him to the Roman congregation, and they described how he saw himself and his approach to following Jesus.

How far Paul had come! Now he was a slave, sent by the one to whom he now offered all faithfulness and allegiance. Paul indeed was a follower of Christ.

What title would you offer that describes your relationship with Jesus? How would others recognize your understanding of your place in Jesus' world?

Thank you for accepting me, dear God, and help
me learn more about how to serve you. Amen.

Monday, September 7

Being Part of the Announcement

Mark 1:14-15

What is the best announcement you can recall hearing?

Announcements are sometimes surprises, other times confirmations of what we have already expected. Our daily world is full of announcements, if we listen: babies born, couples married, financial markets booming or crashing, new restaurants opening, and bad weather coming.

Our two verses from Mark's Gospel are a great announcement. John had been arrested. His ministry was over. The news the world had all been waiting for was here! Not, "Stay tuned for something possible coming sometime next year," but "Now is the time! Here comes God's kingdom!"

As Jesus began his ministry, he announced the kingdom of God, but he did one thing more. Did you read it? He said, "Change your hearts and lives, and trust the good news!" The big announcement came as an invitation, a call, a summons to you and me to respond! God's kingdom is here. Will we change, transform, give up, and take up something new so that our lives and hearts are in line with and are under the call and claim of God's wonderful reign?

When we read Mark's Gospel, it's important for us to understand that the announcement of God's kingdom is new today as well! We are invited to change our hearts and lives and trust this good news ourselves. How will you respond with your life to this big announcement today? Let it happen as you share your love with this lonely world.

Gracious God, thank you for announcing your kingdom.
Help me share in this good news today. Amen.

Are You the One?

Matthew 11:2-5

How do you know Jesus is the Messiah?

John the Baptist, in prison, had heard of what Jesus had been doing. So "he sent word by his disciples to Jesus, asking, 'Are you the one who is to come, or should we look for another?'" Verses 4 and 5 indicate that Jesus pointed out the key to understanding who he was. It wasn't a secret. It was in broad view of the world. Healing the blind, the crippled, the diseased, the deaf, even raising the dead, were all happening by Jesus' hand, actions that had been predicted to be part of the Messiah's life. Now, Jesus didn't come right out and say so, but he did say, "Look around! My actions speak for themselves."

What do we see as we look around our world today? What do we see through our eyes of faith? Have you witnessed healing? Have you seen lives and relationships restored? Have you seen the powerful effects of holy love? When we observe the power of the Holy Spirit, it becomes possible and even makes sense to answer, "He is the Messiah, the one who has ushered in God's reign on this earth, and who has saved my life as well."

What effort would you need to affirm that Jesus is the one? What do you see around you right now, in the lives of those you know, where Jesus has indeed made all the difference in living abundant and hopeful lives?

> Open my eyes, dear God, so that I, too,
> may see the one Jesus Christ. Amen.

WEDNESDAY, SEPTEMBER 9

Ignoring What's There

Hebrews 2:1-5

How has Jesus been revealed to you?

The writer of Hebrews urges us not to ignore or act blind to the message of salvation. Jesus and those who follow him have announced the message repeatedly, and God has "vouched" for the message with "signs, amazing things, various miracles, and gifts from the Holy Spirit." How is it that anyone could miss such an obvious revelation of who Jesus is and the fact that salvation has come to this earth?

Part of what it means to live a new life in Christ is that we acknowledge our need of God and our tendency to walk away from God to sin. By the gift of Jesus Christ, we have been brought back into God's arms, and we pray for each person in the world to know that gracious joy. Once we have offered our hearts and our lives to God, that message and that power should re-create us as new persons. It's for us to spend our lives continuing to learn, observe, and claim the "signs, amazing things, various miracles, and gifts from the Holy Spirit" that God continues to provide.

How would you describe your salvation? How have you experienced God's forgiveness and claim on you? When we let those kinds of questions guide us and lead us daily, then our minds and our eyes are indeed on Jesus, and our lives do reflect the growing awareness of a grace-filled existence, as we simply pay attention to what brings us true life in Christ!

What questions will you ask that will reveal Christ today?

Lead me deeper into my love for you, O God,
as you have loved me with new life. Amen.

Thursday, September 10

Standing on Shoulders

1 Peter 1:7-12

Who will follow you in the Christian faith?

The writer of 1 Peter reminded "God's chosen strangers in the world of the diaspora" (1 Peter 1:1) that a significant faith history preceded them. Indeed, as they received the joy of salvation, in a way, they were standing on the shoulders of the prophets and others who foretold and inquired deep within their hearts about the coming of Christ and what that would mean for this world. They did not see Jesus, at least in this world, but they did proclaim that it would happen, and indeed it has happened. The same is true for us. We've never "seen" Jesus, but our faith invites us to love and trust and to declare his place as Lord of the universe as we wait until Christ comes again.

The big question is who will follow you? Who are you preparing now to stand on your shoulders? Each generation is the final one to know faith in Christ, unless it is shared with the one that follows. We have a powerful opportunity and a sobering responsibility to continue to share and experience the good news of Christ with all we meet. We are called to live in expectation of Christ's coming to this earth, even if we are not alive to experience it here.

What moves you today to share your faith? Who needs to stand on your shoulders and come to know the blessings of salvation and the joy of a life lived in faith? Who are you praying for to know Jesus as you know him?

O Lord, thank you for the privilege of sharing my faith.

Amen.

FRIDAY, SEPTEMBER 11

Staying the Course

Philippians 1:27-29

What does it mean to be "worthy of the gospel"?

Paul instructed Christians to "live together in a manner worthy" of the gospel. Paul wants us to "stay the course" when it comes to being faithful and to exhibit the gracious and loving actions of a community of Jesus. The reason he considered this so important was that all around, there are "enemies" who would be more than happy to take us off course, to destroy our faith and hope in Jesus.

We are called to hold the map and stay the course. This "course," of following Jesus with our whole lives, is not just something we come up with or decide is interesting to do for a little while. This is God's path for you and me. Prayer, study, worship, offering ourselves, caring for this world, and more are all part of the course that we are called to take. It will guide us in a straight direction to live faithfully and strongly and have our trust in God become increasingly strong and unwavering.

This means that our lives are no longer our own. Our plans reflect God's plan and direction for our lives. Our actions live out our faith. Our preferences become our desire to follow Christ. We stop detouring or going off the map when something tries to distract us. We live lives of faith and trust in the outcome that it will be pleasing to God and hopeful for us. How might you keep the course of the Christian faith in your life? Who will join you on this journey? Whom do you trust to hold your map?

Lead me, Lord, and teach me
to follow your way to life. Amen.

Saturday, September 12

The Righteous Truth

Romans 1:15-17

How is God's power lived out in your life?

In today's Scripture, Paul was eager to preach in Rome because he believed the gospel is "God's own power for salvation to all." It is the way in which each of us gets our lives in truth with God. That happens by faith in the story of salvation. The gospel is the righteous instrument leading us back to God.

In Romans 1:15-17, Paul hits this idea hard. He sees the gospel as having the power to save us. Do you understand and believe in that power? Unfortunately, some people understand salvation as something other than the power to transform, instead just adjusting their lives a little. That was not Paul's understanding. The powerful gospel changes who we are.

Can you feel that? This is grace acting in our lives so that we might live by faith ourselves. How does that happen? We know it comes when we release our hold on our lives and take up the gift of faith in God to hold us, lead us, and free us to act as a holy offering for God's use. The power is not what we own; it is God's power in us, to live righteously and to love fully. It is a gift, just as we know salvation itself is not what we earn, but a gift of God.

How have you accepted that gift for yourself? How have you shared the power of the gospel to change others' lives, too?

Bring me right with you, O God,
and let me live out the gospel. Amen.

Sunday, September 13

Restored!

Romans 5:6-11

How would you describe your relationship with God?

Paul is clear and concise about what the gospel means and what it means for us personally. Christ died for us "while we were still sinners." This shows how much God loves us since God didn't save nice, good, righteous people who were already right with God but instead saved us, who didn't deserve that gift. Because of that, Paul says, and because of the life we know in Christ, "we now have a restored relationship with God."

That's an interesting use of that word. Paul means that all of humankind is restored, as it once was broken and apart from God. For us, however, it means that we have been restored to a completely new and different relationship. We have been restored to a relationship with God, for which we should be eternally grateful, but we will always know it was restored because Christ died for us.

God's action allowed us to return to God, just as God acts in our lives today to further bring us to holiness of life and heart. We are reconciled into a new eternal life in which we might know and have the blessing of God with us.

As you read Paul's words today, can you feel the depth of Jesus' gift for you? How does that affect how you live with God today? What more might you want to do and be in this new relationship? What role does gratitude play in your life? How might you reconcile with others as God has done for you?

Help me to live humbly and thankfully
before you, O God. Amen.

MONDAY, SEPTEMBER 14

Actions Speak Louder

Proverbs 24:9-12

How do you act when others need you?

Look at our Scripture for today from Proverbs. We aren't sure of the context of verse 11 (persons dragged to slaughter or taken off to death), but when we see something like that happening, it's not the time to show weakness! Instead, we should act out of strength when the situation calls for it. The writer seems to be saying that part of being human involves helping to save or rescue. What is not part of a faithful human's response is, "Look, we didn't know about it." God knows when we fail to live up to what it means to be a human and a faithful person. We aren't talking about heroic actions, just good works, which arise out of our knowledge that the God of the universe knows us.

We don't have to do extraordinary things to live up to our role as someone who occupies a spot in this world. However, we don't have the right to just turn away, to ignore or to make excuses when we see someone in trouble, in distress, or needing what we can offer. Imagine what would happen if we were that kind of role model or example and were able to teach others that essential truth: simply to "love one another." It certainly means that we are people who know God.

Who needs that action from you today? Who needs you to rescue them, to save them, using the strength of character and love that you have? Don't be a hero. Just be you.

O God, fill me with the desire to love
as I have been loved by you. Amen.

TUESDAY, SEPTEMBER 15
Living in Bad Times

2 Timothy 3:1-9

How would you describe the world we are living in today?

Many of the horrible qualities that Paul listed for Timothy in 2 Timothy 3, we can also list for this age. It doesn't sound good. People have given in to their selfish desires and have chosen to live out the worst tendencies of being human. Even loving pleasure instead of loving God and wanting to look religious while denying God's power are all part of the lives of some people.

Even though those behaviors exist and may be common today, that's not who everyone is. Millions of people want to do the right thing; want to care for others; and want to love, forgive, and honor others as cherished people. Some do not, of course, but that's not everyone; those people just probably get more attention by the media. That simply reflects human nature and the tendency to publicize the exciting and horrible actions. We must be careful not to delude ourselves into thinking those actions are never part of our lives. Sometimes we, too, are contrary and critical—and other things.

It would be more helpful to consider how we might live more deeply in the Spirit than getting wrapped up in the condemnation of others. Notice it, be aware of it, and then leave it behind and follow Christ. How might you stand for something of holy character and purpose, even when you see the world sometimes in a mess? What witness could you bear of love, forgiveness, and new life?

Lead me, Lord, in your righteousness,
and teach me to love. Amen.

Figuring Out What Is True

Luke 11:14-20

When did you last have an argument over whether something was true?

Even when he was about the holy and loving work of healing someone, of chasing out a demon from somebody's life, those against Jesus felt the need to slander him by suggesting that the only way he could throw out a demon would be if he were under the leadership of Beelzebub. Jesus' response was perfect. It wouldn't make sense for him to chase out demons if he were under the authority of the demons, he said. Instead, Jesus declared, if he throws out demons by the power of God, then the kingdom of God is already at hand!

What's wonderful to see is that even though Jesus had to go on the debate stage with these persons who wished to diminish his power and authority, his answers always rose above their criticism. Instead of arguing, he simply spoke the truth in a winsome and honest way, bringing light to thorny issues.

What would happen if we were to take that same approach? It's easy to argue. It is far more difficult and more rewarding to simply speak the truth and not necessarily have to have the last word. In the end, the word spoken in love and truth always amounts to the last worthwhile statement in any argument! How could you take that rule of life with you today?

Fill my word with truth, O God,
or help me be silent. Amen.

THURSDAY, SEPTEMBER 17

The Greater Power

Acts 13:34-39

How have you come to know Jesus' forgiveness of sin?

In the synagogue in Antioch, Paul spoke about the incredible difference between Moses' law and Jesus. He compared King David, the highest example of a king of Israel, to Jesus. David indeed was great, but as Paul pointed out, he died and "experienced death's decay." He was human. Jesus, on the other hand, did not stay dead but was raised up by God. It is through the living Christ that our forgiveness comes, which brings us into a right relationship with God more than even following the law of Moses could. We are not in relationship with God due to our obedience to a law or any set of rules but in Jesus. It's not even because of what Jesus taught but because of who he is and what he has done.

God gave the Israelites the law of Moses as a path to righteousness, but with Jesus, the "path" is made by Christ on the cross and in the empty tomb. We should find great joy in knowing that our relationship with God is secure. Our way of living now in the Spirit is also a gift of Christ for us.

I hope that you see and rejoice in the truth of this part of our faith, that what we have is the best we could ever have. How does that speak to your heart? How might that truth of God's love for you move you to live differently in your life?

Paul's words to the people in Antioch were meant as good news and a word of freedom. Have you experienced that good news and freedom in Christ, too?

Holy God, I thank you today for the gift
of salvation through Jesus! Amen.

FRIDAY, SEPTEMBER 18

The Promise

John 5:21-30

What promise do you believe God has given you concerning eternal life?

When Jesus spoke to the Jewish leaders in this encounter recorded in John's Gospel, he made statements about life and death promises of God. The Father promised the Son the powers of resurrection and also of judgment. Therefore, the Son is to be honored and believed just as the Father is honored, and the Son will judge the living and the dead and offer resurrection. This happens because the Father has empowered the Son with such authority.

You are informed and brought into the promise of Jesus in this Scripture. Jesus wants you to understand that the judgment for your life is in his hands. He talks about those who did "good" or "wicked" things in life and whether they go to resurrection of life or judgment. "Wicked" here means living apart from God's will. "Good," then, is not just doing nice things but living according to God's claim and call on us and our trust in Christ.

These are fundamental things we need always to remember. They should change how we act today. This future promise that Christ will bring us from death to life ought to make us bold and courageous to love while we are alive.

What is one thing you might be able to do differently, knowing that your life and your eternal life are in the hands of Jesus Christ?

Thank you for your gift of eternal life, O God,
and for Jesus. Let me so love in my life. Amen.

SATURDAY, SEPTEMBER 19

Set Free

Romans 8:1-5

What are you free to do in your life?

A major distinction of our Christian faith is that we are not saved by works we do, nor by obedience to any law, as though we work our way to heaven. Instead, we are given a new life in the Spirit because Jesus Christ has set us free from being bound to any of that kind of idea or work.

So we are set free! Please understand, however, that "freedom" means we are freed to an entirely different relationship than one in which we try not to make a mistake so that we can work our way to heaven. We are still in a relationship, however, and that means we live an important life with Christ. We give up chasing after "stuff," power, me-first, or even the fear of the future that drives us to insulate ourselves from others and things beyond our control. We are set free from condemnation but not from holy living and not from the command to love as we have been loved. Even when we have not been loved by others, we love because God first loved us.

Freedom is not a license to do whatever we want. It is a path and an open door to experiencing God's joy in us. Our faithful response to that grace that will always keep us and help us to change this world.

So now that you are free, what's on your list? What will take your time and your attention, since you will no longer be focused only on you? Who needs to know the joy that you now feel as you are free in God's Spirit? Who needs the love you have experienced?

Let me live freely for you,
O God, with all my heart. Amen.

SUNDAY, SEPTEMBER 20

A New Attitude

Romans 8:6-11

How can you give up self-centeredness?

Paul is clear that people who carry an attitude of self-centeredness, of selfishness, are on their way to death, are hostile to God and simply cannot please God because their lives are all about themselves. Instead of getting what they want, they just get death.

Once we give our lives over to Jesus and accept the gift of salvation, we no longer live for ourselves, but God's Spirit lives in us and frees us for an abundant life lived with purpose and with the indwelling of the divine. Life in the Spirit brings power! Instead of believing that life is helpless and hopeless, with the Spirit we know that we have unlimited power to love and bring joy to others. The weight of death is lifted off our shoulders, and we are able to proclaim and bear witness to eternal life even in our lives now.

Life in the Spirit brings possibility! No longer bound to being self-centered, we are free to imagine how we might bless the world and give ourselves away with incredible love and hope. We can change lives because our lives have been changed.

Life in the Spirit brings peace. No longer living with regret or complaining because we don't have what we think we want, we have peace with God. We have serenity even when storms rage around us, for God anchors us and calms our jagged hearts with the Spirit.

How will you live in the Spirit today?

Move in me, O Spirit of God,
and bring me alive. Amen.

MONDAY, SEPTEMBER 21

The Only One

Isaiah 45:21-24

Why do you trust in God to save you?

In today's Scripture, Isaiah quotes the Lord speaking to the people of Israel concerning the one they need to bow and confess to: all other gods are simply idols, scraps of wood, stone, and metal made by human hands. The Lord is the one true God. "There's no other God except me . . . there's none besides me!"

How important this is to us in our faith! One God and no other. Granted, we still make our idols today of money, things, or people we seem to worship and bow down to with our hearts. God's Word doesn't change, however. There is no other, and we know it is more than simply "God is out there in the great somewhere, hearing us." God is deeply involved in our lives. God has sworn a solemn pledge to us. We have a place with God, and our joy should be to bow and confess that core truth of our existence, that God is with us, and we are to be with God.

It's not a house of mirrors, where we think one thing is true, and we are tricked. "Turn to me and be saved," God says. God is righteous and a savior for us. Do you need to know what is true? Find that truth and that absolute reality as you trust God with your life.

What do you know to be true about God? What things can you utterly rely on God to be and to do?

I worship you and you alone, my God.
Strengthen my faith. Amen.

TUESDAY SEPTEMBER 22
Speaking the Truth

Psalm 40:1-10

Have you had the opportunity to "stand up" for God?

Proclaiming the good news of God's righteousness, faithfulness, salvation, loyal love, and trustworthiness confirms that the psalmist loved and worshiped God and lived in grateful response to God's gracious gift! His trust was in the Lord, and he found himself thrilled to be able to make that witness and not hold anything back.

This is indeed a psalm that we should bookmark and perhaps even memorize. It is so filled with God's care and the way we can respond to that care that it can be a blueprint for our lives of faith. But do we declare the good news in the assembly? Do we strive never to hold back or hold in the story of God's righteous love for us? Or could it be that we tend to hide God's loyal love for us and that we think it's simply enough to know God loves us instead of sharing that love with the love-lost or lonely world around us?

It's easy to remain silent about God's love for us or use the excuse that somehow others will see God's love for us as they look at our lives, without us saying a single word. Yet we fall short of living a life of gratitude to God if we never tell anyone else about it. My prayer becomes one that asks God to give me strength and courage and then the opportunity to share the good news I know to be true, that Jesus loves me.

What do you know to be true? How can you also simply and gently let this world know what God has done for you? Can you imagine the joy you will feel to share that?

> Fill my mouth and my heart with joyful
> thanks for you, O God. Amen.

WEDNESDAY, SEPTEMBER 23
Stand Firm

2 Thessalonians 2:13-17

How do you know God has chosen you to honor Christ?

Today's reading is five beautiful verses of love, support, and encouragement for the church. "He chose you from the beginning to be the first crop of the harvest," Paul told the Thessalonians. Paul made sure that each word selected built up these new believers and gave them hope and direction on how they could continue to live faithfully.

Wouldn't you love to receive a letter like this? What a treasure it would be for someone you trust and admire to describe your faithfulness and dedication to Christ and then encourage you to remain strong and firm in your faith. We all need that kind of encouragement, to know that someone is there for us in our daily lives and struggles. To know that someone believes in us, in our integrity, and in our faith transforms what is "normal" into holy time. If we are willing to have our eyes opened, we see that each day is a holy day and that others are indeed praying for us to live those days out in abundance and love.

Of course, the next thought is that while it is a wonderful joy to receive encouragement like that, are we willing and able to encourage someone else? Who needs a letter, not a text message or an email, but a regular, handwritten, put-a-stamp-on-it letter that describes what you see as their faith, their love, their "standing firm." Who needs to receive a message from you that will encourage and bless them with the strength to live as a follower of Jesus?

> God, grant me the opportunity to bless
> another as I have been blessed. Amen.

Thursday, September 24

Christic in Me

Galatians 2:15-21

How are you living today that expresses Christ living in you?

Paul told the Galatians that our righteousness with God comes from the grace of Jesus, and that with Jesus' death, so we, too, died. Now Christ lives in us, and our entire lives are to be lived in faith in the gift of Jesus for us. And we say amen. Of course, that's so. Why would we want to adhere to a law to bring us salvation?

Without even thinking, we can fall into a host of behaviors, actions, and beliefs that are completely apart and separate from faith in Jesus Christ. We all have habits and predilections, even silly customs, that are contrary to God's will. While we do not rely on strict adherence to the Law for salvation, in Christ and through the Holy Spirit we are freed for a joyful obedience that will center us in God's will and teach us to live righteously in a world that needs righteousness.

So with eyes and minds wide open, Paul asks us simply to think about in whom we place our trust. How diluted or even distracted is our simple and sure understanding that Christ lives in us, and nothing else in this world or out of it has sway over our lives?

Silly things are silly, and the Law is only the Law. Our hope is built on nothing less than Jesus. How intentional might you be in keeping clear that our trust is in Christ and nothing else in this life?

Help me always remember that
my trust is in you, O Lord. Amen.

Friday, September 25
Keeping the Faith

Revelation 14:9-13

What does it mean to "keep God's commandments"?

As you read today's text, it almost sounds like a horror story, with gruesome and horrible images. Verse 10 is probably the hardest to read. Anyone who "worships the beast . . . will drink the wine of God's passionate anger . . . [and] suffer the pain of fire and sulfur." Why would John write this? Let's be careful and acknowledge that it was not written so that we "good people" could gloat or smile over the idea of a "bad person" (meaning someone not like us) being tortured for all eternity. Let's get rid of the satisfaction in hearing of others' suffering. Instead, the key is verse 12, as the entire book was written for this, too. It was to call "the saints" to endure.

It is far more important as we read this not to get caught up in the punishment of others but instead to place our trust in Christ, even when we are up against terrible things in our lives. Our most important goal each day, one that requires endurance, is to keep God's commandments, to love, do justice, act humbly, forgive, live at peace, and follow Jesus' example in every other way.

Consider how you can keep faith and keep the commandments yourself. What is required of you? How can you ensure that your life, lived in Christ, will earn you the title of "Favored" at the end of your days? What should become part of your life, and what should you shed in order to live that way?

God of love, help me to always live in you. Amen.

The Path to Salvation

Romans 10:5-13

What is your "job" as a follower of Christ?

As Paul wrote to the Romans, he compared the righteousness of someone following the law of Moses to someone having faith in Christ. To try to be righteous by following the Law means that someone has their work cut out for them! It is a huge task. Imagine having to keep the entire Law in order to be seen as righteous. The fact is, it's a losing proposition. We can't do it.

To live as a righteous person through one's faith in Christ, however, is a different path. Paul says we aren't responsible for bringing Christ down from heaven to the earth, nor are we responsible for raising Christ from the dead. Of course, we know those important tasks are in God's hands. Our work? Simply preach the message of faith that we have. Confess that Jesus is Lord as we trust that God has done all of the work of salvation. Trust and speak the gospel and call on the name of the Lord. We find our salvation as we trust in God's work, in Christ's gift of grace, instead of having to work our way to heaven all by ourselves. What a relief, and what a joy to know that life can be lived this way as we trust in God.

You see, we simply cannot do what Christ did in any way, shape, or form, but we can confess it, celebrate it, and accept it as a gift for all time.

Which path do you want to take? Which one do you find yourself on? How is your life becoming more grace-filled as you trust in God? What does a grace-filled life look like?

God of grace, I thank you for
what you have done for me! Amen.

SUNDAY, SEPTEMBER 27

One Depends on Another

Romans 10:14-17

How did you come to hear the good news of Jesus Christ?

Paul built a tower of sorts in today's text. He started at the top. Who can call on Christ if they don't have faith? How can they have faith if they haven't heard of him? How can they hear if there isn't a preacher? And who will preach if they aren't sent? And the one who is sent must have heard Christ's message in the first place and obeyed.

Each step depends on the others. If you pull out one part, it all collapses. Sounds precarious, but think again. The Christian faith and its continuation in this world depend on you and me. Where do we fit in this "tower"?

First, we have been blessed to hear the good news of Jesus Christ, then we believed it, obeyed it, and then listened to Christ's urging of us to share that good news with others. It's not difficult, but it does require us to act. Imagine hearing the news of Jesus and then never sharing it. The tower falls, or worse, others never hear it and never come to know or call on Christ themselves. We dare not do that. So many people are depending on us. Can you see how valuable you are, since you know Jesus? Because your life was changed when someone told you, taught you, showed you faith, what a wonderful gift you can give to others.

This is the most important thing we can do in our lives. This is salvation for this world. Who may be depending on you to hear God's good news? Who needs the love you alone can share and offer?

Dear God, place others in my path
so that I may offer Christ to them. Amen.

Good to Be Near God

Psalm 73:21-28

Where do you recognize God's presence in your life?

The Mosaic covenant was established on Mount Sinai when God brought the Hebrews out of bondage in Egypt. However, as many of the Old Testament prophets declared, the people did not always live up to this agreement and had broken the covenant (Jeremiah 31:31-33).

Christians believe Jesus established a new covenant at the Last Supper with his disciples, as reported by Matthew. "While they were eating, Jesus took bread, blessed it, broke it, and gave it to the disciples and said. . . . This is my blood of the covenant, which is poured out for many so that their sins may be forgiven" (Matthew 26:26, 28).

In Psalm 73, the author reminds us that living in a covenant relationship with God is not always easy, just as the ancient Hebrews discovered. The psalm begins with the author acknowledging that he "almost stumbled" because he couldn't understand why evil sometimes prospered more than good. Fortunately, God had never given up on him. God had held on to him even when he was not holding on to God!

This commitment from God is at the heart of God's covenant renewal as revealed through Jesus Christ. The Book of Matthew concludes with this promise, "Look, I myself will be with you every day until the end of this present age" (Matthew 28:20).

Dear God, thank you for never giving up
on me and staying by my side. Amen.

TUESDAY, SEPTEMBER 29
I Will Keep Your Righteous Rules

Psalm 119:105-112

Are you keeping God's statutes?

The psalmist had sworn to keep God's rules, rules he saw as righteous. He seems to have understood that keeping God's rules didn't mean that nothing bad would ever happen to him. In fact, he had been suffering a great deal. But he believed that God would eventually deliver him from his enemies, and he still offered praise to his Creator.

God didn't make up a set of rules and regulations just to show us who is boss or to make life difficult for us. God's laws are designed for our benefit. My state has a lot of statutes we might call "rules of the road." To be licensed to drive, one must take a test and demonstrate a certain amount of driving competency. The law insists that we come to a complete stop at a stop sign. This law was not enacted by our state legislature simply to delay us. It is intended to keep everyone safe.

The same is true with God's laws. The Bible is like God's "driving manual." We should study it and obey it, not just to please God but because it will teach us how to live safely and successfully. We may not always see the immediate benefit, but time will prove its wisdom.

A friend recently posted something on social media that I thought was worth reposting. He wrote, "For lasting peace and joy, don't do the things that immediately make you happy. Just do what you know is right." The author of Psalm 119 must have understood this.

Dear God, help me "keep your statutes
forever, every last one." Amen.

Wednesday, September 30

Walking the Precise Path

Deuteronomy 5:23-33

Are you keeping your promises to God?

While the book is written from the perspective of an unknown narrator, Moses is the principal character in Deuteronomy. Much of the book is taken up by four lengthy speeches made by the lawgiver. Today's text comes from his second speech, which begins in the previous chapter.

The verses that come right before our text recall how Moses reminded the people that God had made a covenant with them on Mount Horeb (Mount Sinai) and restated the Ten Commandments.

We are still called to live in a covenant relationship with God, and we, too, are called to learn God's laws and obey them. Today's text recalls the response of the people immediately after receiving the Ten Commandments. They asked Moses to "go and listen to all that the Lord our God says. . . . We'll listen and we'll do it." However, God seemed to be skeptical. "If only their minds were like this: always fearing me and keeping all my commandments so that things would go well for them and their children forever!"

We know, unfortunately, that God's skepticism was warranted. The Israelites could have accomplished great things; they soon could have been entering the Promised Land and living the life of their dreams. Yet they repeatedly failed in their goals because they failed to live up to their promises to live by God's laws.

> Dear God, forgive me when I fail t
> o live up to my promises. Amen.

OCTOBER

CONTRIBUTORS:

Gary Thompson
(October 1–October 25)

Clara Welch

(October 26–October 31)

THURSDAY, OCTOBER 1
Faithfully Obedient

Exodus 19:1-8

Are you carrying out God's call on your life?

Throughout the Bible, a tension exists between God's grace and the divine call for obedience. God unconditionally delivered the ancient Israelites from bondage in Egypt, but God also had a purpose for their existence. God gave them a mission. They were called to be a "kingdom of priests," "a holy nation."

While God's love, grace, and mercy were (and are) unconditional, there was an "if" to God's covenant relationship with the chosen people. "So now, if you faithfully obey me and stay true to my covenant, you will be my most precious possession out of all the peoples," God told Moses to tell the people.

God delivered the Israelites out of bondage but called them to make a difference in the world. God saves us and calls us to make a difference in the world, too. Christians are saved by the grace of God, but we cannot disconnect this from our call to obedience, mission, and ministry.

> Dear God, thank you for your saving grace,
> and help me to hear your call on my life and
> carry whatever mission you give. Amen.

FRIDAY, OCTOBER 2

Keeping Our Vows

Exodus 24:3-8

Are you living in a covenant relationship with God and keeping your vows?

As we saw yesterday, Chapter 19 reports about Moses' meeting with God on Mt. Sinai. Chapters 20–23 contain the laws that were to guide this new nation, including the Ten Commandments.

While other nations were ruled by earthly kings, this new nation was to be a theocracy, ruled by God. While other people groups pledged their loyalty and support to their king, the Israelites pledged their loyalty to God. When Moses "told the people all the LORD's words and all the case laws" they "answered in unison, 'Everything that the LORD has said we will do.'"

Exodus reports two ratification ceremonies, the first found in today's text. Here, Moses built an altar, "wrote down all the LORD's words," and sprinkled blood, the sign of life, on the altar and the people. Again the people said, "Everything the LORD has said we will do, and we will obey."

> Dear God, help me keep my vows
> and forgive me when I fail. Amen.

SATURDAY, OCTOBER 3

Our Covenant

Hebrews 9:18-23

Are you keeping your covenant with God?

According to Hebrews, everything about Jesus is better. In Christ, we have a better high priest, a better faith, a better assurance, and a better sacrifice that establishes a better covenant with God. In Chapter 8, the author of Hebrews began to hone his argument that the covenant with God through Jesus Christ is better than the old covenant made with Moses. He then quoted from the Book of Jeremiah.

In today's text, the writer reminded his readers that Moses used blood to ratify the covenant. However, this blood was inadequate. The blood of Jesus is far superior to the blood of goats and sheep. The old covenant called for the repeated animal sacrifices upon an altar. Jesus, on the other hand, was the one final, perfect sacrifice for the remission of our sins.

Like the early Christians, we are tempted to follow the dominant culture rather than the better way of Jesus Christ. Perhaps today is a good day to make a sincere self-examination of the choices we are making.

Dear God, help me make the kind of daily choices
that will honor my covenant with you. Amen.

SUNDAY, OCTOBER 4

Come and Wait

Exodus 24:1-2, 9-12

Are you listening for the voice of God?

Some of us are naturally contemplative and reflective and may be comfortable spending quiet time with God. Others of us are more active in orientation. Personally, I'm more like the latter. I have to be intentional about engaging in contemplative prayer. I must work at listening to God, but even when I am intentional, I want God to speak to my own agenda.

Serving as a pastor, I have always felt that it was important to spend quiet time with God. How could I speak on God's behalf if I had not heard from God? However, sometimes I find this difficult. Sometimes things drown out God's voice. Yet taking the time to wait on God and listening are a prerequisite for knowing what God wants me to say to others on God's behalf.

It is not enough to simply claim that "God told me this." Any assertions about God's voice that don't align with the divine commandments to love God and to love our neighbor should be rejected. How will you wait on God and listen for God's voice today?

> Dear God, give me ears to hear, eyes to see,
> and a mind that understands. Amen.

Monday, October 5

Choosing God

Psalm 51:1-12

Are you calling on God for comfort and support and waiting expectantly for God's help?

Our readings this week lead up to a focus on God's covenant with the people during Joshua's time. Joshua 24 records how he gathered "all the tribes of Israel at Shechem" (verse 1). There, he made essentially his retirement speech. He reminded the people of the mistakes their ancestors had made. He offered a call to commitment (verses 14-15).

Joshua's speech reminds us that we all have a choice. We can choose the ways of God or the ways of the world. David, the author of Psalm 51, had chosen to trust in God. He trusted in God's abundant, faithful love. Even though he was guilty of grave sin and threatened by his enemies, he took refuge in God's "faithful love," "great compassion," and willingness to create in him "a clean heart" and "a new, faithful spirit." He called out to God in the midst of his struggles and waited expectantly for God's deliverance.

Dear God, hear my prayers as I wait
expectantly for your help. Amen.

TUESDAY, OCTOBER 6

Good to Be Near God

Psalm 73:21-28

Do you ever doubt God and God's promises?

The psalm writer confessed that he almost stumbled, but he had progressed from doubt to trust. His doubt had not come so much because of his troubles but because he had so often observed the prosperity of the wicked. However, he had also observed over time that their prosperity was transient and fleeting. On the other hand, God's promised blessings are eternal.

It seems to me that someone who has never had doubts has never done much thinking. Life indeed offers us many reasons to question God's promises. Sometimes the wicked seem to prosper, while the people of God suffer. There are times when it is easy to think that God doesn't care.

But the psalmist declares, "I was still always with you!" This psalmist realized that God was staying close to him even when he wasn't working to stay close to God. Once he had finally fallen back on the traditions he had been taught, he sought God in the sanctuary, and then he discovered a renewed faith.

God, give me a profound sense of your presence
and a life-transforming gift of faith. Amen.

WEDNESDAY, OCTOBER 7
Life and Death

Deuteronomy 30:15-20

Are you doing the things that nurture your faith?

The Israelites had a choice. They could choose to obey and enjoy the blessings of God, or they could choose to disobey and reap the results. Moses assured them that it was a life-or-death decision.

So how do we make sure we don't gradually "fall away"? We might learn a valuable lesson from the cuckoo bird. This bird is a brood parasite. Cuckoos lay their eggs in the nests of other birds that unwittingly raise their young. The baby cuckoo is much larger than the foster mother's own babies. When she arrives with a big, juicy worm, she finds three or four tiny mouths and one humongous cuckoo insisting on being fed. The larger, stronger cuckoo usually manages to get the worm. It continues to grow while the tiny birds wither and die.

Scripture teaches us that we have two natures, and the one we feed is the one that will grow. If we feed our minds and hearts on God's word and allow ourselves to be nurtured by God's people, we will grow spiritually, getting stronger each day.

Dear God, nurture my faith and help me grow
in wisdom, understanding, and obedience. Amen.

Thursday, October 8

What God Has Done

Joshua 24:1-13

Have you counted your blessings lately?

Joshua 24 begins with Joshua rehearsing a history of God's relationship with the Israelites. He reminded them of what God had done for them and encouraged faithfulness and thankfulness. A healthy relationship with God begins with gratitude. The only proper response to what God has done for us is to do what God asks us to do, to pay it forward.

Mother Theresa related that when she and some of the other sisters went out to minister on the streets, Mother Theresa did all she could for a woman in critical condition. As she took her last breath, the woman weakly said, "Thank you." Mother Theresa wondered what she would have said had she been lying on that bed. She was quite sure she would have been drawing more attention to herself, perhaps saying, "I am hungry. I am dying. I am in pain." But this poor woman said none of that. She simply expressed her gratitude.

Dear God, I confess that I, too,
often take your blessings for granted.
Thank you for all your marvelous gifts. Amen.

Friday, October 9

Choose Today

Joshua 24:14-21

Are you keeping the promises you've made to God?

After Moses led the Israelites out of Egypt, Joshua led them into the Promised Land. By Joshua 24, he was retiring, but concerned about the future. Based on his experiences, he believed that God would continue to bless the people if they would remain faithful. On the other hand, based on his experiences, he knew that the people had not always been faithful.

Joshua reminded his people that their future was up to them. They could choose to serve the Lord and enjoy God's blessings or they could choose to serve other gods and reap the destruction that sin produces.

When given this unambiguous alternative, the Israelites responded, "God forbid that we ever leave the LORD to serve other gods! The LORD is our God." However, as the story continues, we discover that it was not long at all until they did just that. What about you? Are you being obedient to God? Are you keeping your covenant?

Dear God, help me recognize my broken promises.
Forgive me and give me the power
to overcome temptation. Amen.

SATURDAY, OCTOBER 10

Staying True to God

Joshua 24:22-28

Does your covenant with God need renewal?

Joshua recognized that remaining faithful in our relationship with God is never easy. He had doubts that the Israelites would succeed. However, remaining faithful means much more than being obedient. Being faithful means loving God and others.

Being a faithful Christian is not simply living by a moral code because God is going to punish us if we don't. Being a faithful Christian is about living in a covenant relationship with God and our neighbors. It means listening to God's voice and responding as an obedient child responds to the guidance and supervision of wise parents.

Today's text should remind us of the holiness and the righteousness of God and God's love. Scripture teaches us that God offers divine grace while at the same time is the ultimate judge who calls us to account. Pray for the kind of relationship with God that grows out of gratitude and recognition that God is our Creator and the source of all that is good.

Dear God, I seek to renew my covenant with
you as I renew my commitment to faithfulness. Amen.

SUNDAY, OCTOBER 11

Death of the Covenant Generation

Judges 2:6-12

What do you do to keep your covenant with God?

The Book of Judges seeks to demonstrate the catastrophic consequences of being unfaithful to God. When God's people failed to be faithful and obey divine precepts, God withdrew divine protection and blessings. When they repented and chose to follow a faithful leader, God blessed them.

The cycle of sin and repentance reported in the Book of Judges is actually a spiral downward. Each time the people fell away from God, they fell deeper into their cycle of sin. This, of course, is the very nature of sin and the human condition. Each time we give in to temptation, our resistance is weakened, and it becomes easier to give in the next time.

Joshua's concern about his people breaking their covenant with God was legitimate (Judges 2:20-22). God has promised to watch us. However, we cannot expect God's protective hand to keep us safe if we insist on going our own way, doing our own thing, ignoring God's warnings and God's wisdom.

Dear God, help me remain faithful
and keep my covenant with you. Amen.

Monday, October 12

More Desirable Than Gold

Psalm 19:7-11

Are you placing your faith in God's truths?

In our text for today, the psalmist insists, "The LORD's laws are faithful, making naïve people wise. The LORD's regulations are right, gladdening the heart. The LORD's commands are pure, giving light to the eyes." Yet so many people ignore these realities, naively thinking they are smarter than God. Many disregard God's "regulations," missing out on the joy that comes by the wisdom of divine principles.

Verses 7-10 recall terms used to refer to God's law. The conclusion is that God's laws are without defect and bring peace, joy, and meaningful life to those who live by these principles. God's precepts are true and can be trusted.

So much of what the world claims as true is actually illusory, erroneous, false, distorted, even perverse. God's laws are true and will never mislead or deceive us. They are truth and the truth will set us free.

"Make your ways known to me, LORD;
teach me your paths. Lead me in your truth—
teach it to me—because you are the God
who saves me. I put my hope in you all day long"
(Psalm 25:4-5). Amen.

TUESDAY, OCTOBER 13

Rejoicing in the Lord

Psalm 89:1-18

How do you rejoice in the Lord?

God, who created the world, can restore it. "Heaven is yours! The earth too! The world and all that fills it—you made all of it! North and south—you created them!" Psalm 89 says. The good news is that the Creator and Sustainer of the universe loves creation and always keeps promises. God has made a covenant with us, and God never breaks covenant.

Psalm 89 begins, "I will sing of the LORD's loyal love forever." The Hebrew word translated by the CEB "loyal love" is *hesed*. The NIV translates it "great love," while the NRSV renders it "steadfast love." The King James reads, "For ever."

The word *hesed* means to be merciful and faithful, to love as one loves a close family member. It is an extremely important word in the Old Testament and is used to refer to the essence of God's character. It is this "loving kindness" that the author is praising in Psalm 89.

Dear God, I join the psalmist in giving thanks for your loving kindness and filling me with your love. Amen.

WEDNESDAY, OCTOBER 14

Sweeter Than Honey

Psalm 119:97-104

Do you often read and meditate on God's word?

The author of Psalm 119 didn't have all the Scripture we have today, but he sought to take full advantage of what he had. He constantly meditated on words from God; he thought of it as God's instruction manual. He sought God's wisdom and guidance. The author was convinced that knowing God's word and obeying God's laws kept him on the right path. It gave him the wisdom to outwit his enemies and to remain safe from those who would do him harm. "Your commandment makes me wiser than my enemies because it is always with me," he said.

The Bible is more complete than what the psalmist had available. It is a comprehensive revelation of God's will and ways. This book has been given to us for our benefit. It is a precious gift that we can't afford to take lightly or ignore. God grieves when we fail to take advantage of this gift, and we often suffer consequences when we act apart from its teachings.

Dear God, give me the kind of love and understanding
of your word expressed by the psalmist. Amen.

Thursday, October 15
The Power of Scripture

2 Timothy 3:14-17

Do you study God's word with an open mind, allowing the Holy Spirit to speak?

Paul says Scripture is "inspired by God and is useful." The Greek word translated "inspired" is the Greek word *theopneustos* from *theos*, God, and *pneō*, to breath or blow. The NIV renders the verse, "All Scripture is God-breathed and is useful for teaching, rebuking, correcting, and training in righteousness." This verse is the only place this term is used in Scripture. It contrasted the divine or supernatural with the natural or physical world.

Paul believed Scripture is inspired and contains the truth. It can be trusted when properly understood. Psalm 119:160 reads, "The sum of your word is truth; and every one of your righteous ordinances endures forever" (NRSV). We discover God's truth in the "sum" or "totality" of God's Word. We should be careful about using only short passages or single verses or phrases to support our beliefs. That can lead to wrong conclusions. We need to read and study the whole of God's word, not just certain passages.

Dear God, teach me your truths. Amen.

FRIDAY, OCTOBER 16

A Lamp Shining in a Dark Place

2 Peter 1:19-21

What do you use to help you understand the Bible?

Paul declared that the Bible "is inspired by God and is useful for teaching, for showing mistakes, for correcting, and for training character" (2 Timothy 3:16). The author of 2 Peter insisted that it is "a most reliable prophetic word."

Each Sunday, I pass many churches of various denominations. These denominations are convinced that the Bible is inspired by God. However, these denominations exist largely because of the differences in our interpretation of Scripture. We don't all agree on what God is saying through the Bible.

Most Methodists believe that we should use what we sometimes refer to as "the quadrilateral" to help us interpret Scripture. John Wesley believed in the centrality of Scripture, but he supported orthodox tradition, reason, and human experience as guides to understanding God's Word. How do you read the Bible? How is it like "a lamp shining in a dark place" for you (2 Peter 1:19)?

Dear God, help me grow in my
understanding of the Bible. Amen.

Saturday, October 17

A Great Celebration

Nehemiah 8:1-12

What are you doing to grow in God's word?

The books of Ezra and Nehemiah give accounts of Ezra's and Nehemiah's return to Jerusalem. Nehemiah went to Jerusalem to rebuild the city's wall. When this was finished, Ezra led the people in a covenant renewal service where he read what the Common English Bible calls the "Instruction scroll."

Those gathered to hear Ezra listened with great interest but had difficulty understanding what they heard. The text tells us "they read aloud from the scroll . . . interpreting it so the people could understand what they heard." When the people "understood what had been said to them," they had "a great celebration."

No person can fully understand God's Word. We all need other people in our lives who will help our understanding. In addition, we need to seek the help of the Holy Spirit. And we can celebrate that God helps us to understand the message of Scripture and what it means for how we live.

Dear God, continue to give me greater
understanding of your word. Amen.

Great Rejoicing

Nehemiah 8:13-18

How has obedience to God transformed your life?

God had allowed the Israelites to be taken into captivity because of their disobedience. Because of God's mercy, they were allowed to return to their homeland. Today's text from Nehemiah tells us that "they found written in the Instruction that the LORD had commanded through Moses that the Israelites should live in booths during the festival of the seventh month." This was their first test, and they passed it with flying colors.

Simply hearing and knowing God's Word is not enough. The joy and peace of a transformed life comes through obedience. Like each of us, the Israelites as a people struggled with obedience to God's instruction and failed miserably at times. But on this occasion, they obeyed what God had commanded, lived in booths, "and there was very great rejoicing." May the same be true for you, that obedience to the Lord leads you to a joy-filled life.

Dear God, help me know the joy
of obedience to your word. Amen.

Monday, October 19

Hope for the Future

Zechariah 9:9-12

Are you a prisoner of hope?

The Book of Zechariah is complex, ambiguous, and even obscure. The first eight chapters encouraged the exiles to return to their homeland and to "make just and faithful decisions; show kindness and compassion to each other!" (Zechariah 7:9). Chapter 9 begins what some refer to as "Second Zechariah."

While Zechariah 9:11 was clearly referring to the return of the Jews from Babylonian captivity and God's covenant with Moses and the ancient Israelites, this text was a favorite of the early church, which understood the passage to be a reference to Jesus. The author of Matthew, of course, was referring to this passage when he wrote, "Look, your king is coming to you, humble and riding on a donkey" (Matthew 21:5).

The early church found comfort in the fact that God had kept covenant with their ancestors, delivering them from bondage in Babylon. Just as the Jews in captivity were "prisoners of hope," so too were the early Christians who placed their faith in a new covenant through Christ.

Dear God, make me a prisoner of hope. Amen.

Strangers No More

Ephesians 2:11-14

How do you understand your relationship with God in terms of a covenant?

"With his body," Paul wrote to the Christians at Ephesus, Christ "broke down the barrier of hatred" that divided Jews and Gentiles. And even more, "he made both Jews and Gentiles into one group." This is good news to those who were "called 'uncircumcised' . . . without Christ . . . aliens rather than citizens of Israel, and strangers to the covenants of God's promise." Those formerly with "no hope and no God" had and have today the opportunity for reconciliation with God and peace. How? Those "who were once so far away have been brought near by the blood of Christ."

Christians have traditionally understood Jesus to be the descendant of David who will sit on the throne forever. The author of Ephesians makes the argument in our text for today that Jesus has now brought Gentiles into this covenant relationship with God. Because of Jesus, we are no longer "strangers to the covenants of God's promise."

Dear God, deepen my covenant relationship
with you, your people, and with all creation. Amen.

Wednesday, October 21
Jesus and the Law

Matthew 5:17-20

Are you building your life based on God's laws?

Matthew wanted to show how Jesus was a radically different Messiah from the warrior-king most expected. Jesus came to establish a new covenant between God and God's people. The Sermon on the Mount demonstrates the nature of this new covenant. It presents a view of a new covenant that demands a greater righteousness than that required by the Mosaic covenant. This calls for ethical behavior that leads to a kingdom characterized by love for all God's people.

What Jesus says in Matthew 5:17-20 might seem to conflict with what he has to say on other occasions. However, we know that Jesus often used hyperbole to make a point. When we look at the whole of Jesus' teaching, we see that his teachings were based on a foundation provided by the Mosaic law. Like a gardener who grafts a new, more beautiful plant on to older, perhaps hardier root stock, Jesus built on the laws found in the Old Testament.

> Dear God, help me live by your laws so that
> I can experience the new life that comes
> from being a part of your kingdom. Amen.

THURSDAY, OCTOBER 22
Living in God's Kingdom

Hebrews 12:18-24

Are you living as if you are in God's kingdom?

Christians are sometimes accused of being so heavenly minded that they are no earthly good. The author of Hebrews insisted that a person cannot be of much earthly good unless he or she is "heavenly minded."

Many Christians think of heaven and the kingdom of God only as transcendent realities somewhere "out there" and primarily in the future. However, the Bible presents a different picture. Jesus proclaimed the kingdom of God as a present reality (Luke 17:20-21). The author of Hebrews insisted that Jesus is the perfect High Priest, the mediator between God and humankind. Jesus is the perfect sacrifice offering, the way to God and the divine kingdom through a better covenant.

For Christians, God's kingdom is not far away nor in the distant future. Eternal life has already started, and we are to be living into Christ's purposes today. What can you do this day to bring about God's kingdom here on earth?

> Dear God, thank you for allowing me
> to be a part of your kingdom. Amen.

FRIDAY, OCTOBER 23

Prepared to Act

Luke 22:7-13

Are you prepared to carry out God's call?

I don't want to believe that my life is all predetermined. I believe in the Armenian, Wesleyan notion of free will. However, I do understand why some people think differently. Some passages in Scripture seem to support a more deterministic view of life and suggest that there are indeed forces at work over which I have no control.

Luke 22 is one of those passages. The third verse of this chapter tells us that "Satan entered Judas." Does this mean that "the devil made him do it"? In today's text, Jesus knew that a certain man would be carrying a water jar. It was like a great drama was unfolding, and people were simply players with assigned roles.

But the Bible teaches us that we are responsible for our actions. The disciples were urged to be prepared for what was coming. We don't always understand the various forces at work around us, but we are called to be prepared to do our part.

Dear God, help me prepare physically, mentally,
and spiritually for what you call me to do. Amen.

The Last Supper

Matthew 26:26-30

Do you remember?

The Eucharist looks backward to the death of Jesus and to his life as one who often ate with sinners. Communion also looks forward to the kingdom of God coming in its fullness. Communion points inward, too; it is a time of self-examination (1 Corinthians 11:27-28). When we share in the Lord's Supper, we are also encouraged to look upward. Paul reminds us, "It is Christ who died, even more, who was raised, and who also is at God's right side. It is Christ Jesus who also pleads our case for us" (Romans 8:34).

Finally, participating in Communion with our family in Christ reminds us to look outward to the whole of God's creation. Jesus once described what we sometimes call the final judgment of the nations, where everyone will be divided like a shepherd divides sheep from the goats. God doesn't look at what we believe, but how we live out those beliefs.

How does Communion direct your life in Christ?

> Dear God, help me to look backward, forward,
> inward, upward, and outward, to remember
> you and what you have done for me. Amen.

SUNDAY, OCTOBER 25

Transformed and Empowered

Luke 22:14-20

Are you empowered by Christ and his Holy Spirit?

The idea of a new covenant leads us to ask what is better about this covenant. This question has, of course, been debated ever since the time of Jesus. The prophet Jeremiah predicted that this new covenant would be written on our hearts, not tablets of stone (Jeremiah 31:33). The old covenant was based on God's loving-kindness—God's grace and compassion. It instituted a set of laws based on justice and mercy. However, there was nothing in the old covenant that provided the power the people needed to keep their part of the bargain. The Israelites were simply unable to remain obedient.

The new covenant comes with a built-in power system: the Holy Spirit. We depend on God's power working within us (2 Corinthians 3:1, 4-6). Paul wrote, "The Lord is the Spirit, and where the Lord's Spirit is, there is freedom. . . . We are being transformed into that same image from one degree of glory to the next degree of glory" (verses 17-18).

Dear God, transform me into the person
you created me to be. Amen.

MONDAY, OCTOBER 26

Starting in the Parking Lot

Psalm 95:1-11

How do you enter your place of worship?

Psalm 95 is part of a collection of enthronement psalms as it celebrates God as king. It was likely sung on a festival day, with a choir leading the Israelites in singing as they processed to the Temple.

The Israelites praised God as "the rock of our salvation" and acknowledged that God is "the great king over all other gods." They celebrated the relationship between "the LORD, our maker" and themselves, "the people of his pasture, the sheep in his hands." As the procession entered the Temple, the worshipers were invited to bow down and "kneel before the LORD," acts of worship that show humble adoration before God.

When we arrive at our places of worship, it is unlikely we will be met by a choir to lead us in singing as we walk across the parking lot! Yet as we make our way to the sanctuary, we can remember God's gifts of salvation and creation and offer praise and thanksgiving in our own way. We can enter the worship space with receptive hearts.

Holy God, accept my songs and shouts of joy as
I worship you with praise and thanksgiving. Amen.

TUESDAY, OCTOBER 27

Receding Water

Genesis 8:15-22

What everyday spaces are sacred for you?

In our Christian churches, the altar is usually a table made of wood or stone where the elements of Holy Communion are consecrated. In Old Testament times, an altar was a raised place or structure. Sacrifices were often offered there as an act of worship. The term *ad hoc* is Latin and is translated "for this." An *ad hoc* altar then was not permanent, but was constructed for a specific purpose at a specific time.

We can imagine Noah's delight when God said he, his family, and the animals could leave the ark. His response was to build "an altar to the Lord. He . . . placed entirely burned offerings on the altar." We imagine Noah's thankfulness that he and his family were saved.

We can call on God for help and offer praise and thanksgiving wherever we are. Have you ever thought about the spaces where you offer these prayers as being sacred, *ad hoc* places of worship? Our faithful worship is pleasing to God, no matter where we are!

Holy God of new beginnings, thank you for
your continuing faithfulness in my life. Amen.

WEDNESDAY, OCTOBER 28

Sacred Spaces on the Journey

Genesis 12:1-8

Where have you been moved to worship during your life journey?

Abram built altars and worshiped the Lord as he journeyed through Canaan. One of these altars was at "the sacred place at Shechem, at the oak of Moreh." Abram built another altar where he "pitched his tent with Bethel on the west and Ai on the east." He soon "settled by the oaks of Mamre in Hebron. There he built an altar to the LORD" (Genesis 13:18).

When Abram built these altars and worshiped the Lord, he was initiating Israel's worship in various areas in the Promised Land of Canaan. When the people of Israel took possession of the Promised Land, they associated the various established sacred sites with the patriarchs Abraham, Isaac, and Jacob.

Sometimes we may establish a place of worship that will serve future generations without us realizing it. Our faithfulness can set an example, as Abram's did. What worship and devotion habits do you practice? How do they shape others' faith?

Faithful God, thank you for accepting
my faithful worship wherever I am. Amen.

THURSDAY, OCTOBER 29

The Backstory

Genesis 28:1-7

In what ways have you been the bearer and the recipient of God's blessings?

The route from Beer-sheba to Paddan-aram would have taken Jacob past Hebron, Bethel, and Shechem, places where his grandfather Abraham built altars. As Jacob set out on his journey, was he wondering about what it meant for him to be one of the bearers of "Abraham's blessing"? Or was he thinking more about the issues at hand: the many miles that stretched before him and the revenge his brother was planning against him? After all, he had tricked his brother out of both his birthright and blessing. Was he someone God would choose to participate in God's plan to bless "all the families of the earth" (Genesis 12:3)?

With our backstories of imperfection and disobedience, we may not believe that God would choose us to participate in the divine plan to bless others. Yet, God does choose us! God also calls other imperfect people to remind us of God's blessings in our own lives.

Holy and redeeming Lord, open my eyes to the
ways I may share your blessings with others. Amen.

FRIDAY, OCTOBER 30
Jacob Sets Up an Altar

Genesis 28:10-22

Where are the sacred spaces where you have experienced God's presence?

Jacob would not have known that he had chosen a sacred place to rest for the night, for he was just passing through. After a life-changing dream, he woke up and "thought to himself, 'The LORD is definitely in this place, but I didn't know it.'"

When Jacob woke from his dream, he responded to God's presence with terror and awe. He set up the stone as a pillar, anointed it to show it was holy, and "named that sacred place Bethel," which means "house of God." In time, Jacob's *ad hoc* altar became an important worship center for his descendants, the beneficiaries of God's promise.

The places where we have special experiences of God's presence, as Jacob did at Bethel, become especially significant for us, and we may hold them in our hearts as sacred. Where are the sacred spaces in your life? How have you experienced God's presence, love, and compassion in those spaces?

> Ever Faithful God, thank you for always being with me and watching over me everywhere I go. Amen.

Saturday, October 31

Pouring Water

1 Samuel 7:2-6

How do you express your deep yearning for God?

Today's passage tells us, "The whole house of Israel yearned for the Lord." Samuel was serving as the leader of God's people during this time. The Israelites "knew that Samuel was trustworthy as the Lord's prophet" (1 Samuel 3:20). Samuel instructed them to do two things. First, "get rid of all the foreign gods." Second, "Set your heart on the Lord! Worship him only!"

The people's worship at Mizpah included pouring water, fasting, and confession. The drawing and pouring of water as an act of repentance is not mentioned anywhere else in the Bible, but we can draw our own conclusions as to its meaning. Water quenches our thirst and cleanses. The place where the Israelites poured water as an act of worship in Mizpah became a holy altar, a sacred place.

What acts of worship reassure you of God's continuing presence in your life? How does the image of pouring water help satisfy your thirst for God?

Loving God, I yearn for you. I open
my heart to your holy presence. Amen.

NOVEMBER

CONTRIBUTORS:

Clara Welch
(November 1-November 29)

Stan Purdum

(November 30)

ALL SAINTS DAY, SUNDAY, NOVEMBER 1
A Stone Named Ebenezer

1 Samuel 7:7-13

Where do you set up an Ebenezer?

In this short account, the historian tells us that Samuel set up two *ad hoc* altars. The first altar was a place of prayer and sacrifice. Samuel offered prayers of supplication and "an entirely burned offering to the LORD" as he asked God to "save" the Israelites "from the Philistines' power." The second *ad hoc* altar was a place of thanksgiving. Samuel set up a stone to commemorate the place where God intervened on behalf of Israel. Samuel "named it Ebenezer," which means "stone of help."

We have visited several biblical *ad hoc* altars this week, places of worship established for specific times and purposes. Noah built an altar to honor God for God's gifts of salvation and a new beginning. Abram and Jacob honored God for the gifts of God's continuing presence and promises of blessing. Samuel honored God for God's gifts of forgiveness and deliverance.

When Samuel set up his Ebenezer "stone of help," he explained, "The LORD helped us to this very point." His stone was a visible sign and gave him the opportunity to invite others to worship.

When have you worshiped God at an *ad hoc* altar? In other words, what spaces have become sacred for you as you offered prayers of supplication, thanksgiving, and praise? When have you had the opportunity to invite others to worship with you?

> Merciful God, thank you for hearing my cries for
> help and giving me everything I need. Amen.

MONDAY, NOVEMBER 2

Smoldering Altars

Psalm 74:1-12

What sustains your hope in God during disaster?

The author of Psalm 74 described the burning of God's "sanctuary" and "all of God's meeting places in the land." He cried out, "God, why have you abandoned us forever?" It is likely the psalmist was describing the fall of Jerusalem and the destruction of the Temple in 587 BC, when the people of Judah were exiled to Babylon. The prophets had warned the people that God would punish them for their disobedience. When the Temple was ransacked and the people were forced to leave, their feelings of abandonment were strong and real.

The psalmist asked, "Why does your anger smolder at the sheep of your own pasture?" Yet he and the people of Judah knew the cause of God's anger. The prophets had warned them many times to turn away from idols and worship only the Lord. The people did not heed the prophets' words, and God destroyed the "sanctuary" and "meeting places."

The psalmist had not lost all hope, though. His lament that "none of us know how long it will last" seems to indicate he believed it would eventually end. He proclaimed, "God has been my king from ancient days—God, who makes salvation happen in the heart of the earth!" He held on to hope that God would make "salvation happen" again! When we face despair and loss, we too can trust God to see us through. God will never abandon us. God "makes salvation happen" again and again.

Merciful God, thank you for your
continuing presence and love. Amen.

TUESDAY, NOVEMBER 3
Shepherds and Farmers

Matthew 9:35-38

How are you part of the answer to Jesus' plea for more workers for God's harvest?

Matthew summarizes the ministry of Jesus in verse 35: "Jesus traveled among all the cities and villages, teaching in their synagogues, announcing the good news of the kingdom, and healing every disease and every sickness." Jesus' observation that the crowds were "like sheep without a shepherd" was a negative commentary about the religious leaders who were not caring for the people, their flock.

Jesus said, "I am the good shepherd" (John 10:11). Jesus has compassion for everyone who is "troubled and helpless." He came to announce "the good news of the kingdom" to all humankind and to invite all of us to live in God's kingdom, both here on earth and in the eternal life to come. When Jesus observed the crowds that followed him, he said, "The size of the harvest is bigger than you can imagine, but there are few workers." He instructed his disciples to "plead with the Lord" for more workers.

How has God called you to be one of these workers? How has God called you to be a shepherd and reach out to the "troubled and helpless" with compassion? How has God called you to be a farmer and cultivate seeds of faith to "harvest" followers of Christ?

Loving God, help me serve you as a faithful farmer
and a compassionate shepherd. Amen.

Wednesday, November 4

Healing Love

Matthew 12:9-14

How is your church a place of love, healing, and hope?

Jesus brought up the question of what to do when a sheep "falls into a pit on the Sabbath." The natural response is to "pull it out." Yet the Pharisees disagreed with Jesus' decision to heal the "withered hand" of a fellow human being on the Sabbath, a day when no work is to be done. In the Pharisees' view, the hand could have been healed the following day. Jesus overrides this viewpoint by proclaiming, "The Law allows a person to do what is good on the sabbath."

When Jesus healed the man's hand on the sabbath, he was showing love for the man. He offered us an example of love for God and neighbor taking precedence over everything else. In so doing, he gave the man hope and new life.

As Christians, we are called to be love in the world. We show our love for God by extending love to all God's children. Love is not always easy. Throughout his life and in his death, Jesus showed us that love sometimes requires sacrifice; love sometimes calls us to care for people who are not easy to love.

How does your church extend love to its members and the community? What challenges does your church face as it seeks to be a place of healing and hope? How does your congregation share the light and love of Christ?

> Loving God, thank you for loving me. Open my
> heart to love others in the name of Christ. Amen.

THURSDAY, NOVEMBER 5
Having Spoken Openly

John 18:19-24

In what ways is your church a place where the good news of Jesus Christ is shared openly?

After Jesus was arrested, the chief priest had another concern: Had Jesus been teaching his disciples a different message in secret? With this in mind, "the chief priest questioned Jesus about his disciples and his teaching," so he could interview the disciples as well. Jesus had nothing to hide. He replied, "I've spoken openly to the world. I've always taught in synagogues and in the temple, where all the Jews gather. I've said nothing in private." In other words, the chief priest could question anyone who had listened to Jesus' teachings, and he would receive the same answers.

Jesus came "so that everyone who believes in him won't perish but will have eternal life" (John 3:16). Jesus told his disciples, "The size of the harvest is bigger than you can imagine" (Matthew 9:37). People need to hear the good news of Jesus before they can believe in him. Seeds of faith need to be planted before there can be a harvest of believers. So Jesus spoke "openly . . . in synagogues and in the temple, where all the Jews gather"; he taught on the hillsides when crowds of people flocked to hear him.

How does your church openly share the teachings and love of Christ? In what ways does your congregation extend invitations to the people in your community to come hear the good news of Christ? How do you speak openly about your faith in God?

Loving God, show me opportunities to openly witness to
your love and grace in my life. Amen.

Proclaiming Moses, Proclaiming Christ

Acts 15:14-21

What is proclaimed aloud in your church every week?

James declared, "Moses has been proclaimed in every city for a long time, and is read aloud every Sabbath in every synagogue." James was referring to the Law of Moses. The Jews lived their lives in relationship to God according to these Laws. After Jesus' death and resurrection, his followers preached the gospel to both Jews and Gentiles. They were in agreement that Gentiles were to be included in the church. Barnabas and Paul told of "all the signs and wonders God did among the Gentiles through their activity." James shared the Lord's words spoken through the prophet Amos (Amos 9:11-12) in verses 16-17. The question Jesus' apostles faced was whether or not Gentiles were required to keep the Mosaic Law, including circumcision and food laws.

James suggested the Gentiles be told "to avoid . . . idols . . . immorality . . . and consuming blood." He prefaced this suggestion by saying, "We shouldn't create problems for Gentiles who turn to God." The NIV reads, "We should not make it difficult for the Gentiles who are turning to God."

How do you feel when you worship with your congregation? Are there expectations that make it difficult for you when you turn to God, or that may discourage new believers? How is the message of Christ's love and grace proclaimed? How does your congregation pray and work together to resolve differences?

> Loving God, thank you for your steadfast
> love and amazing grace. Amen.

SATURDAY, NOVEMBER 7

Jesus' Authority

Luke 4:31-37

How do you place your trust in Jesus' authority?

Imagine what it would have been like to hear Jesus deliver the sermon at your place of worship each week. Luke writes that the people "were amazed by his teaching because he delivered his message with authority." It is interesting to see how his authority affected his various listeners. Some people received his teaching and followed him. The Pharisees saw his authority as a threat to their own authority.

The demons and unclean spirits knew exactly who Jesus was, "the holy one from God." The demon in the "man in the synagogue" cried out his question, "Have you come to destroy us?" The answer for the demon was yes. Jesus came to destroy evil in the world. Jesus came to bring healing and hope to all people. The people who witnessed this dramatic exorcism on that long-ago sabbath day "were all shaken." They marveled at Jesus' "authority and power" and reported what they had seen and heard to others.

Jesus calls us to obey the commandments to love God and neighbor. We experience the effects of evil in our world when people choose instead to act out of selfishness and greed. The apostle Paul declared, "Let love be genuine; hate what is evil, hold fast to what is good; love one another" (Romans 12:9-10, NRSV).

How do you "hold fast to what is good"? How do you express your trust in Jesus' authority and power?

God of power and love, thank you for Jesus,
who spoke with authority and showed us
that we can place our trust in you. Amen.

Jesus Preaches in the Synagogues

Luke 4:38-44

What happens when the gospel of Jesus Christ is proclaimed at your church?

What happened when Jesus taught in the synagogues? In the reading for November 3, we noted that Jesus criticized religious leaders who did not fulfill their responsibility to take care of the people. When he healed the man's withered hand on the sabbath (Matthew 12), he angered the Pharisees, who accused him of breaking sabbath law. Jesus revealed his authority and power in the synagogue when he healed the man who "had the spirit of an unclean demon" (Luke 4:31-37).

Today's reading tells us that after Jesus exorcised the demon in the synagogue, he "went home with Simon," where he healed Simon's mother-in-law. There, he continued his ministry into the evening, healing and casting out demons. Then, at "daybreak . . . Jesus went to a deserted place." These times of solitude and prayer (Luke 5:16) sustained him as he remained faithful to his calling and traveled to "other cities [and] continued preaching in the Judean synagogues."

What happens when the good news of Jesus Christ is taught in your church? Do people hear the invitation to serve and care for others? Are people open to new insights? Have people experienced physical and spiritual healing through Christ's power and authority? What Scripture passages about the teachings of Jesus have had the most impact on your life?

> Holy God, open my mind and heart to the teachings
> of Jesus so that I may be a faithful follower. Amen.

MONDAY, NOVEMBER 9

Christ Builds His Church on Rock

Matthew 16:13-20

How does your faith in Christ serve as a rock that supports your church?

How do you answer Jesus' question, "Who do others say that I am?" I think about what I learned from my parents, Sunday school teachers, and youth counselors as I form my response. Who are the "others" who told you about Jesus? What did you learn about Jesus from them?

Jesus' next question to his disciples was more personal. "And what about you? Who do you say that I am?" Peter spoke up: "You are the Christ, the Son of the living God." Look closely at Jesus' response: "No human has shown this to you. Rather, my Father who is in heaven has shown you."

We come to faith in part through the teaching, preaching, and example of others. We grow stronger in our faith through our personal experiences of God's presence, power, and love. These experiences may happen at any time, perhaps when we are watching a sunset, undergoing medical treatments, or serving someone in need. When has God revealed God's self to you?

Jesus called "Simon son of Jonah" by the name Peter, which means "rock." He declared, "I'll build my church on this rock." Jesus built his church on a strong foundation that remains firm against all the forces of evil in the world.

How do you serve your church as a faithful witness of Christ's presence and love?

Holy and Redeeming God, help me continue to grow in faith
so I may contribute to the growth of your church. Amen.

341

Tuesday, November 10
The Church Proclaims God's Grace

Acts 20:17-28

What is your hope for the people you serve in Christ?

Paul gave his life to preaching and teaching the gospel as he worked to establish and nourish young churches. During his missionary journeys, he testified "about the good news of God's grace" and urged his listeners to "turn to God and have faith in our Lord Jesus." The church grew as Paul and the other apostles proclaimed the good news of Christ to both Jews and Gentiles. The church continues to grow as believers answer the call to serve.

We may feel intimidated when we compare ourselves to the likes of Peter and Paul. We may feel hesitant to engage in ministry when, as Paul indicated, we may find ourselves responding "with tears in the midst of trials."

Paul reminded the elders of the church in Ephesus of the presence of the Holy Spirit and the call "to shepherd God's church, which he obtained with the death of his own Son." We are each gifted with different talents and abilities. Even if we're no Peter or Paul, we can testify to God's love and grace through our own changed hearts and lives. We can serve as shepherds and care for God's people.

What is your hope for the people in your church? In what ways do you feel called to proclaim God's grace and "shepherd God's church"? Paul relied on the presence and power of the Holy Spirit. The Holy Spirit is present with us for guidance, strength, and courage.

Loving God, show me ways to shepherd your church so that others will grow in faith and experience your grace. Amen.

WEDNESDAY, NOVEMBER 11
The Body of Christ

1 Corinthians 12:3-18

What gifts and abilities do you bring to the body of Christ?

Paul tells us that, "There are different spiritual gifts . . . different ministries . . . different activities." These different gifts, ministries, and activities have an important thing in common: each one is from "the same spirit . . . the same Lord . . . the same God." These spiritual gifts are "given to each person for the common good."

It is important to remember that the goal is "the common good." God does not bestow these spiritual gifts to bring honor and glory to the people who possess them. God gives these gifts for the sake of the church, so that collectively the members of the church will have everything needed to be an effective witness for Christ in the world.

Paul writes, "We were all baptized by one Spirit into one body." When students take their first biology class, they learn just how complex the body is. Not only are there different parts like eyes and ears, but each eye and ear contains numerous smaller parts. Eyes, ears, hands, feet, head, and heart work together so the entire body may function.

The church makes its best witness for Christ when all the parts are working together. Paul declared that no one part is more important than another. God "gives what he wants to each person" and "has placed each one of the parts in the body just like he wanted." This is worth remembering when we doubt our own ability or the ability of another person to contribute to the work of the church.

Holy Spirit, guide me to use my gifts to
contribute to the work of the church. Amen.

Transforming Relationships

Romans 12:3-18

In what ways do you express genuine love for Christ?

Even though Christ's followers have different gifts and contribute in different ways to the life of the church, we all have the same call, which is to love God and love each other. It is not enough to go through the motions of love. Paul said, "Love should be shown without pretending." He offered a list of instructions about how to express genuine love for others. Let's consider Paul's instructions as questions rather than statements. For example:

Do you "hate evil, and hold on to what is good"? Do you show honor to others? Are you enthusiastic and "on fire in the Spirit as you serve the Lord"? Are you "happy in your hope"? Do you "stand your ground when you're in trouble"? Do you "devote yourself to prayer"? Do you "contribute to the needs of God's people, and welcome strangers"? Are you "happy with those who are happy"? Do you "cry with those who are crying"? Do you, to the best of your ability, "live at peace with all people"?

It is not always easy to love others with a genuine, Christlike love. The church will do well if it follows Paul's instructions.

In what ways have your life and relationships been transformed through the love of Christ? When have you seen the transforming power of Christ at work in the lives of others?

Loving God, let my love for Christ and others be genuine.
Thank you for your transforming presence in my life. Amen.

FRIDAY, NOVEMBER 13

A Community of Believers

Acts 2:42-47

In what ways is your church like the early church described in Acts?

The early Christians were bound together in their love for Christ. Their community life included shared meals, worship, and prayers. They met in the Temple and in each other's homes because they did not have their own church buildings. The early Christians also shared a missionary focus. They took care of each other even when it meant selling their own "property and possessions" and giving the proceeds to the needy. They also "demonstrated God's goodness to everyone." Luke emphasizes here that God was working through the early church. The members of the body of Christ "devoted themselves" to faithful living. Yet it was God who powered the miracles and increased the number of believers.

In what ways do believers in your church devote themselves to prayer, praise, and worship? How is the Word proclaimed? When do you gather around the table and share a meal together? How does your congregation respond to the needs of its members and demonstrate "God's goodness to everyone"?

The early church met openly in the Temple. In what public places do members of your church gather? How has God worked through the members of your congregation to perform "many wonders and signs" and added to the number "being saved"?

Loving God, help me devote myself to
being a faithful follower of Christ. Amen.

Gathered in Christ's Name

Matthew 18:15-20

When have you experienced a restored relationship through repentance and forgiveness?

What do you do when a brother or sister in Christ "sins against you"? Do you get angry? Do you turn away and give up on the friendship? Or do you "go and correct them when you are alone together" as the Scripture for today instructs? But what if the person does not listen? That could put us in an uncomfortable position. We may prefer to start with verse 16 and "take . . . one or two others" with us from the outset.

In Jesus' day, Gentiles were considered to be sinners and outsiders because they did not follow the Law of Moses. Tax collectors were seen as sinners and outsiders because they cheated the people for their own gain. Jesus said that if the "brother or sister" who sins against us will not accept correction, then "treat them as you would a Gentile or tax collector." Is Jesus really giving us permission to turn away and treat the one who sins against us as an outsider? Remember that Jesus forgave the tax collector Zacchaeus (Luke 19:1-9). He offered the Samaritan woman living water and eternal life (John 4:13-14). Jesus offered love and forgiveness to everyone. He calls us to do the same.

It may not be easy to correct another person or to confess our own sin when we have hurt someone. Yet through repentance and forgiveness, we can restore relationships within the church and bring others into the fellowship of believers. We can trust Jesus to be with us as we follow his example of love and forgiveness.

God, help me forgive others as
you forgave me. Amen.

Don't Stop Meeting Together

Hebrews 10:19-25

Why do you meet together with other believers?

A habit is a pattern of behavior that we repeat with some regularity. We may find it is just as hard to break a bad habit as it is to start a good habit. When we have established a good habit, it is best if we don't slack off, because reestablishing the habit can be difficult. The author of Hebrews advises against getting out of the habit of meeting regularly with other believers.

Jesus opened the way for us to "draw near" to God in a way that was not possible before his death and resurrection.

We are invited to enter God's presence with confidence and certainty that we have been made righteous through Christ. We can confess our faith in Christ with unwavering hope, knowing that God is reliable and the promise of eternal life is sure.

We draw near to God and meet with other believers for our own benefit so we may grow stronger in our faith and nurture supportive friendships. We also meet together for the benefit of the church, "for the purpose of sparking love and good deeds" and to "encourage each other." Verse 24 in the NRSV says "to provoke one another to love," and the NIV reads, "spur one another on toward love."

How do you experience the love of Christ when you meet with other believers? How does your church spark love and "spur one another on" to share the love of Christ with others?

Loving God, help me be a faithful member
of the body of Christ. Amen.

Serve the Lord With Celebration

Psalm 100:1-5

In what ways is your worship of God an act of service?

When the ancient psalmist proclaimed, "Serve the LORD with celebration!" he was inviting the people to worship. The NRSV reads, "Worship the LORD with gladness." Have you ever thought about worship as service to God? The Hebrews lived in a time when the nations were ruled by kings. The people were expected to bow down before their kings with reverence and respect. The kingdoms of Israel and Judah were ruled by earthly kings, yet the people understood God to be their supreme ruler. This is clearly expressed in the collection of psalms known as the "Enthronement Psalms."

The author of Psalm 100 is inviting the people to praise God in a way that is similar to the way they praised their kings. The invitation has seven components: "Shout triumphantly"; "Serve" and "Come"; "Know"; "Enter" and "Thank him!" and "Bless his name!" The invitation to "enter his gates . . . his courtyards" calls to mind the Temple.

The psalmist declares our reasons for worship. First, we "Know" God as our Creator, the one who "made us" and cares for us as a good shepherd cares for his sheep. Second, we have experienced God's goodness; we trust God's loyal love and faithfulness that will last forever. We can respond to God's amazing love and faithfulness through the "service of worship." The invitation to "bless his name" means to bow in homage and show reverence and respect. We are invited to enter the sanctuary with thankful hearts, reflected in our offerings of triumphant praise, celebration, and joy.

Lord, I worship you with praise, thanks, and joy. Amen.

TUESDAY, NOVEMBER 17

Pilate Questions Jesus

John 18:33-38

What questions do you want to ask Jesus?

Pilate asked Jesus, "Are you the king of the Jews?" Jesus did not look like a king. He wore a simple robe and was taken "to the Roman governor's palace . . . early in the morning" after having been bound, questioned, and slapped by Jewish leaders the night before. If Jesus had been a king according to the world's standards, none of that would have happened, for he would have had guards to fight and protect him.

Jesus did not answer Pilate, but instead asked another question. Jesus asked Pilate if he had drawn his own conclusions about Jesus' kingship or if he was repeating what he had heard from others. This is a question all believers need to answer for themselves. Jesus had asked his disciples similar questions: "Who do people say that the Son of Man is?" and "Who do you say that I am?" Simon Peter spoke up and exclaimed, "You are the Messiah, the Son of the Living God" (Matthew 16:13-16, NRSV).

Pilate excused himself from answering, saying, "I'm not a Jew, am I?" Jesus did not deny his kingship but explained, "My kingdom doesn't originate from this world. . . . I . . . came into the world for this reason: to testify to the truth." The truth is the word of God (John 17:17) with God's promises of hope, salvation, and eternal life. Jesus said, "Whoever accepts the truth listens to my voice." Pilate was not interested in listening. He asked, "What is truth?" and then "returned to the Jewish leaders" without waiting for an answer. In what ways do you listen and accept the truth Jesus proclaims?

Holy King, open my heart to your truth. Amen.

The King of Kings

1 Timothy 6:11-16

How do you "grab hold of eternal life" (1 Timothy 6:12)?

Today's passage begins with a warning: "But as for you, man of God, run away from all these things." What are these things we are supposed to run away from? A quick look back at verses 9 and 10 tells us Paul was talking about the "harmful passions" that lead people to love money in place of loving Christ. Paul warns us to run away from the lure of wealth and pursue a faithful relationship with Christ. Sometimes we need to do battle against self-centered desires and keep our focus on Christ. How do we do this? By pursuing "righteousness, holy living, faithfulness, love, endurance, and gentleness."

Paul reminded his readers of Jesus' unwavering love for God and humankind. Jesus knew the pain and suffering of the cross was before him, but he did not back down when questioned. He said to Pilate, "I was born and came into the world for this reason: to testify to the truth" (John 18:37). The truth is the word of God and the promise of eternal life.

Paul proclaimed, "Grab hold of eternal life—you were called to it." When we "pursue righteousness, holy living, faithfulness, love, endurance, and gentleness," we are grabbing hold of eternal life. It is awesome that this is God's hope and plan for us. We "Grab hold of eternal life" when we follow the example of Jesus and stand firm in faith in spite of opposition. How do you pursue righteousness and holy living? How do you reflect the love of Christ?

King of kings, I come before you with
reverence, awe, and a thankful heart. Amen.

Thursday, November 19

Our King, Forever and Always

Revelation 1:4-8

How does God's continuing fulfillment of divine promises bring you hope?

The Book of Revelation is apocalyptic in nature as it offers a vision of the end times. John's vision is filled with symbolic imagery and passages that offer a splendid picture of worship at God's heavenly throne. John opens the letter with a traditional greeting, "Grace and peace to you from . . ." He then mentions three senders. The first sender is God, "the one who is and was and is coming." The second sender is "the seven spirits that are before God's throne." These seven spirits may symbolize God's active presence in the world.

Third, John writes that "Grace and peace" are also "from Jesus Christ—the faithful witness" to God's truth. He is "the firstborn from among the dead," meaning he is the first to give his life for the faith and be born to eternal life. He is "the ruler of the kings of the earth" who exercises authority and judgment over all earthly powers.

John's revelation emphasizes Christ's love for humankind, portrayed so vividly in the sacrifice of himself on the cross. Jesus fulfills God's promise to the Israelites in the desert, "You will be a kingdom of priests for me and a holy nation" (Exodus 19:6). The Book of Revelation is a book of hope and an assurance of God's promise of everlasting life.

Holy Lord, thank you for Jesus,
our salvation and our hope. Amen.

351

FRIDAY, NOVEMBER 20
The Lamb of God

John 1:29-36

What does Jesus as "The Lamb of God" mean to you?

The day after John the Baptist had been baptizing "across the Jordan in Bethany" (John 1:28), he "saw Jesus coming toward him and said, 'Look! The Lamb of God who takes away the sin of the world!'" He may have been thinking of the Paschal or Passover Lamb. This imagery of Jesus as the sacrificial lamb continues in the New Testament Letters. Peter proclaimed, "you were liberated by the precious blood of Christ, like that of a flawless, spotless lamb" (1 Peter 1:19). The apostle Paul declared, "Christ our Passover lamb has been sacrificed" (1 Corinthians 5:7). The author of 1 John wrote, "the blood of Jesus . . . cleanses us from every sin" (1 John 1:7) and "there is no sin in him" (1 John 3:5), thus Jesus is worthy to be the sacrificial lamb for humankind. When John saw Jesus the following day, he again proclaimed, "Look! The Lamb of God!" (John 1:36).

As we grow in our faith, learn more about the Bible, and experience God's loving presence in our lives, the power and truth behind John the Baptist's identification of Jesus as "The Lamb of God" can take on more meaning for us. John's Gospel reports that "two disciples heard what he [John the Baptist] said, and they followed Jesus." How do you respond to Jesus' loving sacrifice and the gifts of forgiveness and salvation? What prayers and passages of Scripture continue to call you to faith in Christ?

O Lamb of God, that takest away the sins
of the world, grant us thy peace. Amen.

SATURDAY, NOVEMBER 21

God's Heavenly Throne

Revelation 4:1-11

How do you "give glory, honor, and thanks" (Revelation 4:9) to God as you live your daily life?

John was not able to offer an exact description of God. He compared God's glory with things he knew in creation, in this case radiant gemstones. We imagine brilliant color. Jasper comes in a variety of colors; carnelian is red or orange, and emerald is green. Against this colorful backdrop, we see the "white clothing and . . . gold crowns" of the twenty-four elders, "seven flaming torches" and "something like a glass sea, like crystal." Throughout history, humankind has built beautiful churches and cathedrals around the world, but none of them compare to the beauty and majesty of God's heavenly throne. John described a place of continual worship. The "four living creatures" who "never rest day or night," along with the twenty-four elders, continuously proclaim that God is holy and worthy of our worship.

Psalm 19:1 declares, "Heaven is declaring God's glory; the sky is proclaiming his handiwork." Another psalmist called, "Shout joyfully to God, all the earth! . . . Come and see God's deeds; his works for human beings are awesome" (Psalm 66:1, 5).

How do you join earth and heaven in the continual worship of God? When we love God's children and care for creation, we are giving glory and honor to God. How are these acts of love and care also acts of worship? In what ways do you express continuous gratitude to God?

Holy are you, Lord God Almighty. Help me live my life
in a way that brings glory and honor to you. Amen.

SUNDAY, NOVEMBER 22

Who Is Worthy?

Revelation 5:1-14

How do you worship the Lord and the Lamb?

Did you ever have the idea that you needed to "measure up" to earn someone's approval or love? We live in a culture that sends the message that acceptance is dependent upon success. It is easy to transfer this way of thinking to our relationship with God; that is to say, we may believe that we need to "measure up" to receive God's love and gift of salvation. If that were the case, we would all be in trouble! None of us, on our own, can stand before God as righteous.

In Revelation 5, John describes his vision of Jesus as the Lamb. John "saw a scroll . . . with seven seals" in God's "right hand," the hand of authority. An angel asks, "Who is worthy to open the scroll and break its seals?" The answer is Jesus Christ, the sacrificial Lamb who takes "the scroll from . . . the one seated on the throne." Christ has authority and knowledge over all creation.

John witnessed powerful and joyful worship, as the four living creatures and 24 elders were joined by "many angels" and then by "everything everywhere" in proclaiming words of praise "to the one seated on the throne and to the Lamb."

Only the flawless Lamb of God is worthy to be the sacrifice and atone for our sin before God. God's love and acceptance of us, sin and all, is clearly shown through God's Son. Through Christ, we "measure up" and are assured that we are indeed worthy of God's love and salvation!

Holy Lord and holy Lamb, blessing, honor, glory,
and power belong to you. Amen.

Monday, November 23

It Is Good to Proclaim God's Love

Psalm 92:1-15

How do you proclaim God's loyal love and faithfulness?

The psalmist proclaims, "It is good to give thanks to the Lord." This is a timely passage for us as we look ahead to celebrating Thanksgiving Day later this week. The psalmist also declares, "It is good . . . to proclaim (God's) loyal love in the morning." As we begin each day, it is comforting to know that God's love for us is steadfast and unwavering. Then we're told, "It is good . . . to proclaim . . . (God's) faithfulness at nighttime." It is good to reflect on the gifts and blessings we have received from God during the day and to offer thanks and praise before we sleep.

The Israelites thought of the Temple as "the Lord's house" and the place where they were closest to God. We, too, feel God's presence in our churches, yet we learned from Jesus, who came to live among us, that the heart, not the place, is most important to God. Jesus said, "The time is coming—and is here!—when true worshippers will worship in spirit and truth" (John 4:23). The psalmist reminds us that God's loyal love and faithfulness are always with us, and that, "The righteous . . . will bear fruit even when old and gray."

This is a beautiful promise, a promise that gives us hope and calls us to worship with the psalmist, saying, "The Lord is righteous. He's my rock. There's nothing unrighteous in him."

Holy Lord, thank you for your loyal love and faithfulness
that are with me all day, every day. Amen.

God Called Them "Humanity"

Genesis 5:1-5

How does the fact that you are part of humanity that is blessed by God influence the way you live?

Humanity, all humanity, is created by God! The ancient historian tells us that "On the day God created humanity, he made them to resemble God." This echoes the statement in the creation story where the first thing we learn about humanity is, "God created humanity in God's own image, in the divine image God created them" (Genesis 1:27). From the very beginning, God set humans apart from the rest of creation and invites us into a special relationship with our Creator.

Humanity has continued to experience God's loyal love and faithfulness through the generations. Genesis 5 includes "the record of Adam's descendants," beginning with his son Seth and "other sons and daughters" and ending with Noah and his three sons (verse 32). Luke, in his Gospel account of Jesus Christ, concludes his genealogy of Jesus with "son of Seth son of Adam son of God" (Luke 3:38). With the birth of Christ, God makes it clear that the divine favor and benefits will continue for eternity. All humanity is related. The relationship of "son of God" or "daughter of God" is part of each of our genealogies.

How does the fact that you have been blessed by God influence the way you live? In what ways are you mindful that everyone you meet is a blessed and beloved child of God?

Loving God, thank you for claiming me as your child.
Thank you for blessing me with your
steadfast love and faithfulness. Amen.

Wednesday, November 25
You Created Me

Job 10:8-12

What do you say about God by affirming God is your Creator?

One of the things we learn from Job is that it is perfectly acceptable to express our questions, burdens, and heartache before God. Job declared, "I will let loose my complaint; I will speak out of my own bitterness" (Job 10:1). Job did not turn away from God. God did not turn away from Job but listened to his complaint. If there are times we do not feel comfortable expressing our true feelings before the Almighty, we can remember that God already knows our bitterness and sorrows. God invites us to express our feelings in prayer and open our hearts to God's response.

Job acknowledged God as his Creator: "Your hands fashioned and made me." When we affirm that God is our Creator, we affirm what we know about the creation of humanity. God "made them to resemble God . . . He blessed them" (Genesis 5:1-2). God's blessing, love, faithfulness, and favor are always with us. When we face trials and hardship, we can do so with the sure knowledge that God remains with us. Job affirmed God's love for him, saying, "Life and kindness you gave me, and you oversaw and preserved my breath."

Remember, we can share both our joys and our sorrows with our Creator, trusting in God's faithful presence and enduring love.

Almighty God, thank you for hearing my prayer
and remaining with me always. Amen.

Thanksgiving Day, Thursday, November 26
We Belong to God

Isaiah 44:1-5

What blessings has God poured into your life?

This passage from Isaiah is a prophecy of hope. The people of Israel endured punishment for their unfaithfulness and disobedience. Then, through the prophet Isaiah, God called, "But now hear this, Jacob my servant, and Israel, whom I have chosen."

God identified God's self to the people of Israel as their Creator, "The Lord your maker, who formed you in the womb and will help you." God promised to "pour out water" and to "pour out my spirit." Water and God's spirit are both life-giving. We imagine fields turning green with new growth. We imagine weary people looking forward to a brighter future. God promises, "I will pour out my spirit . . . and my blessing" on future generations. Verse 5 looks forward to a time when the people of Israel will be faithful to God, saying, "I am the Lord's."

Sometimes we, like the nation of Israel, endure suffering that results from our sinful actions. Other times, like Job, we suffer hardship due to circumstances beyond our control.

As you celebrate this Thanksgiving Day, be mindful of the ways God pours out blessings into your life, especially the unexpected blessings that come during challenging times. Proclaim with a thankful heart, "I am the Lord's."

> Thank you, God, for your abundant
> blessings and steadfast love. Amen.

FRIDAY, NOVEMBER 27

The Life Breath of God

Ecclesiastes 11:1-5

How do you give thanks for God's breath, which gives life?

One of the ways we celebrate God's gift of the Savior is to give gifts to others. The author of Ecclesiastes offers words of wisdom on this subject. He wrote, "Send your bread out on the water. . . . Give a portion to seven people, even to eight." The image of "bread out on the water" is an ancient metaphor for extending charity.

One of the themes in the Book of Ecclesiastes is the mysterious nature of God. The Teacher points out that we do not understand the beginning of life, "how the breath comes to the bones in the mother's womb" (verse 5, NRSV), and we do not know what will happen during our lives on earth. He even inserts a word of doom and gloom: "You don't know what disaster may come upon the land." This is true, of course, but we do not need to live in fear. We know that God is always with us, through all the challenges we face.

In spite of the mystery, the Teacher points out that we can depend on certain things to happen with regularity. He encourages us not to sit by and idly "observe" but to be at work within the parameters of what we do know.

During the season of Advent, we are presented with many opportunities to share. We may purchase warm clothes for the homeless and toys for needy children, for example. We may "Give a portion" of our financial resources to various outreach ministries. How will you "Send your bread out on the water"?

Loving God, thank you for your breath, which gives me life.
Open my eyes to the ways I may help others. Amen.

SATURDAY, NOVEMBER 28
Created in God's Image

Genesis 1:24-28

How do you resemble your Creator?

Genesis 1 tells about God's creation of "the heavens and the earth" (verse 1). On the sixth day, God created "livestock, crawling things, and wildlife," then God created humanity. Our Creator said, "Let us make humanity in our image to resemble us." Thus, humanity is different from everything else God made. God gave humanity instructions to "Take charge of" the other living creatures. As the bearers of the divine image in the world, we are called to have loyal love for God and all God's creations and to remain faithful to God's call to care for creation.

Humanity has fallen short of fulfilling this call, however, so God came to us in human form to show us how. Jesus is the perfect bearer of God's image in the world. Jesus is the perfect example of what it means to "take charge of" and care for creation. Jesus is the perfect example of living a life of love and faithfulness.

Humanity will never bear God's image in the world perfectly, as Jesus did. Thankfully, God does not call us to perfection. God calls us into relationship. Many times over, Jesus forgave the sins of the people. He taught us that God will forgive our sins and that we are called to forgive the sins of others. We are called to bear God's image, to "take charge of" all created things with love and faithfulness. We are thankful for the gift of Jesus to show us the way.

Creator God, thank you for Jesus, who shows me how
to be the bearer of your image in the world. Amen.

First Sunday of Advent, November 29
Marvelously Set Apart

Psalm 139:13-18

How do you express love and thanks to your Creator?

The author of Psalm 139 affirms the special attention God gives to humankind. We hear joy in his voice as he declares, "I am . . . wonderfully made" (verse 14, NRSV). God created him "in a secret place" where only God could see. Even before his birth, God was forming days and plans for him. The psalmist expresses his sense of wonder as he acknowledges "your plans are incomprehensible to me!"

All of humankind is "marvelously set apart" as we are created in God's image. Each one of us is special to God, known to God even before the day of our birth.

God's greatest expression of love for us is the gift of the Son, Jesus Christ. How will you celebrate this season of Advent? As the season progresses, we sometimes find ourselves feeling overwhelmed by the items on our "to-do" list, and we may lose sight of the manger in Bethlehem. Remember the words of the psalmist: you are "marvelously set apart." Remember that even though God's "plans are incomprehensible," we, like the psalmist, can say, "If I came to the very end—I'd still be with you." When the angel told Joseph of Jesus' coming birth, he said Jesus would be called Emmanuel, which "means 'God with us'" (Matthew 1:23).

God made us in the divine image. God sent Jesus to assure us of God's love and to reconcile us to God forever.

Everlasting God, thank you that I am marvelously
set apart as your beloved child. Amen.

361

Monday, November 30
Hoping Against Hope

Romans 4:17-24

When have you given up hope too soon?

Paul here is talking about believing God's promises. As an example, he referred to Abraham, whom God had told he would become the "father of many nations" (verse 17, referencing Genesis 17:5). Abraham was childless, and his wife, Sarah, was beyond child-bearing years. Nonetheless, because he believed God, Abraham became a father (and Sarah a mother). As the NRSV puts verse 18, "Hoping against hope, he believed that he would become 'the father of many nations'" (NRSV).

"Hoping against hope." Now there's a phrase for us. It means hope despite apparent impossibility—that's what "against hope" means. Hope is when there is little reason to expect things to come out as we want them to. Hanging on when some might accuse us of mere wishful thinking.

The message from Abraham's story is not "just keep hoping no matter what," but "trust what God tells you." That's hard to do when circumstances seem to render a desired outcome improbable. But if it were easy, Paul would not have described it as "hoping against hope."

There is always the danger of false hope. It is possible, especially when strong emotions and terrible loss are involved, to grasp illusions and call them real. But when matters are still unresolved, if our choices are between hoping too much or too little, the story of Abraham suggests that we would do well to err on the side of excessive hope.

O God, let my faith be like Abraham's, trusting you even
when the promised outcome seems impossible. Amen.

DECEMBER

CONTRIBUTORS:

Stan Purdum
(December 1-December 29)

Michelle Morris
(December 30-December 31)

Tuesday, December 1
God Said "Go!"

Genesis 12:1-9

When has God called you out of your comfort zone?

Today's reading tells of Abram, who will later be known as Abraham, receiving a call from God to set out on a trip to visit some spiritually significant sites in Canaan. Well, no, that's not what God said. God called Abram to a journey all right, but there's no mention of religious tourism. In fact, the divine instruction that came to Abram was as much about where he shouldn't remain as it was about where he should travel: "Leave your land, your family, and your father's household," the Lord said to Abram, "for the land that I will show you,"

Centuries later, the writer of Hebrews referred to this story as an example of faith, saying, "By faith Abraham obeyed when he was called to go out to a place that he was going to receive as an inheritance. He went out without knowing where he was going" (Hebrews 11:8) The salient point is that Abram obeyed God and hit the road. Abram's obedience eventually led him to a greater understanding of God.

God may not call you to a new location, but perhaps to move out of your comfort zone, to do some new thing that God will show you. It is good for us to remember that obedience, listening, worshiping, selflessness, and remaining open to new understandings of God can make all our journeys and changes of direction into spiritual pilgrimages.

Help me to be aware, Lord, of when you
tell me to go, and make me obedient. Amen.

Abraham's God and Mine

Psalm 47:1-9

For what do you praise God today?

Psalms 47 is an "enthronement psalm," a praise hymn celebrating God's rule over the nations. In Israel, it was most likely used on festal occasions when Israel again declared that God was its king. Verse 2 declares that God is "awesome," which reminds me that it wasn't too long ago that "Awesome!" was the youth culture's exclamation of choice to express that the teen was really impressed by something. But, of course, as the psalmist is using the word, it means "inspiring awe" or "worthy of awe," and the psalmist knew no superlative could improve it.

Theologians have another word to express this: *transcendence*. That word is from a Latin term meaning "to surpass," and it refers to the "beyondness" or "otherness" of God and to God's being above creation and outside of human comprehension. In other words, God is wholly other than what we are, which is what Psalm 47 communicates.

But theologians couple another word with transcendence to further describe God's nature: *immanence*. That is derived from a Latin word that means "to remain in" or "dwelling in." It is a way of saying that God is near to every one of us, closer to us even than is our own breath. Jesus referred to the immanence of God when he talked about God's care for the birds of the air and the lilies of the field (Matthew 6:26-28), and then added, "Are you not much more valuable than they?" (NRSV).

O God who is both far above me and
very near me, receive my praise! Amen.

Thursday, December 3
Changing Because of Scripture

Acts 7:1-8

How has what you've read in the Bible shaped your life?

Today's reading is the start of a speech by Stephen, in which he used key points in Israel's history to accuse fellow Jews of being unfaithful to their tradition by refusing to hear the gospel of Jesus Christ as good news for them. What Stephen was attempting to do with his review of Israel's history as recorded in Scripture was to get his listeners to use that Scripture as a means of self-criticism and change their ways. Obviously, he was unsuccessful, but the principle still holds: Scripture can work that way for us. Here are three reasons why:

First, the Bible is a finger pointing to God. Being a Christian does not mean primarily believing in the finger, but in believing in the God to which the finger points. Second, the Bible is a lens through which we view God. The lens is not perfect, and to some degree, it distorts what we see, but it is still the clearest view of God that we have. Third, the Bible is, as Peter dubbed it in one of his letters, "a lamp shining in a dark place" (2 Peter 1:19). A lamp does not eliminate all darkness, but it enables us to find our way through it.

All of this brings us down to one final point. We cannot benefit from the Bible unless we have some knowledge of what's in it. We need to read it.

Thank you, Lord, for revealing yourself to me
through the Bible. Awaken my spirit and speak to
me as I read it about where I need to change. Amen.

Friday, December 4

Faith and Authority

Matthew 8:5-13

To what degree is your connection to God a leap of faith?

This short healing story invites us to think about the linkage between faith and authority. The centurion who went to Jesus seeking healing for his desperately sick servant identified himself as "a man under authority." In indicating that Jesus' authority over illness was such that he could accomplish the healing from a distance, the man was making a statement of faith in him. Jesus was impressed by this and said so in verse 10. He then told the man, "Go; it will be done for you just as you have believed." And indeed it was. The servant was healed "that very moment."

We, too, are making a statement about faith and authority when we affirm such things as our belief that God is sovereign over this world or even when we sing, "He's got the whole world in his hands." The affirmation that God has "the whole world in his hands" is a conclusion that can be reached only by faith, for there is no incontrovertible evidence.

We live our lives trusting the authority of Christ, seeking to keep him as the sovereign of our lives. In big things, like prayers for healing or help in troubles, we acknowledge that Christ has the power and authority to help us. But even in the minutiae of our daily lives, we trust Christ's authority. After all, we never know what the result will be of even the smallest decision we make.

Where do you need to trust Christ's authority in your life?

Thank you for the way faith
connects me to you, O Lord. Amen.

SATURDAY, DECEMBER 5

God's Promises and Our Hope

Hebrews 6:13-20

On what specific promises of God is your hope built?

Hebrews speaks of our need for patience, saying that God's promises mean "that we, who have taken refuge in him, can be encouraged to grasp the hope that is lying in front of us." Hope is long-term patience. If promises are immediately fulfilled, there's no need for patience or hope, but if they are not and you still believe fulfillment is coming, then hope is a term for that expectancy.

Another way to say this is that Christianity has a "tomorrow factor." Tomorrow—maybe some distant tomorrow—things will be better than today. While the tomorrow factor is helpful to many, it is also what turns some off to Christianity. They listen to that and say, "Why Christianity is just like all the other philosophies—based on a someday hope instead of immediate solutions." In other words, they see Christianity as primarily wishful thinking. Perhaps you've felt that way yourself sometimes.

But here's the thing: Christians have a sense of how to get to tomorrow. That comes from the confidence we have in the One who holds the future and in the belief that wishful thinking is not wasted thinking, but rehearsal for how it is going to be when God's kingdom becomes a full reality in this world.

Thank you for your promises, O Lord,
and the living hope they engender. Amen.

SUNDAY, DECEMBER 6

Resurrection Faith

Acts 26:1-8

How does the Resurrection play out in your daily life?

Our passage for today includes Paul's opening statements in his defense before Roman governors, Festus and Agrippa. After identifying himself as a faithful Jew and even as a Pharisee, he stated that he was on trial "because of the hope in the promise God gave our ancestors." Paul understood that promise as something different from what most Jews would. The original promises God made the ancestors had to do with progeny and land (for example, Genesis 15:5), but as we continue to read Paul's defense, it appears the divine promise he meant was Jesus' resurrection. Paul may have intended that the fact of the Resurrection validated the claim that Jesus was that Messiah.

Paul asks rhetorically, "Why is it inconceivable to you that God raises the dead?" If indeed God is God, such an act would certainly be within the divine ability. From Paul's perspective, the Resurrection makes perfect sense. What's more, the Resurrection explains the remarkable turnaround in Paul's life, from persecutor to preacher. It makes sense of his own conversion and calling. Without God's Resurrection power, what became Christianity would have fizzled out.

The Resurrection also means that we cannot dismiss Jesus as simply a "great teacher" or "moral example." The Resurrection shows him as the authoritative revealer of God's truth, so that to know him is to know God in a more personal way.

Let the Resurrection empower
my hope in you, O Lord. Amen.

MONDAY, DECEMBER 7
Abraham's Blessing to Us

Galatians 3:6-14

How are faith and righteousness connected?

Paul and Barnabas had preached the gospel of Jesus Christ in Galatia during Paul's first missionary journey, and Paul and Silas had done the same in the northern part of that province during his second missionary journey. After Paul left that area, some rival apostles arrived and began insisting that Paul's converts needed to adopt the Law-based practices of the Jews and, if they were male, be circumcised. Paul's letter came as a confrontational retort of that teaching and a restatement of "the truth of the gospel" (2:5).

Paul stated his premise plainly in Galatians 2:16: "We know that a person is justified not by the works of the law but through faith in Jesus Christ" (NRSV). Paul elaborated further on that premise in today's passage, citing in verse 6 the statement from Genesis 15:6 that "Abraham believed God and it was credited to him as righteousness." And thus, "all who believe are the children of Abraham."

Where we can connect with this passage is in verse 11, where Paul cites Habakkuk 2:4, that the righteous "live on the basis of faith." As Paul saw it, Abraham's acceptance of God's call was a model of the kind of faith we need today. Thus, in Paul's thinking, the "blessing of Abraham" is the faith that brings us to Jesus.

O Lord, let my faith guide
me in righteous living. Amen.

Skywalk Faith

Hebrews 11:1, 6-16

What can be "seen" only by faith?

Have you ever walked out on the famous Skywalk Bridge in Grand Canyon National Park? Its deck floor is clear glass and it juts out into thin air more than 700 feet above the canyon floor. It's beautiful and terrifying at the same time. In your mind, you know the glass will support you, and that the structure is completely safe. But your gut doesn't quite embrace what your mind believes.

Glass-bottomed bridges are a good metaphor for faith. Faith is "the proof of what we don't see," Hebrews 11:1 says, and walking on glass means we're not seeing that which supports us. What we do see are the dangers below, and they can be terrifying. We grasp the "railings" that give us comfort (God's Word) or perhaps we crawl on our knees (prayer).

We can take heart from the fact that faith is, in truth, a way of seeing that looks beyond appearances. In Hebrews 11, the writer tells of Abraham "looking forward to a city that has foundations, whose architect and builder is God." Abraham wasn't looking with his physical eyes, of course, but with the eyes of faith. In other words, faith is not something we somehow drum up with gumption and by stifling the clamor of doubts and other voices. Rather, faith is a way of seeing that what's under our feet, though it appears transparent, is the solid rock of Christ.

> Help me to keep my spiritual eyes open,
> Lord, that I might "see" and believe. Amen.

WEDNESDAY, DECEMBER 9

Loving the Lord's Instruction

Psalm 119:161-168

What has the Bible taught you recently?

If you were around in the 1960s and 1970s or perhaps listen to an "oldies" music station, you may remember the singing group "Peter, Paul and Mary." The taller of the two men in the group was Noel Paul Stookey. As a young man, he became a follower of Jesus.

Seeking fulfillment inn his life, Stookey read the Bible seriously, reading the entire New Testament and parts of the Old. The reading was slow going, but as he pursued it, he found that something real happened in his life. By 1968, Paul was reading the New Testament. Following a Peter, Paul and Mary concert in Austin, Texas, a young man approached Paul backstage and said that he wanted to talk to him about the Lord. Paul was prepared to listen. And he gave his heart to Jesus that night.

The Bible—the "Instruction" (Psalm 119:163) of the Lord has that kind of power. When studied, taken seriously, and lived out, God's Word does indeed change lives. Are you studying God's instruction seriously, to be changed by it? Or do you think you know it all already?

Let me be attentive to your instruction, O Lord. Amen.

Thursday, December 10

A Theological View of Life

Psalm 71:14-20

If God is the source of good things, where do troubles come from?

Psalm 71 is a prayer for help and a statement of confidence in God—and something more: a theological perspective on life. The psalmist declares, "You've taught me since my youth, God, and I'm still proclaiming your wondrous deeds!" But what the psalmist says in verse 20 gives a view of God that is less common today: "You, who have shown me many troubles and calamities, will revive me once more." That God is the source of our "troubles and calamities" is not something we commonly affirm. It is, however, consistent with the psalmist's belief that God is sovereign and Lord of all of life.

When thinking about who is in control of the world, most of us Christians believe in the sovereignty of God, though we might not express it that way. That is, while we may not see our suffering as coming directly from God, we may understand God as allowing it to come to us. If this is God's world, and God is sovereign, then the fact that troubles come to us must, logically speaking, be by God's permission.

However, we should also note from verse 20 that while the psalmist believed even his troubles came from God, he also believed that in the final analysis, God wills that life prevail. Thus, the psalmist said, "You, who have shown me many troubles and calamities, will revive me once more."

O God, despite the troubles I've been through,
revive me again, that I may always trust you. Amen.

FRIDAY, DECEMBER 11

God Is Doing a New Thing

Isaiah 43:14-19

When have you realized God was doing something new?

Isaiah was referencing the Exodus crossing of the Red Sea when he spoke of God making "a path in the mighty waters" and extinguishing the "chariot and horse, army and battalion." But in verse 18, the prophet broke with the traditional use of Israel's history by saying, "don't ponder ancient history." The Lord was saying, "Look! I'm doing a new thing; … I'm making a way in the desert …." In other words, whereas before, the Lord made a way through the sea, now the Lord was making a way through the desert, the land between Babylon and Judah, doing a new thing.

The principle of old ideas breaking down and new ones breaking through is still a major way that we grow spiritually as individuals and that the church grows in its understanding of what it means to be the body of Christ in the world. It is not that we usually go looking for some new concept. Instead, we usually hold tightly the ones we are already comfortable with until we reach some point where they become flawed, inconsistent, or unworkable—or until some new light is shed on the subject and we come to see that God is the one shedding it.

It takes new information, arguments from experience, some brave persons pioneering a new way, and a growing conviction that God is the one nudging us toward newness that helps the church see the new things God does. Are you open to learning from God in this way?

Give me, Lord, the ability to recognize when you are
doing a new thing, so that I don't stand in your way. Amen.

Saturday, December 12
God Brings Salvation Near

Isaiah 46:8-13

What bearing do the past works of God have on your faith?

Given that in yesterday's reading the prophet told his hearers not to "ponder ancient history," and instead accept that God was doing "a new thing" (Isaiah 43:18, 19), today's reading seems at first glance to be a contradiction. But the prophet was simply coming at his message from another direction. One value of the Bible for us is that it enables us to "remember" the former things God did. Biblical history is a witness to the power of God today.

In Judaism, storytelling is a predominant way each new generation is invited to personally step into the stream of salvation history. The rabbis seldom re-tell a biblical tale using the word "them"; instead, they use "us." Historical stories become vital and significant to each new generation of Jewish children because they are personally brought into the biblical tales.

We Christians are also inheritors of that history. The God of the Bible is our God, too. The God who brings deliverance near brings it near for us. Re-telling the stories of God's work in the past invites us to open our lives to God today, so that a new story of God's faithfulness can be told tomorrow.

Give me the insight, O God, to move
into the Scriptures so that I embrace them
as my stories. And help me to write new chapters of
your faithfulness through the witness of my life. Amen.

SUNDAY, DECEMBER 13

On Having a Forehead of Bronze

Isaiah 48:2-11

When has something good happened to you that had to be either a remarkable coincidence or an action of God?

The Jews were in exile in Babylon, and the prophet, speaking for God, was telling them that eventually God would return them to their homeland. Here, however, God took a different tone with the people, accusing them of having "foreheads of bronze," which in today's language might translate to being "blockheads." God's point was that when the "new thing" happened—their release from captivity—they weren't to write it off as the work of some idol.

In verse 3, God stated, "Past things I announced long ago; from my mouth I proclaimed them. I acted suddenly, and they came about." God was saying that if the people looked at their history, Israel's God had long ago established a reputation for announcing what was to happen and then bringing it to pass. In other words, past prophecy and its fulfillment were evidence of God's ability to bring about the new thing God had promised.

We, too, sometimes behave as though we have "foreheads of bronze." For example, have you ever prayed for more patience, and then, when circumstances required you to be patient, you failed to recognize that those circumstances may have been God answering your prayer? Or have you ever wondered whether a sudden good thing that befell you was an act of God or a coincidence? Be open to seeing God's acts in daily ways.

Help me to recognize your acts
in my life, O Lord. Amen.

Glimpsing the Kingdom to Come

Isaiah 65:17-25

Of what value are impossible dreams?

Isaiah 65:17-25 describes a kind of utopia, where people live long and trouble-free lives and everything is as we would wish it to be. Even the wild animals dwell in peace with one another. But the very word *utopia* denotes an imagined place that is not achievable among humankind. No group of people has achieved utopia, including the postexilic Jews to whom this passage from Isaiah was originally addressed. So of what value is a biblical passage such as this?

This prophecy, if it is to have power, must refer to a state still to come. But if its fulfillment was to be far beyond the lifetime of any of those alive when the prophecy was spoken, why was it even given at that point? One reason is that utopian visions tend to make us work to effect immediate changes in the real world.

We who worship God benefit from glimpsing God's intention for the future. Yes, we have a long way to go. Yes, it seems hardly possible that humankind can get there. Yes, we have lots of reasons for pessimism. But without the vision, what do we have? Make the best of things now and wait for heaven? No, not good enough, and here's why: Jesus tells us that with his coming, the kingdom is already begun; it's not fully here, but it began with his first coming. And for us who follow him, the vision of the kingdom of God elicits action in the here and now. We work with Christ in the Holy Spirit to bring about God's Kingdom here on earth.

Thy kingdom come, O Lord, thy will
be done, in me and through me. Amen.

TUESDAY, DECEMBER 15

God's Servant

Isaiah 42:1-9

What does it mean to live righteously?

Bible scholars call verses 1-4 of Isaiah 42, along with three other passages from Isaiah (49:1-6; 50:4-9; 52:13–53:12) "songs of the suffering servant." These passages refer to an agent specially called by God to a role where suffering is the price paid for doing God's will.

This servant, says verse 1, "will bring justice to the nations." The Hebrew word interpreted as "justice" in this verse (and again in verse 3) is *mišpāt,* and it has two meanings. One is the judicial meaning, in the sense of "judgment." However, the Bible rarely speaks of justice in the "just deserts" meaning. The more common biblical meaning of *mišpāt* is "true religion" or "righteousness." Thus, when God says that the servant "will bring justice to the nations," the image is not that of arriving with a fiery sword to slay the wrongdoers of earth but coming with the compassionate righteousness on which the wholeness of earth and humankind depends.

As followers of Jesus, we are to continue doing justice today, working for the well-being of the community, including those at the bottom. How do we do that? Many people have put their faith into action. Some who work for God's justice help by giving money. Some help by pitching in with a hands-on effort; some help by speaking up for those on the margins of society. Some help in other ways. It is useful to remind ourselves that when, out of our devotion to God, we care for the well-being of others, we are being righteous.

O God, open my eyes, heart, and imagination
that I may do justice and live righteously. Amen.

WEDNESDAY, DECEMBER 16
An Unembarrassed Witness

1 Peter 3:13-17

What does your faith in Christ mean in your everyday life?

In this passage, Peter advises his fellow Christians, "Whenever anyone asks you to speak of your hope, be ready to defend it." The hope to which he refers is one's faith in Christ, but the Greek word translated "defend it" is *apologia*, which can also be rendered as "an answer." And that may be a better rendering for us who live in free societies, where we're seldom called on to defend our faith, but may be asked by an interested person to explain it.

What would be your response if someone asked you why you trust Christ? You might think, "Why me? I'm no professional." But you're the one with whom the inquirer has enough of a connection to raise the topic. And while you may not have formal training, you can tell the person what your faith means to you.

Surely in moments like that, where someone is asking for information, we can be unembarrassed witnesses for Christ. It doesn't need to be an in-depth theological treatise. We just need to say something about what Christ means to us. Perhaps something like, "Because Jesus is in my life, I no longer _____." Or "Because Jesus is in my life, I've been able to let go of _____." Or "Because Jesus is in my life, my outlook is more positive," and then tell why. How can you prepare yourself to "speak of your hope"?

Lord, enable me to speak plainly about my faith in
Christ when asked by an interested person. Amen.

Thursday, December 17

When Challenges Come

Acts 4:8-20

When has someone challenged you about your faith in Christ to the point that you felt you had to defend it? How did you respond?

We said yesterday that the Greek word *apologia* can be rendered in English as "an answer" regarding our faith or "a defense" for it. Today, we have an example of a defense of the faith. After healing of a crippled man in the Temple (Acts 3), Peter and John were arrested, brought before the authorities (Acts 4:1-3), and asked, "By what power or in what name did you do this?" (verse 7). Jesus had earlier told the disciples, "When they bring you before the synagogues, rulers, and authorities, don't worry about how to defend yourself or what you should say. The Holy Spirit will tell you at that very moment what you must say" (Luke 12:11-12).

Peter and John were prepared, and the Holy Spirit indeed inspired their response. Peter answered with the words in Acts 4:8-12. Referring to Jesus, Peter said, "Salvation can be found in no one else. Throughout the whole world, no other name has been given among humans through which we must be saved." Peter and John were fishermen, not trained public speakers. Yet they inspired and persuaded many.

Sometimes our conversations with people give us opportunities to provide answers to their questions. At other times, like Peter and John, we may have to offer a "defense" of our faith. When we do, we can, like they did, rely on the power of the Holy Spirit to give us words that will convince, persuade, and offer hope.

Give me courage, O Lord,
to speak up for you. Amen.

FRIDAY, DECEMBER 18
Divine Reassurance

Isaiah 7:10-17

What confidence for the future does your faith support?

Matthew 1:22-23 quotes Isaiah 7:14 to show that Jesus' birth was a fulfillment of prophecy. But in its original context, 7:14 referred to the birth of a son to a woman who was pregnant at that time. The Lord was speaking to King Ahaz by way of Isaiah. Judah was being threatened by an alliance between Aram and Israel, the northern Hebrew kingdom. The Lord's message to Ahaz was that the alliance's plans would fail, and their threat against Judah would come to nothing.

Ahaz, however, wasn't convinced, so the Lord told him to ask for a sign. Ahaz refused the offer, saying he wouldn't "test the Lord." But Isaiah saw that remark as a lack of faith on Ahaz's part—a refusal to be reassured. Isaiah gave Ahaz a sign from the Lord anyway. Pointing to a pregnant young woman, Isaiah declared that she would give birth to a boy, whom she would name Immanuel. Furthermore, said Isaiah, "Before the boy learns to reject evil and choose good" (that is, learns right from wrong), "the land of the two kings you dread will be abandoned." (This is not to say that Matthew was wrong, but only that in its original setting, the statement had a "right now" meaning.)

Perhaps you know someone like Ahaz who refuses to be reassured, or perhaps you have some of that same unwillingness to be reassured. It can be a good thing to question optimism that seems unwarranted, but faith in God is still "the reality of what we hope for, the proof of what we don't see" (Hebrews 11:1).

I trust myself into your hands, O Lord. Amen.

SATURDAY, DECEMBER 19

Darkness and Light

Isaiah 9:2-7

In what ways do the terms "darkness" and "light" describe your situation?

Isaiah lived in the southern Hebrew kingdom of Judah during the time that the northern Hebrew kingdom of Israel was being overrun and destroyed by the Assyrians. It seemed likely that the Assyrians would turn their attention to Judah next. Isaiah uttered these words in our passage to talk about their present time and contrast it with a future to come, thanks to the arrival of a new Davidic king.

Isaiah lists three hope-filled assurances. First, "the yoke that burdened them . . . and the rod of the oppressor" will be permanently broken, for the king will deliver them from their enemies. Second, "the boot[s] of the thundering warriors . . . will be burned, fuel for the fire," and war will be no more. And third, "A child is born to us, a son is given to us, and authority will be on his shoulders. He will be named Wonderful Counselor, Mighty God, Eternal Father, Prince of Peace."

Christians have seen this passage as a reference to an eternal king, the Messiah, Jesus Christ. That's why Matthew quotes some of this passage from Isaiah when talking about Jesus (see Matthew 4:12-16). We are currently in Advent, and this passage from Isaiah is a traditional Advent reading. This passage is written in poetic form. As poetry, this hope can be named and stated in a way that touches the heart. It helps us grasp what Advent is about—the fact that our hope for enduring peace, joy, love, and the kingdom of God is not a pipe dream. And our hope in Jesus Christ is not misplaced.

Thank you, Lord, for the light that is Jesus. Amen.

The Genealogy of Jesus, Part 1

Matthew 1:1-8

How does your family tree influence who you are today?

Here you are, all set to start reading about Jesus, and the first thing you encounter is a list of his ancestors. It does not make for exciting reading: "Abraham was the father of Isaac. Isaac, the father of Jacob. Jacob, the father of Judah. . . ." Many readers skip this part.

If we do that, however, we miss some important themes that Matthew introduces by beginning this Gospel the way he did. One refers to the common understanding among the Jews of that day that the promised Messiah would be a descendant of King David. By listing David among Jesus' progenitors, Matthew clearly communicates that fact: Through his earthly father, Joseph, Jesus was a descendant of David. That does raise a question, though, for Matthew goes on after verse 18 to tell us that Joseph was really Jesus' adoptive father. So how was Jesus a descendant of David?

By tradition, if a Jew formally adopted and named a child, that child became his child in every sense of the word.

Clearly, Matthew was satisfied that Jesus was the heir of David's throne. What's more, Jesus is called "Son of David" numerous times in Matthew (for example, 12:23; 15:22; 21:15). Matthew was not claiming that Jesus was the son of David because the two were genetically connected, but because the two were divinely connected. It was God's plan to present Jesus that way. Matthew began his Gospel with a genealogy not to show biological connections, but to highlight God's purposes.

Show me your purposes for me, O Lord. Amen.

The Genealogy of Jesus, Part 2

Matthew 1:9-17

What barriers keep you from fellowship with Christ?

Jesus was born into a patriarchal culture. In all things legal, religious, and economic, men were in charge. They were also the ones whose ancestry was usually recorded. Women were subjugated. Thus, in this genealogy of Jesus, 39 times we encounter the phrase, "was the father of." It's surprising, therefore, that Matthew makes five departures in the 42 generations he lists. In those five cases, he tells us not only the name of the father, but also the name of the mother.

The five are Tamar, the mother of Perez and Zerah; Rahab, the mother of Boaz; Ruth, the mother of Obed; Bathsheba, the mother of Solomon (although she is mentioned only as having been "the wife of Uriah"); and Mary, the mother of Jesus.

There is something irregular about how each of these five became part of Jesus' family tree. Three and possibly four of the women were not Hebrews. The stories of these women sometimes involve seduction, adultery, and even sexual assault. While there was nothing wrong with her behavior, Mary's neighbors considered her scandalous because she became pregnant outside of marriage (Luke 1:26-45).

While we cannot know for certain what Matthew had in mind, here are four possible lessons: The coming of Christ transcended the barrier (1) between races and nationalities, (2) between male and female, (3) between the married and the unmarried, and 4) between saint and sinner. Jesus' lineage reassures us that God has a plan and use for all of us.

Thank you that Jesus came for all, O Lord. Amen.

Naming the Christ Child

Matthew 1:18-25

What affirmations about God are in Jesus' birth?

The child born to Mary receives two important names in today's reading. Before Jesus was born, an angel appeared to Joseph, informing him that the child Mary was carrying was conceived by the Holy Spirit, that he should not be afraid to take Mary as his wife, and what to name the child—Jesus. The name "Jesus" means "God is salvation." Matthew went on to make his own observation—that the child fulfilled Isaiah's prophecy. Matthew quoted Isaiah 7:14: "Look! A virgin will become pregnant and give birth to a son, And they will call him, Emmanuel." Matthew hastens to tell us that Emmanuel means "God with us."

Thus, between his given name, Jesus, and his symbolic name, Emmanuel, this child born to Mary makes two important affirmations about God—that God saves us and that God is with us. God created us to have close association and communion with God. But to have that connection, we must change and become fit for it. Among the things that make us unfit are our sins and self-centeredness, but when we turn to God, God makes it possible through Jesus for us to become fit for communion with our Creator. That is salvation.

So, even in the naming of Jesus, we find two powerful testimonies to remind us of how God comes to us, if we will allow it. God comes with salvation and is present with us where we are, no matter what we go through.

Thank you, Lord, for these two good messages
about you in the naming of Jesus. Amen.

WEDNESDAY, DECEMBER 23

Impatient Faith

Isaiah 63:7-14

What does it mean to wait on the Lord?

Our reading from Isaiah 63 is a prayer of yearning, recalling God's past deeds on behalf of the Israelites, but noting that God seemed absent now. The mood of the prayer can be summed up in 64:1: "If only you would tear open the heavens and come down!" That mood, in a nutshell, is the tone of Advent. Advent hymns, like "O Come, O Come, Emmanuel," emphasize the sense of waiting for something that has not yet happened, something that will eventually change everything for the good.

We may come to Advent with a kind of resignation that leads us to not really expect things to get much better. If we feel that way, there's another verse from this prayer we should listen to: Isaiah 64:4. "From ancient times, no one has heard, no ear has perceived, no eye has seen any god but you who acts on behalf of those who wait for him!" That's an expression of faith that while we are waiting for the fulfillment of faith's promise—even if we are tired of waiting—God nonetheless works on behalf of those who wait.

Waiting is hard. But Advent reminds us that waiting for God's mastery to be revealed is not a time of inactivity, but of preparation, creativity, and vitality.

Enable me to wait and not lose faith, O Lord. Amen.

Thursday, December 24, Christmas Eve
The Power of Belief

Luke 1:39-45

How easy is it for you to trust in God?

Today's reading opens with Mary making haste to visit Elizabeth. When she entered the house and greeted Elizabeth, the child in Elizabeth's womb "jumped for joy" and "Elizabeth was filled with the Holy Spirit." She began to speak an oracle, proclaiming Mary "blessed above all women."

Elizabeth's oracle regarding Mary ended with, "Happy is she who believed that the Lord would fulfill the promises he made to her." That puts before us the power of faith, and a central message of the New Testament: Belief is blessed. If only one will trust, there are no limits to what God may bring to pass.

Consider how often Jesus referred to belief. Here are just three examples:

- "Have faith in God" (Mark 11:22).
- "It will happen for you just as you have believed" (Matthew 9:29).
- "Don't be afraid; just keep trusting, and she will be healed" (Luke 8:50).

Trust, of course, does not come automatically, and there is plenty in life that works against it. Life's difficulties, discouragements, and allures pull heavily away from belief. But it comes with a surrender of oneself to the spirit of God.

Strengthen my faith, O Lord. Amen.

Friday, December 25, Christmas Day
The Great Reversal

Luke 1:46-53

What new understanding of what is important in life did Jesus bring?

The key point in Mary's song was that the coming salvation would be a great reversal. God, sang Mary, would bring down the mighty and lift up the lowly. God would fill the hungry and send the rich away empty-handed. God's mercy will be for those who fear God. The church understands this song as an expression of the kind of salvation Jesus would bring. It was a salvation the proud and powerful would not welcome, because it would bring justice, calling them into account for their unjust ways. For the humble and lowly, however, and for those suffering injustice, that salvation would be good news.

We should take a moment to understand this concept of a great reversal, for what Mary is saying in this song is that the redemption of the oppressed and the humbling of the powerful is frequently a sign of God's activity in the world. That Jesus was born in a stable instead of in a palace or the first-century equivalent of a hospital on Upper East Side is itself an indicator of God at work.

And we have experienced the inner sense that the things the world uses as markers of greatness and power—wealth and might—are not the things that really matter in life. That is part of the great reversal.

Through what God began with the birth of Jesus, a new understanding of what matters in life has taken hold.

> Lord, help me to see and affirm
> heavenly values in this life. Amen.

SATURDAY, DECEMBER 26

The Companion

John 14:15-26

How do you discern the voice of the Holy Spirit?

This passage comes from Jesus' discourse to his disciples at the Last Supper. He knew he would be leaving them, but promised them "another Companion, who will be with you forever." This Companion was the Holy Spirit. The Greek word translated by the Common English Bible as "Companion" is *paraklētos*, which is often rendered as "Comforter," but also by a range of English words including Counselor, Helper, Intercessor, Advocate, Strengthener, Friend, and Standby. Literally, *paraklētos* means "one called alongside to help."

While as a "spirit," the Holy Spirit often seems to believers as having less "personality" than God the Father and Jesus the Son, it is revealing that the writer of 1 John used the same word, *paraklētos*, to refer to Jesus. In 1 John 2:1, that writer said, "I'm writing these things to you so that you don't sin. But if you do sin, we have an advocate [*paraklētos*] with the Father, Jesus Christ the righteous one."

Thus, what Jesus was telling his disciples during that final week was that while he would no longer be with them physically, by the Spirit, he would be with them still. In that way, Jesus' statement to his followers renders unnecessary such questions as "Is the voice of God inside me God the Father, the God the Son, or God the Holy Spirit?" In fact, the answer to that question is "Yes." The Spirit brings the presence and resources of Jesus himself to us.

Help me to discern the voice of
your abiding Spirit, Lord. Amen.

Sunday, December 27
Of Trouble and Hope

Romans 5:1-5

How easy do you find it to be hopeful about the future?

"We even take pride in our problems, because we know that trouble produces endurance, endurance produces character, and character produces hope." Paul had written that sentence in developing his claim that our faith gives us peace with God through Christ. It is easy to feel hopeful when things are going well. But hope is not for easy times. Hope is necessary when things are not going well. How do we become the type of people who take pride in problems because of the hope that is eventually produced?

Endurance is the first virtue that follows trouble in Paul's chain towards hope. Endurance can only be learned through practice; we must endure hard times to learn how to endure hard times. This is not just waiting out the hardships, but refusing to give in to them, continuing to live godly lives and exercise righteousness in contrast to unrighteous situations. Thus, we grow into the women and men of character that Jesus intends for us to be. The hope we have and proclaim is not in our own abilities, but in what Christ has done in us.

The reality of starting with trouble and ending with hope is a major biblical theme that helps us find our footing today. Our faith is not blind to the troubles of life, and we cannot pretend to always live victoriously. Our only claim is that present circumstances, however bleak, are never the last word. That word belongs to God, and it is one of salvation and deliverance.

Lord, let my troubles lead
not to despair, but to hope. Amen.

The Old Testament and Jesus

Luke 24:44-53

When has Scripture spoken directly to you?

The disciples had not recognized in Scripture "everything written about [Jesus] in the Law from Moses, the Prophets, and the Psalms." Nor had they seen it written that "the Christ will suffer and rise from the dead on the third day." The disciples can hardly be blamed for that, however. There are very few Old Testament references to resurrection at all, let alone to Jesus' raising. It took some enlightened explanation for the early followers of Jesus to understand that certain verses did indeed forecast the miraculous event.

If we can imagine not having the New Testament, would we recognize those verses as predicting the resurrection of Jesus? Probably not. Later, however, it became a common practice in the early Christian community for believers to read the Old Testament with new eyes, discovering Jesus on pages where they had not previously seen him. We have the added advantage of the New Testament, and yet, like the disciples during Jesus' post-resurrection appearance, we sometimes fail to grasp the significance of the biblical knowledge we possess.

We are blessed with knowledge of the scriptures, but we should never start thinking we know it all already. Our situations might change, and while God's Word remains the same, we find in our new experiences fresh guidance, wisdom, comfort, and more in these old words. Make reading the Bible your lifelong habit, and you'll never regret it.

Let the Scriptures, O Lord, be a place to rendezvous with
Jesus and hear what he has to say to me today. Amen.

Tuesday, December 29

How We Got the Gospel

Acts 1:1-9

Who first told you about Jesus?

Jesus' Ascension is as decisive as it is dramatic. It marks not only the ending of Jesus' time on earth, but also the beginning of the period when people would learn to see Jesus with the inner eyes of faith. According to Acts, Jesus told his disciples that the Holy Spirit was shortly to come upon them, and that they were to be his witnesses, extending to all the earth. Then all at once, Jesus was lifted into the sky and disappeared. His followers continued staring skyward, straining to see what else might happen. Suddenly, "two men in white robes" appeared and asked, "Why are you standing here, looking toward heaven?"

The implied instruction in their question was "Stop standing here staring and start looking around you. That's where your witnessing is to begin." Jesus' last words to his disciples were about their mission. Starting in Jerusalem, but moving rapidly outward to the very "ends of the earth," they were to teach and testify about Jesus and the gospel. Those first believers did that, and that's the reason that you and I are Christians today. Those first believers started the process that eventually made the gospel available everywhere.

Christ's Ascension comes to us with the message of those two angels: Don't stand here focused only on the mystery of Christ disappearing into the sky. Instead, open your eyes to see both the work of global outreach and the opportunity to tell your neighbor and your household about Jesus.

Thank you, Lord, for the faithfulness of your first followers,
and for allowing the gospel to reach me. Amen.

Holy Splendor

Psalm 93:1-5

How does the Christmas season overwhelm us with "splendor"?

This short and sweet psalm packs two central themes into five verses. This psalm speaks to the eternal and to the splendor of life with God. The psalmist mentions three things as eternal (or nearly so): the throne, the Lord, and the holiness decorating the Lord's house. An eternal house, with eternal décor, for an eternal God.

The splendor of God is on display in the majesty of God's robe and clothing of strength and in the firmness of the throne. The psalm closes with an interesting turn of phrase, that holiness decorates God's house for all time, bringing the two themes of splendor and eternity together.

Imagine what holiness looks like. Can we? I suspect for each of us, holiness looks different. The psalm doesn't load us down with description, but allows us to use our own experience. Holiness could be represented by a stained-glass window, or it could be someone taking the hand of a homeless person. What if it is all those things? What if the holiness that decorates God's home is made up of the things that allow us to grow close to God?

Is the splendor around you this Christmas season focused on projecting an image of a perfect holiday celebration? Then it is not holy. May this season instead draw you intimately toward a life in relationship with Jesus Christ, and through Christ with a world of neighbors to love.

Eternal God, let me spend my brief time here focused
on you and the people I am called to love. Amen.

Thursday, December 31, New Year's Eve
Walk the Walk

Psalm 84:1-12

How would your view on life change if you viewed it as a pilgrimage to God?

The draw of any pilgrimage for me is the intention of growing closer to Jesus Christ. The worship on such pilgrimages is a deliberate choice—not something we do just because that is what we are supposed to do or are in the habit of doing. Today's psalm describes the journey of faith as a pilgrimage. In fact, this speaker says of those who put their faith in God that "pilgrimage is in their hearts." They are walking along, eyes on reaching God, and experiencing the refreshment of water, the strength of faith, and the protection of the Lord.

What is stopping me from being on a pilgrimage for and with God? What if I were intentional about imagining that every breath I take and every step I make is both made with God and toward God?

I tell you what would happen. First, there are some steps I would not take. I would stop myself from doing the shameful things that I hope God does not see. I would also, though, grow closer to God. I would learn to love God better. I would be in real relationship with God.

When I imagine taking a pilgrimage, I always imagine it as a solo journey. I am just not sure I could stand anyone else being with me for that long in those conditions. Now, though, I am imagining a companion. I am imagining walking with Jesus. May I hold on to that image every day of my life.

Lord Jesus, let me walk with you.
Let me walk with you always. Amen.

Continued from page iv.

NOTES

_____

_____

_____

_____

_____

_____

_____

_____

_____

_____

NOTES

NOTES

_____

_____

_____

_____

_____

_____

_____

_____

_____

_____

_____

NOTES

_____

_____

_____

_____

_____

_____

_____

_____

_____

_____

NOTES

_____

_____

_____

_____

_____

_____

_____

_____

_____

_____

NOTES

_____

_____

_____

_____

_____

_____

_____

_____

_____

_____

NOTES

_____

_____

_____

_____

_____

_____

_____

_____

_____

_____

_____

_____

NOTES

NOTES

_____

_____

_____

_____

_____

_____

_____

_____

_____

_____

NOTES